READING LUKE

A New Commentary for Preachers

CHARLES H. TALBERT

SPCK

First published in the USA in 1982 by The Crossroad
Publishing Company, 370 Lexington Avenue, New York,
N.Y. 10017, as *Reading Luke: A Literary and
Theological Commentary on the Third Gospel*.

This edition first published in Great Britain in 1990 by
SPCK, Holy Trinity Church, Marylebone Road,
London NW1 4DU

ACKNOWLEDGEMENTS

Quotations from the Bible are taken from the Revised
Standard Version unless otherwise specified. A quote from
the Gospel of the Hebrews comes from *Gospel Parallels*
(RSV). Quotations from the early church fathers are from
The Ante-Nicene Fathers. Citations from Greek and Roman
authors are found in the Loeb Classical Library.

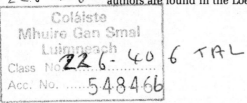
British Library Cataloguing in Publication Data

Talbert, Charles H.
Reading Luke.
Bible N.T. Luke — Critical studies
I. Title
226.406

ISBN 0-281-04494-5

Printed in Great Britain by
Courier International Ltd, Tiptree, Essex

To
the memory of Eleanor Mills
Prayer Warrior Extraordinary

CONTENTS

PREFACE

This volume was begun during the spring semester, 1979, when I enjoyed a Reynolds Research Fellowship from Wake Forest University. Its progress has been facilitated by a series of grants from the Graduate Council of Wake Forest University, and by the untiring assistance of Mrs. Anne Francis, secretary to the Department of Religion. That several good friends read all or part of earlier drafts resulted in numerous improvements; the flaws remaining are my responsibility.

Two sources of encouragement deserve special mention. First, I benefitted greatly from the constant stimulation provided both by colleagues in the Society of Biblical Literature's Luke-Acts Seminar which began in 1979 and the earlier Luke-Acts Group, 1973–78, on the one hand, and by my peers in the Catholic Biblical Association's Luke-Acts Task Force, in which I have participated since research for this book began, on the other. Second, the students of Wake Forest University who took my exegetical course on the Gospel of Luke in 1978, 1980, and 1981 have been, in many ways, my teachers. Both colleagues in the professional societies and students in my classes deserve my thanks.

As always, without the support of my wife, Betty, and my children, Caroline and Richard, such an effort would have been impossible.

GETTING READY
TO READ THE GOSPEL

E very reading of a gospel is from a particular angle of vision. It is imperative, therefore, at the outset, to understand the angle assumed in the commentary. The following paragraphs are devoted to this end.

This volume reflects the widespread loss of confidence in the two-source theory that has occurred during the past fifteen years. The anonymous author of the third gospel, a Christian of the second generation and of unknown provenance, who writes on the basis of what the first generation delivered (cf. Heb 2:3–4 for a similar perspective), mentions other reports of the things "fulfilled among us" that were written before his attempt. In the past some have suggested that Mark and Q were among those reports and were used by the evangelist as his primary sources. Since 1963, however, there has been a prolonged assault on the two-document hypothesis. Although the alternatives proposed have not proved convincing, enough difficulties with the priority of Mark and the existence of Q have emerged to render the two-source theory's position as an "assured result" of criticism suspect. It is, therefore, a questionable control on redaction critical work.

> Employing Mark as a control today is about as compelling as using
> Colossians and Second Thessalonians to describe Paul's theology.
> It may very well be legitimate to do so, but so many have problems
> with the procedure that such an assumption narrows considerably
> the circles with whom one can converse. (C. H. Talbert, "Shifting
> Sands: The Recent Study of the Gospel of Luke," *Interpretation*
> 30 [1976]: 393–94)

This commentary will not assume the two-source theory, nor any other source theory, for that matter. Although the movement beyond the study of the Lukan alterations of Mark is both necessary and proper, this does not prevent the comparison of Luke's narrative development with that of the other gospels, including Mark, when they run parallel. This procedure need not assume Luke used any of the other gospels any more than a comparison of Mark and John assumes the former's dependence upon the latter. In this volume comparisons of Luke with other gospels will be made, but without assuming any source theory.

The commentary will investigate the third gospel with a type of redaction criticism heavily influenced by nonbiblical literary criticism.

> From the standpoint of current American redaction criticism, each gospel represents an intricately designed religious universe, with plot and character development, retrospective and prospective devices, linear and concentric patternings, and a continuous line of thematic cross-references and narrative interlockings. The art of interpretation consists in analyzing the complexities of the narrative construction and to comprehend [sic] individual parts in connection with the total architecture. (Werner Kelber, "Redaction Criticism: On the Nature and Exposition of the Gospels," *Perspectives in Religious Studies* 6 [1979]: 14)

The thrust of this approach is on understanding large thought units and their relationship to Lukan thought as a whole rather than focusing on the individual pieces of the narrative. Given this approach, the present volume does not follow the word-by-word, phrase-by-phrase, verse-by-verse method of traditional commentaries. Nevertheless, the thrust of this approach is also on the close reading of the text of the gospel itself. Similarly, although the interpreter's dialogue with the gospel is carried on in light of the history of research, this commentary makes little reference to secondary literature. The aim is not to direct one through the maze of scholarship but to make one feel at home in the biblical text itself. The closest parallel to the type of approach attempted here for the third gospel is Part III, "Argument and Structure," of C. H. Dodd's *The Interpretation of the Fourth Gospel* (Cambridge: Cambridge University, 1958).

This book operates from a perspective indebted to genre criticism. Luke-Acts belongs to the ancient biographical tradition. Ancient biographies can be separated into two different categories: literary (e.g., Plutarch's *Lives*) and cultic. Cultic biographies are those produced by and used within religious or semireligious communities, such as philosophical schools, and usually treat the career of the community's founder as the value norm for devotees and the object of their reverence and worship. Among such lives was a type in which (a) the life of the divine hero was followed by (b) a narrative of successors and selected other disciples. The two components (a + b) were parts of a single work. Such biographies are known both from the later literary collections made of the individual cultic legends (e.g., Diogenes Laertius, *Lives of Eminent Philosophers*) and from fragments of the early and original documents (cf. Ingemar Duering, *Aristotle in the Ancient Biographical Tradition* [Goeteborg: Goeteborgs Universitets Aersskrift, 1957], who has collected the fragments of a pre-Christian biography of Aristotle). The function of such a biography with an a + b pattern in a philosophical school was legitimation. On the one hand, such a biography would legitimate the founder's successors at the time of the document's writing by showing the line of tradition from the founder to them and by showing the continuities between what they did and said and what the founder did and said. On the other hand, this type of biography would legitimate the founder's positions by showing the line of tradition from his time to the time of the document's writing: that the founder really did and said these things can be known with certainty because a line of tradition guarantees it.

Of all the types of literature in antiquity, this variety of biography is most like what one finds in Luke-Acts: that is, the life of the founder of a religious community followed by a narrative about his successors and selected other disciples—both in one work. Here also is a literary genre with some similarity in function to that of Luke-Acts. At least one aim of the Lukan work is to say the true tradition is that which came from Jesus through the Twelve to Paul and from him was passed to the Ephesian elders (Acts 20). This Lukan motif would inevitably function as legitimation in the same twofold way the philosophical biographies did.

This concern for legitimation reflected in the literary genre of Luke-Acts is also found in the preface with which the gospel begins:

> *Since many* have undertaken to *write* a *report* of the things that have been fulfilled among us, as those who were from the beginning eyewitnesses and ministers of the word have delivered them to us, *so also* it seemed to *me* a good thing, since I have followed everything carefully from the first, to *write* an orderly *account* for

> you, most excellent Theophilus, so you may have certainty about
> the matters of which you have been instructed. (my translation)

The author writes, he says, to give Theophilus certainty (*asphaleian*).

There are at least three major themes running through Luke-Acts that would contribute to this legitimation: the fulfillment of prophecy, the occurrence of miracles, and the martyrdom of the hero. Excursus A treats the first and shows how fulfilled prophecy functioned in antiquity as a legitimation technique. Excursus B takes up the second and likewise indicates how miracles served in antiquity to give certainty. The section of this commentary covering 23:26–56 focuses on the legitimating function of martyrdom in Mediterranean antiquity.

The example of Justin Martyr offers evidence of the persuasive power of fulfilled prophecy, miracle, and martyrdom on behalf of the Christian cause. In two places in his extant writings Justin tells of his conversion to Christianity. (1) In his *Dialogue with Trypho the Jew*, 7, Justin tells how he walked by the seashore prior to becoming a Christian and met an old man, a Christian, who said to Justin,

> There existed, long before this time, certain men more ancient than all those who are esteemed philosophers, both righteous and beloved by God, who spoke by the Divine Spirit, and foretold events which would take place, and which are now taking place. They are called prophets. . . . Their writings are still extant . . . and *those events which have happened, and those which are happening,* compel you to assent to the utterances made by them, although, indeed, they were entitled to credit on account of the *miracles* which they performed.

Here Justin says fulfilled prophecy and miracle were catalysts in his becoming a Christian. (2) In *II Apology*, 12, Justin again returns to his conversion:

> For I myself, too, when I was delighting in the doctrines of Plato, and heard the Christians slandered, and saw them fearless of death, and of all other things which are counted fearful, perceived that it was impossible that they could be living in wickedness and pleasure.

As a result of Christian suffering and martyrdom, Justin says (13) that he, "with all [his] strength strive[s] to be found a Christian."

Taken together, martyrdom, miracle, and fulfilled prophecy were persuasive to Justin. There is no reason to think Justin was the exception in his time and place. He and his contemporaries would have heard the evangelist eagerly as he told the story of Jesus and the early church, with emphasis on the martyrdoms of Jesus and Stephen, the miracles of Jesus and the apostles, and the numerous fulfilled prophecies of every sort that dominate the two-volume work. Luke's narrative would have given certainty to Christian and non-Christian alike because it appealed to the persuasiveness of a selfless commitment (martyrdom), of power (miracle), and of being right and having roots (fulfilled prophecy). This narrative of Jesus and the early church is a legitimation document: its story is told with a persuasiveness intended to give certainty.

Certainty was essential if the Lukan biography of Jesus was to serve its practical purpose. Ancient biography, even of a literary type, often aimed at instruction in values (cf. Plutarch, "Cleomenes," 13), which, it was believed, could be most graphically communicated when shown incarnated in living personalities. Hence biographies often became hagiographies. As D. R. Stuart has put it, Aristoxenus' life of Pythagoras and the Pythagoreans consisted of

> preachments in which he sought to glorify the master and the ideals for which the master stood, and to correct the vulgar errors according to which popular belief had deformed the Pythagorean way of life. Thus his treatment . . . had much of the color of a saint's life. (*Epochs of Greek and Roman Biography* [Berkeley: University of California, 1928], pp. 158–59)

The emulation of the hero's way of life was the goal of such biography, but this was not understood as simply a blind and unthinking repetition of acts performed by the great person. Rather one was expected to learn from the hero how to order one's own life. Without necessarily performing the same actions, the reader of such biographies was expected to emulate the values of the hero in his or her own context (A. J. Gossage in *Latin Biography,* ed. T. A. Dorey [London: Routledge & Kegan Paul, 1967], p. 49). If the third gospel is biography, then the work and words of Jesus are narrated with the intent that they be emulated—not in a mechanical way but with imagination and conviction, and not through one's own strength but through the power of the Holy Spirit. That the evangelist repeatedly portrays Jesus as a model for disciples conforms to the preceding assessment of the gospel as a type of ancient biography. From this angle of vision the present commentary unfolds.

For the reader who wants to supplement this volume's approach with the resources of a traditional type of commentary, the following are recommended: Joseph A. Fitzmyer, *The Gospel according to Luke, I–IX* (Anchor 29; Garden City, N.Y.: Doubleday, 1981); I. H. Marshall, *The Gospel of Luke* (New Inter Gk NT Comm; Exeter: Paternoster Press, 1978); and Frederick W. Danker, *Jesus and the New Age according to St. Luke* (St. Louis: Clayton Publishing House, 1977).

MAKING A BEGINNING

1:1–4

G enre studies show that much can be learned about a text first by seeing how it participates in a given genre and secondly by noting how it differs from the genre. This certainly is true of Luke's preface in 1:1–4.

We begin with an examination of the components of ancient prefaces. Although not all are exactly alike, there is a significant number that correspond to one another in remarkable ways. In these prefaces taken from history and biography there are seven components, all or most of which appear regularly. (1) There is often a statement about the author's predecessors, usually about their inadequacies. Diodorus Siculus writes, "A study of my predecessors in this field has inspired me with the strongest feelings of approval for their purpose. At the same time, I hardly feel that the full possibilities of instruction inherent in it have been realized in their works." Philo writes in his *Life of Moses*, "Greek men of letters have refused to treat him as worthy of memory, possibly out of envy, and also because in many cases the ordinances of the legislators of the different states are opposed to his." Luke 1:1 contains this component also: "many have undertaken to compile a narrative." If there is any criticism of his predecessors implied, it is muted. It may very well be that his predecessors encouraged the evangelist to write by their example. If we take *epeidēper* as causal, then "inasmuch as" would mean "because," and Luke would be using the work of previous writers positively to justify his own venture. The absence of explicit critical comments about his predecessors sets Luke apart from most Greco-Roman prefaces.

(2) A preface usually tells the work's subject matter. Polybius writes,

> The events which he has chosen as his subject are sufficiently extraordinary in themselves to arouse and stimulate the interest of every reader, young or old. What mind . . . could feel no curiosity to learn the process by which almost the whole world fell under

the undisputed ascendency of Rome within a period of less than fifty-three years.

Philo, *Life of Moses*, states, "I purpose to write the life of Moses." Luke's "the things which have been accomplished among us" reflects this component. In view of the strong emphasis in Luke-Acts on the fulfillment of prophecy (see Excursus A), *peplērophoremenōn* should most likely be translated "fulfilled" instead of accomplished (cf. also Col 4:17 with 2 Tim 4:5): the things about which his predecessors wrote and now Luke also (1:3) writes are things which are fulfillments of prophecy.

(3) There is customarily some statement about an author's qualifications for writing: either knowledge of the subject due to being an eyewitness, or his having good sources, or having the linguistic ability to handle the primary materials. Diodorus Siculus writes,

> My home is Agyrium in Sicily, and my intercourse with the Latin-speaking settlers in the island has given me a thorough command of the Latin language, so that I have been able to derive accurate information of all the transactions of the Roman dominion from the national records, which have been preserved from an early date.

In his *Life of Moses*, Philo says, "I will . . . tell the story of Moses as I have learned it, both from the sacred books . . . and from some of the elders of the nation; for I always interwove what I was told with what I read, and thus believed myself to have a closer knowledge than others of his life's history." Luke 1:1–4 tells both about the sources of the author's material and about his own care in working. The source of what has been delivered (as tradition—cf. 1 Cor 15:3; 11:23) to us who live after the first generation (cf. Heb 2:3; Eusebius, *H.E.* 3:39) is "those who from the beginning were eyewitnesses (cf. Acts 1:21–22; 10:37; 11:15; 13:31; i.e., the apostles) and ministers of the word" (cf. Acts 6:4; 26:16; i.e., people like the Seven and Paul). Four terms characterize the author's description of his care in working. The term *parakolouthēkoti* should be translated "investigated" (as in Demosthenes, *De Cor.* 53) instead of "followed" as in the RSV: "All things" in the origins of Christianity have been investigated—"accurately" and "from the first." The evangelist sets forth his credentials, as was the Mediterranean custom. One who has read widely in Mediterranean literature knows, however, that claims of reliability cannot be taken at face value. Lucian, in his *How To Write History*, 29, complains that those who have never set foot outside their city begin with such words as, "Ears are less trustworthy than eyes. I write then what I have seen, not what I have heard." In spite of claims to historical accuracy in the letter of Aristeas' preface, what follows is largely fiction. A reader must evaluate such claims in terms of the accuracy of the narrative which follows.

(4) A statement of the plan, arrangement, or table of contents of the work is a normal part of prefaces in antiquity. Diodorus writes,

> My first six volumes contain transactions and legends previous to the Trojan War. . . . In the eleven volumes that follow I have recorded the general transactions of the world from the Trojan War to the death of Alexander; while in the succeeding twenty-three volumes I have found room for all transactions between that date and the commencement of the Celto-Roman War.

Philo uses a secondary preface to begin the second volume of *Life of Moses*, and says, "The former treatise dealt with the birth and nurture of Moses; also with his education and career as a ruler . . . ; also with the works which he performed . . . ; further with the troubles which he successfully surmounted. . . . The present treatise is concerned with matters allied and consequent to these." In 1:3 Luke gives his plan: it will be an "orderly account," which obviously does not refer to a chronological scheme of arrangement given the subsequent narrative. That an orderly account need not be chronologically arranged is evident from Suetonius' statement in his "Life of Augustus," 9: "I shall now take up its various phases one by one, not in chronological order, but by classes, to make the account clearer and more intelligible." Furthermore, when Ovid, *Metamorphoses*, 7:520, says he will not ramble but present things in their order, he means his work will be organized.

(5) A comment about the purpose of the writing was an inevitable component of an ancient preface. Dionysus of Halicarnassus writes, "My subject . . . is to eradicate these erroneous suppositions from the public mind and to implant the truth in their place in treating of the founders of Rome and of her early institutions and transactions." He continues, "It is my hope that the discovery of the truth may induce a proper appreciation of Rome in the minds of my readers." Philo says in *Life of Moses*, "I hope to bring the story of this greatest and most perfect of men to the knowledge of such as deserve not to remain in ignorance of it; for, while the fame of the laws which he left behind

him has traveled throughout the civilized world and reached the ends
of the earth, the man himself as he really was is known to few." The
third evangelist sets forth his purpose at the beginning of 1:4: "that
you have certainty" ("know the truth"). This stated purpose presupposes either doubts about Christianity or perversions of it. If the readers of Luke-Acts were non-Christians, the narrative would be designed
to provide what was necessary for them to come to faith. If, as is more
probable, the readers were already Christians, the narrative would provide what was necessary either for their certainty so they would remain Christians, or for their proper Christian stance so they would
represent what was truly Christian in their lives.

(6) Sometimes the author's name is given. Thucydides' *History* begins, "Thucydides of Athens has written the history of the war between the Peloponnesians and the Athenians." This component is
missing from the Lukan preface.

(7) Sometimes the official addressee of the work is named. Josephus, *Against Apion,* writes, "I suppose that, by my books of the Antiquities of the Jews, most excellent Epaphroditus, I have made it evident to those who peruse them, that our Jewish nation is of very great
antiquity." The identity of "most excellent Theophilus" is unknown,
the Lukan preface telling us only that he has been informed of the
things relating to Christian origins. As in Acts 18:25, Rom 2:18, 1 Cor
14:19, Gal 6:6, *katechethes* (informed—vs. 4) may very well refer to
Christian instruction of converts. If so the official addressee was a
Christian. This need not be the case, however.

Luke 1:1-4 fits nicely into the genre of ancient prefaces, containing
six of the seven components widely found in prefaces of histories and
biographies. Certain characteristics of ancient prefaces also need to be
noted. (1) The style was often highly rhetorical. This is certainly true
of 1:1-4. The preface is one sentence which falls into two halves, each
with three members or *cola.* The sense of each of the first three members stands in a corresponding relation to the sense of the latter three:
(a) "many" in opposition to "also to me"; (b) "to compile a narrative"
parallel to "to write an account"; (c) eyewitness tradition echoed in the
"certainty" in vs. 4 (cf. Friedrich Blass, *Philology of the Gospels* [Am-
sterdam: B. R. Grüner, 1969—reprint of 1898 edition], chap. 2). (2)
The style was often in marked contrast to that of the rest of the document. This is certainly true for Luke where the excellent Greek of 1:1-
4 stands in marked contrast with the semitizing style of 1:5ff. The

exalted style of 1:1–4 simply conforms to cultural expectations for a rhetorical beginning. The same can also be said for 1:5ff. with its semitizing style, as it was a cultural expectation that a narrative would reflect the style of the people described. (3) The length was sometimes out of proportion to the body of the work. This prompted Lucian, in his *How To Write History*, 23, to satirize many prefaces as "the head of a Colossos of Rhodes on the body of a dwarf." The Lukan preface is by contrast a model of brevity. (4) The subjects treated were sometimes quite alien to the contents of the main work. Only a careful reading of the gospel and Acts can determine whether the narrative in fact is aimed at giving certainty or causing one to know the truth as opposed to error. (5) When a writing contained more than one volume or book, a secondary preface was often used (e.g., Philo, *Life of Moses*, II; Josephus, *Against Apion*, has a preface to the whole work at the beginning of Book 1 and a brief recapitulation at the beginning of Book 2. Cf. also *Ant.* 13:1). Acts 1:1–2 functions as such a secondary preface: "In the first book, O Theophilus, I have dealt with all that Jesus began to do and teach. . . ."

When one recognizes that 1:1–4 belongs to the genre of ancient prefaces, while at the same time differing from them in some regards, certain inferences can be made. (1) Regarding genre. Since prefaces were used for many different genres in antiquity, this preface cannot be used to deduce the genre of Luke-Acts. (2) Regarding historicity. Since extravagant claims of accuracy often accompanied fictitious accounts, we cannot determine Luke-Acts' historical accuracy from claims made in the preface. (3) Regarding purpose. Since the topics treated in a preface sometimes differed from those dealt with in the subsequent narrative, the preface's statement about purpose cannot guarantee the aim of what follows. It is, however, worth testing in one's reading of Luke-Acts whether the narrative was written so someone might know the truth about Christian origins. Truth could, of course, be understood either in the sense of accurate information or in the sense of certainty about Christianity.

Luke 1:5–4:15

PROPHECIES OF FUTURE GREATNESS

INTRODUCTION

Following the preface of 1:1–4, 1:5—4:15 comprises the first major unit in the third gospel, which is followed by the formal opening of Jesus' public ministry, the frontispiece (4:16–30). Luke 1:5—4:15 depicts the life of Jesus prior to his public career, and constitutes a coherent unit within the gospel. Two strands of evidence make this clear.

The first strand is the literary organization of the unit, which consists of three episodes dealing with John the Baptist and Jesus. Episode One, 1:5–38, involves the annunciations of the births of John and Jesus. The material focusing on John the Baptist (1:5–25) corresponds to that of Jesus' story (1:26–38). Luke 1:39–56 serves as a transition from the two annunciations of Episode One to Episode Two, the narratives about the births and early lives of John and Jesus (1:57—2:52); the section focusing on the Baptist (1:57–80) again corresponds to the material dealing with Jesus (2:1–52). Episode Three, 3:1–4:15, also treats John and Jesus in corresponding ways: 3:1–20 treats the adult ministry of the prophet John; 3:21—4:15 presents the prelude to Jesus' public career. Each of these three episodes is built around a series of correspondences between the story of John and of Jesus which reflects the Lukan artistry; each is concerned to portray Jesus' superiority over John the Baptist. In all three episodes John is depicted as a prophet (1:16–17; 1:76; 3:1–6), not the Messiah (3:15ff.), whereas Jesus is pictured in all three as the Davidic Messiah (1:32–33; 1:69; 2:4, 11; 3:23–38) and Son of God (1:35, 2:49; 3:22). The artistry and the internal coherence argue for the treatment of 1:5—4:15 as a single thought unit in the narrative.

The second strand is the literary genre. In Mediterranean antiquity there was, in biographical writing, a genre constituted by an account of the prepublic career of a great person: in this convention one found an account of the hero's career, before the public activity was begun, which included material on family background, perhaps a reference to

15

a miraculous conception, along with omens and other predictions of future greatness, including childhood prodigies. A representative example of this genre may be found in Suetonius' *Lives of the Twelve Caesars,* in his biography of Augustus.

In the "Life of Augustus" there is one section (94) set aside for "an account of the omens which occurred before he was born, on the very day of his birth, and afterwards." In this unit one finds fourteen omens: (a) portents interpreted by predictions (6 of 14 items) which belong in the same general category as 1:41–45; (b) dreams (3 of 14 items)—e.g., a man dreamed of the savior of the Roman people, then on meeting Augustus for the first time, declared he was the boy about whom he had dreamed (cf. 2:25–35); (c) prophecies (2 of 14 items)—verbal anticipations of the child's greatness and destiny (cf. the prophecies of Luke 1—3); (d) childhood prodigies (2 of 14 items), which claim such childhood exploits were regarded as omens of the youth's destiny (cf. 2:41–51; 4:1–13); (e) reference to a miraculous conception by Apollo (1 of 14 items), though the treatment of Augustus' family belongs to another section of the narrative about his prepublic life. The main thrust of the material in the genre of the prepublic life of a great person was on anticipations of the hero's destiny. It is certainly the case in this example from Suetonius.

In 1:5—4:15 one finds also that the thrust of the material is on anticipations of Jesus' destiny. These anticipations are given in various forms. (1) There are two angelophanies: (a) 1:26–38, the angel Gabriel comes to Mary not only to announce the miraculous conception but also to tell of the child's destiny; (b) 2:8–20, an angel appears to the shepherds in the field announcing the birth of one who will be a savior, Christ the Lord. (2) There are four prophecies: (a) 1:67–79 is a prophecy by Zechariah when he was filled with the Holy Spirit (vs. 67); (b) 2:25–35 gives the prophecy of Simeon, to whom it had been revealed that he should not taste death before he had seen the Lord's Christ (vs. 26); (c) 2:36–38 tells of the prophetess Anna, who spoke of Jesus "to all who were looking for the redemption of Jerusalem" (vs. 38); (d) 3:16–17 gives John the Baptist's messianic preaching, in which he prophecies the coming of the mightier one. (3) Closely related to the series of four prophecies is 1:41–45, which consists of a portent followed by a prophetic interpretation. (4) Luke 3:21–22 has similarities to 1:41–45. It too has a prophetic event followed by a verbal interpretation. The descent of the Holy Spirit in the form of a dove upon

Jesus would be regarded as a prophetic event by Mediterranean readers. The voice from heaven, the *bath qol*, was the interpretation of its prophetic meaning. (5) Both 2:41–51 and 4:1–13 display the young Jesus as a prodigy whose wisdom astounds the rabbis and defeats the devil. (6) The genealogy of 3:23–38 traces Jesus' lineage through David, through the father of the human race, Adam, to God. When a Greco-Roman reader confronted 1:5—4:15, it would be recognized as a conventional mode of expression, belonging to the genre of an account of the prepublic career of a great person. That it fits into a widely-used genre of biographical writing in Mediterranean antiquity is the second argument for its being taken as a coherent unit in the gospel.

If 1:5—4:15 belongs to this genre, how does it function in the gospel? The clue is the function of the genre in ancient biography. Suetonius' "Life of Augustus" again offers a representative statement when we are told,

> Having reached this point, it will not be out of place to add an account of the omens which occurred before he was born, on the very day of his birth, and afterwards, *from which it was possible to anticipate and perceive his future greatness and uninterrupted good fortune.* (94) (my italics.)

The genre functioned as a foreshadowing of the character of the public career of the biographical subject. If this was the purpose of the genre in the Greco-Roman biographies, this is how a reader/hearer of Luke would most probably have taken the material of a similar nature in 1:5—4:15. The first section of the gospel, then, should be read as anticipations/prophecies/foreshadowings of the future career of Jesus. This material would foretell/foreshadow the type of person Jesus would be in his public ministry, which in Luke's narrative begins at 4:16 (cf. C. H. Talbert, "Prophecies of Future Greatness: The Contribution of Greco-Roman Biographies to an Understanding of Luke 1:5—4:15," in *The Divine Helmsman*, ed. J. L. Crenshaw and Samuel Sandmel [New York: KTAV, 1980], pp. 129–41). Given this the reader should expect to find introduced in the section many themes that will be developed later in Luke-Acts.

JESUS, GOD'S ACT

1:26–38

L uke 1:26–38 is the first half of Episode One (1:5–38), which portrays the annunciations of the births of John the Baptist and Jesus. The two halves closely correspond to one another because the core of both is a theophanic birth announcement like those found in the OT.

In the Jewish scriptures there is a stereotyped pattern for theophanies. When the purpose is to announce a birth (e.g., Genesis 16; 17; Judges 13), the pattern is slightly altered to accommodate this objective. Components of the theophanic birth announcement pattern include: (1) God/the angel appears (Gen 16:7; 17:1; Judg 13:3)—cf. Luke 1:11, 26; (2) the immediate reaction of the person (Gen 17:3)—cf. Luke 1:12, 29; (3) the name of the person (Gen 16:8; 17:5)—cf. Luke 1:13, 28, 30; (4) reassurance (Gen 17:4ff.)—cf. Luke 1:13, 30 (note in Gen 15:1; 21:17; 26:24; 46:3; Judg 6:23, the reassurance is "Fear not."); (5) announcement of the birth (Gen 16:11; 17:16, 19; Judg 13:3)—cf. Luke 1:13, 31; (6) the name to be given (Gen 16:11; 17:19)—cf. Luke 1:13, 31; (7) a prediction of the child's future destiny (Gen 16:12; 17:19, 21; Judg 13:5)—cf. Luke 1:14–17, 32–33; (8) an objection (Gen 17:17–18)—cf. Luke 1:18, 34 (note Gen 15:8, "How am I to know?" and Judg 6:15, "How can I deliver Israel?"); (9) a sign or reassurance (Gen 17:21b; cf. also Gen 15:9, 17; Judg 6:17ff.)—cf. Luke 1:19–20, 35–36; (10) the response (Gen 16:13; cf. also 17:23; 26:25; 35:14; Judg 6:24)—cf. Luke 1:22–23, 38. Luke's two annunciations in 1:5–38 correspond to this stereotyped pattern (cf. G. F. Wood, "The Form and Composition of the Lucan Annunciation Narratives," STD thesis, Catholic Univ of Amer, 1962).

In such a form the emphasis is not on the parent(s), but on the child as the fulfillment of the divine promise. So in 1:26–38, where the birth of Jesus is announced in the typical OT pattern, the emphasis is not on Mary but on Jesus. The christological thrust of Episode One has two foci. The first focus is on Jesus' relation to John the Baptist. The

18

paralleling of the two annunciations conveys continuity between Jesus and John in salvation history. The attempt to establish continuity between Jesus/the church on the one hand and Israel on the other is a major concern of Luke-Acts. It is no surprise to find it foreshadowed here in the links between the annunciations of the births of Elizabeth's son and Mary's son. At the same time the evangelist wants to demonstrate the superiority of Jesus over John. Whereas John will go before the Lord "in the spirit and power of Elijah" (vs. 17), Jesus will "reign over the house of Jacob forever" as the Davidic king (vss. 32–33). Again, since this superiority of Jesus over John is a theme that recurs in the third gospel, it is no surprise to meet the anticipation of it here.

The second focus of Luke's christological concern in this section is on the unusual character of Jesus' conception. Verses 32–33 proclaim he will be the Davidic Messiah, explaining why vs. 31 specified his name would be Jesus ("Yahweh saves"). Verse 35 indicates how this will come to pass: he will be conceived of the Holy Spirit. It is because of his conception by the Holy Spirit that Jesus is Son of God (note the "therefore"). Since Son of God is used for Adam in 3:38, and for the risen Christ in Acts 13:33, this title in Luke-Acts may be employed for one who lives because of God's direct, creative intervention.

It is important to clarify what is not being said here. Luke does not address the issues that arose later in church history, such as (a) *virginitas in partu* (a miraculous birth of the child; i.e., giving birth with Mary's physical organs remaining intact), and (b) *virginitas post partum* (the perpetual virginity of Mary). With Matthew, Luke speaks only of Mary's *virginitas ante partum* (virginity before giving birth; i.e., she conceived Jesus without the involvement of a man): Jesus was miraculously conceived by the Holy Spirit (1:35). It is by virtue of this miraculous conception in the womb of the virgin Mary that Jesus is the Son of God.

The miraculous conception, or virgin birth as it is usually called, has functioned theologically in various ways in Christian history. Three examples illustrate this. (a) In the second century, Ignatius of Antioch confronts a docetic problem. Faced with a denial of Jesus' humanity, Ignatius places most of his emphasis on the birth of Jesus as a sign of his humanity (Eph 7:2; 18:2; Ign Trall 9:1; Ign Smyrn 1:1). The first witness after Matthew and Luke to the virgin birth, then, appeals to Jesus' birth of the virgin Mary as evidence of his real humanity. (b)

Augustine is the source from which a dominant interpretation of Jesus' virgin birth entered medieval Christianity. For Augustine, all people are sinful and need Christ's redemption. We have all inherited original sin which has been passed to us by means of sexual propagation. In order for Christ to be Savior from sin, he must be sinless. For him to be sinless he must not inherit Adam's sin as the rest of us have and do. For this to be so Jesus could not obtain his human nature by means of sexual procreation. Hence the conception by the Holy Spirit is the means by which Jesus avoided the taint of original sin and could be the sinless Savior of all. (c) Protestant Orthodoxy saw the indisputable proof of the truth of Christianity in the miracles of Jesus and in the fulfillment of biblical prophecy in Jesus' career. Understanding the virgin birth as a biological miracle and as the fulfillment of Isa 7:14, these Christians understood the virginal conception as the proof of Jesus' divinity and thereby of the truth of Christianity. Their watchword became, If you deny the virgin birth as a biological miracle, you deny the divinity of Christ (cf. Hans von Campenhausen, *The Virgin Birth in the Theology of the Ancient Church* [Naperville, Ill.: Allenson, 1964], and Thomas Boslooper, *The Virgin Birth* [Philadelphia: Westminster Press, 1962]). Given the various ways the miraculous conception has functioned theologically in Christian history, how does it function for Luke?

To discern the function of the miraculous conception in Lukan thought, it is necessary to note two things. In the first place, the function of the genre of the prepublic career of a famous person to which 1:5—4:15 belongs (see the Introduction to Luke 1:5—4:15) was to answer the question, how are we to explain the hero's later life? In the gospel, as in other Greco-Roman biographies, a miraculous conception story functioned to explain the hero's later greatness: Jesus was what he was because he was divinely begotten.

In the second place, one must be aware of the christology employed by Luke-Acts. Even before Paul three different christologies circulated in the early churches: two-foci, exaltation, and epiphany (cf. R. H. Fuller, *The Foundations of New Testament Christology* [New York: Scribner's, 1965]). Whereas the Gospel of John tells the story of Jesus in terms of an epiphany, Luke-Acts employs an exaltation christology: Jesus in his earthly life is the descendent of David and heir to the promises of the Jewish scriptures. By virtue of his resurrection he is raised to the exalted status of God's Son with power. In the present he rules from heaven as Lord over all, intervening on behalf of his people to deliver and protect them. A diagram would look like this:

Son of God with power

Resurrection

Son of David

Exaltation christology functioned to express the church's experience of Jesus Christ in a twofold way: as the present Lord who rules from heaven, and as the historical figure whose story is normative for us. How is it that Christ can function in these two ways? In this schema the explanation for Christ's present reign from heaven is his resurrection from the dead; the explanation for his unique earthly life is his miraculous conception. Christology and genre agree. Jesus' earthly life was what it was because of his miraculous birth.

It was theologically important to begin with the virgin birth because exaltation christology was subject to perversion by those of a legalistic bent. "He was obedient unto death; wherefore God highly exalted him," could easily be understood to say it was Jesus' merit that caused his exaltation. "The Spirit of the Lord is upon me to preach and heal," could be interpreted to mean that because Jesus was more righteous, more prudent, and more wise than anyone else, he was anointed with the Holy Spirit at baptism to carry on God's work. If Jesus' earthly life could be understood in terms of merit, however, then so could the lives of his followers. The result would be the very type of problem Paul opposed in Galatia. In an exaltation schema, then, it was theologically important to begin with a miraculous conception. In that way any interpretation of the earthly life of Jesus and of his followers in terms of merit would be excluded. The greatness of Jesus' life was not a human achievement, but the result of divine intervention. Jesus' career was not the result of the perfection of human striving and effort; only God could produce a life like his. Jesus was God's act. As Luther put it, "Just as God in the beginning of creation made the world out of nothing, so His manner of working continues unchanged" (*Luther's Works,* ed. J. Pelikan [St. Louis: Concordia, 1956], 21:299). If we are to view the miraculous conception of Jesus as Luke viewed it, we must see it as an affirmation of God's grace that excludes all human merit.

MARY, IDEAL BELIEVER AND
SOCIAL PARADIGM

1:39–56

L uke 1:39–56 is a transition between Episode One, the annunciations of John and Jesus (1:5–38), and Episode Two, the births
and early lives of the Baptist and Mary's son (1:57—2:52), and consists
of two hymns (vss. 42–45; vss. 46–55) joined by a narrative introduction (vss. 39–41) and conclusion (vs. 56). The first hymn, that of Elizabeth (vss. 42–45), eulogizes Mary as an ideal believer; the second,
Mary's (vss. 46–55), clarifies the links between what God has done for
one individual and what he will do for the structures of society at large.

Elizabeth's hymn has a narrative introduction, vss. 39–41, which
sets the stage for what follows. When Mary visits Elizabeth, Elizabeth's babe leaps in her womb. Here, as in Gen 25: 21–23, the story
of Rebecca's children, the idea is that the movement of the unborn
babe foreshadows his future lot and that of Jesus. The hymn itself
(vss. 41b–45) offers twofold congratulations to Mary ("Blessed are you,"
vs. 42; "Blessed is she," vs. 45). Each expression of congratulations is
followed by the grounds for Mary's being blessed. First, Mary is to be
congratulated because her child will be the Lord (vs. 43), as evidenced
by the unborn babe's leaping for joy in Elizabeth's womb (vs. 44).
Even in the womb John recognizes the messianic Lord. This prenatal
cognition attests the fulfillment of Gabriel's prophecy to Mary in 1:31–
33, 35. Second, Mary is to be congratulated because of her response
to God's word (vs. 45): "Blessed (*makaria*) is she who believed that
there would be a fulfillment of what was spoken to her from the Lord"
(1:45). Mary hears and believes God's word. Here Luke foreshadows
in capsule form his distinctive understanding of Mary which runs
throughout his narrative: Mary is the model disciple.

(1) In 1:38 Mary is depicted as a believer for whom God's word is
enough: "Behold, I am the handmaid of the Lord; let it be to me according to your word." Augustine caught the Lukan intent when he

22

said that Mary, full of faith, conceived Christ first in her heart before conceiving him in her womb (*Sermon* 215:4). Her belief led to an absolute self-surrender to the divine purpose.

(2) Luke 8:19–21, the climax of a unit beginning at 8:1, carries on the same theme. The distinctive Lukan point of view can best be seen when 8:1–21 is compared with its Markan counterpart, Mark 3:19b–35, a unit which begins (vs. 21) and ends (vss. 31–35) with references to Jesus' family. Very likely vs. 21 and vss. 31–35 originally belonged together. In their Markan context they function to indicate that Jesus' family, no less than the scribes who came down from Jerusalem (3:22), do not understand or believe. Consequently, 3:31–35 speaks negatively of Jesus' human family, distinguishing them from his true, eschatological family. This true family is composed of those who do the will of God, which by implication Jesus' natural family does not do. In Luke, however, Jesus' mother and brothers are not outsiders (8:19; Mark 3:31); the controversy context is abandoned by Luke, the parable of the sower (Mark 4:3–8) is moved to the beginning of the unit (8:4–8), and its interpretation (8:11–15) ends with the comment about the good soil being "those who, hearing the word, hold it fast in an honest and good heart, and bring forth fruit with patience" (vs. 15), and 8:21 becomes a commendation of Jesus' natural family for meeting the criterion for inclusion in the eschatological family of God—"My mother and brothers are those who hear the word of God and do it." Mary, in the third gospel, belongs to the good soil, as do Jesus' brothers. (Contrast John 7:1–9 which indicates that Jesus' brothers did not believe in him prior to Easter.)

(3) In 11:27–28, and only in Luke, the physical fact of Mary's motherhood is said to give no special status in Jesus' eyes. Rather than deserving congratulations because her womb bore Jesus and her breasts nourished him, Mary's status is due to her proper response to God's word.

(4) Acts 1:14 shows continuity between the pre- and post-Easter community of Jesus' disciples. Mary's presence indicates her place in the primitive church at the time of Pentecost. The evangelist has thereby portrayed Mary as a "disciple" from the time of Jesus' conception to Pentecost.

(5) The positive picture of Mary and Jesus' natural family in the narrative helps to explain 4:24. Whereas Mark 6:4 has Jesus say about his rejection in Nazareth, "A prophet is not without honor, except in

his own country, and *among his own kin,* and *in his own house,"* 4:24's version simply says, "Truly, I say to you, no prophet is acceptable in his own country." Any note of rejection on the part of Jesus' family is removed; Mary especially stands as a true believer (R. E. Brown et al, *Mary in the New Testament* [Philadelphia: Fortress Press, 1978], and P. J. Bearsley, "Mary the Perfect Disciple: A Paradigm for Mariology," *Theological Studies* 41:461–504 [1980]).

Regarding Mary's significance for the church, the evangelist portrays her as the prototype of the Christian believer: she hears God's word, holds it fast in an honest and good heart (2:19; 2:51), and brings forth fruit with patience. Here foreshadowed in the virgin mother is the Lukan understanding of what it means to be a disciple of Jesus; she hears God's word, believes it, and surrenders herself totally to it: "Let it be to me according to your word" (1:38). If we are to view Mary as Luke did, then we must see her as a model for disciples. This Marian model holds not self-knowledge or insight but self-surrender or abandonment to God's will to be the essence of discipleship.

Verses 46–55 are a hymn of Mary, as the overwhelming weight of textual evidence and the structure of the section demand, and not of Elizabeth, as a few old Latin witnesses claim. The hymn contains two stanzas which praise God for his mercy: vss. 46–50 and vss. 51–55. Verses 49–50 and vss. 54–55 both refer to God's mercy and signal the end of their respective stanzas.

Stanza one of Mary's song speaks of God's mighty act for one woman only: the emphasis is on the gracious initiative of God. The virgin sings of nothing except her low estate (vs. 46) and the grace of God which was upon her far above any merit of hers (vss. 49–50). If Elizabeth's hymn focuses on Mary as a model of faith (vs. 45), Mary's own song of praise focuses its first stanza on God's grace for her, a grace to which she responded in faith.

Stanza two of the Magnificat expands the horizon to speak of God's social revolution through eschatological reversal. In both stanzas God's surprising concern for the lowly is revealed. God's regard for one humble woman becomes the sign of his eschatological act for the world. In the one small event the greater event lies hidden (R. C. Tannehill, "The Magnificat as Poem," *Journal of Biblical Literature* 93:263–75 [1974]). In Luke's understanding God's social revolution, like the conception of Jesus, is not the perfection of the human by human striving but the result of the divine breaking into history. The reference is eschatological and refers to the Last Day.

The third evangelist here foreshadows his views about the relation between Christ and human culture. On the one hand, it is certainly not Luke's view that there is an identity between God's will for human life and cultural realities. Stanza two of Mary's song proclaims God will ultimately overturn the values and structures of this world's culture. For this evangelist Christ cannot be identified with culture. On the other hand, Luke is no advocate of social action to transform culture, in the sense that we know such action today. Jesus did not go to the top (to Caesar or Pilate) to get things changed; nor did he go to the left (to the Zealots). He went instead to the poor and sinners, offering forgiveness and deliverance, and calling them into a community whose life was to embody God's will. Only God, from Luke's perspective, is able to achieve a just society in the Last Day. In the meantime the evangelist presents Jesus and his church not as having a social ethic for society at large but as trying to have one in their own life together. In the Lukan mind the first duty of the church is to be the church, to be a community which, through the way its members deal with one another, demonstrates to the world what social relations directed by God are. So understood, Jesus and the disciples fulfill their social responsibility not by being one more power block among others but by being an example, a creative minority, a witness to God's mercy. "The church therefore does not fulfill her social responsibility by attacking directly the social structures of society, but by being itself it indirectly has a tremendous significance for the ethical form of society." This statement by a contemporary Christian ethicist accurately reflects the Lukan view (Stanley Hauerwas, "The Nonresistant Church: The Theological Ethics of John Howard Yoder," in *Vision and Virtue* [Notre Dame: Fides Publishers, 1974], p. 212). In Luke-Acts Jesus and his church do not attempt to change society at large by attacking it directly by whatever means—violent or nonviolent—but by subverting its values as they live communally out of God's will before the world (S. Hauerwas, "The Politics of Charity," *Interpretation* 31:262 [1977]). The ultimate transformation of society's structures generally awaits the kingdom of God at the eschaton.

Mary's song reflects her confidence in this ultimate victory of God and the reversal of human values. Following prophetic precedent vss.

51–55 use verbs in a past tense to describe future acts of God. That God has acted for Mary in the present gives such an assurance he will act in the future for the world, this ultimate intervention can be spoken of as though it were already accomplished. This is similar to Rom 8:28–30 where Paul speaks not only of predestination and justification as past but also of the Christians' glorification, a future event, because he is so certain of its reality. To read the Magnificat in terms of Lukan thought, therefore, is to see an individual's (i.e., Mary's) experience of God's grace as prototypical of the way God will ultimately deal with the world at large.

For Luke it is the same God who acts redemptively for an individual and for society at large. It is the same God who acted in the past, who acts in the present, and who will act in the future. If it is the same God, then his acting partakes of the same character: gracious intervention to create anew.

JOHN, PROTOTYPE OF
THE CHRISTIAN EVANGELIST

1:14–17, 57–80; 3:1–20; 7:24–35

The first three passages are from the three episodes of 1:5—4:15; the fourth is from the Galilean ministry (4:16—9:50). Luke 1:14–17 is the prediction about John's future role made by the angel in the context of his birth annunciation in Episode One (1:5–38). Luke 1:57–80 is part of Episode Two (1:57—2:52) and deals with the birth and early life of John the Baptist. It corresponds very closely with the account of Jesus' birth and early life in 2:1–52. The core of 1:57–80 is the Benedictus (1:67–79), the prophecy of Zechariah about John's future role. Luke 3:1–20 also focuses on the Baptist: his person (vss. 1–6), his mission (vss. 7–17), and a summary of the end of his career (vss. 18–20). Luke 7:24–35 gives Jesus' words concerning John in the context of the Galilean ministry. If the first two passages present prophecies about John's future role, the last two offer examples of the fulfillment of those prophecies in John's career and Jesus' assessment of it. Taken together these four units give the Lukan understanding of John the Baptist.

The distinctiveness of this picture of the Baptist can best be seen in the context of the understanding of John in the Gospel of Mark and in the fourth gospel. In Mark John the Baptist is viewed as Elijah who is to come first to restore all things. This can be seen in 1:6 where the Baptist's attire is similar to that of the prophet Elijah (2 Kgs 1:8), and in 9:11–13 where the identification with Elijah is explicitly made. Mark 9:13 also states that John, Elijah *redivivus*, suffered and was martyred, a reference to 6:14–29 (cf. Pseudo-Philo, *Biblical Antiquities* 48:1; Rev 11:4–13, which may enshrine a Jewish tradition). In this way John's fate anticipates that of Jesus. In the fourth gospel, John the Baptist explicitly denies he is the Christ (1:20), or Elijah (1:21), or the prophet (1:21). Nor is he the forerunner, for the Word was before John (1:15, 30). Rather the Baptist is portrayed as a witness (1:7,

27

8, 32, 34), the voice of Isa 40:3 which cried, "Make straight the way of the Lord" (1:23). How is the Baptist portrayed in the third gospel?

Luke 1:14–17, the angel's prophecy to Zechariah, clarifies several things about John. (1) He will be a prophetic figure "filled with the Holy Spirit, even from his mother's womb," who will work in "the spirit and power of Elijah." (2) He will go before the Lord. (3) He will "make ready for the Lord a people prepared."

A hymn attributed to the Spirit-filled Zechariah (1:68–79; esp. vs. 67), makes essentially the same prediction about John in its second stanza. The Benedictus falls into two parts: vss. 68–75, 76–79. Part one is a blessing of God (cf. 2 Cor 1:3–4; Eph 1:3–14). The reasons God is praised are two. First, he has been faithful to his promise to David (cf. 2 Sam 7:11b–16) by raising up a Davidic king (vss. 68b–70; cf. 1:32–33; 2:4). The result of this is Israel's salvation from her enemies (vs. 71). Second, God has also been faithful to his promise to Abraham (Gen 12:1–2, 15; cf. Luke 1:55; Romans 4). This will allow God's people to serve him all of their days without fear (vss. 72–75). In vss. 68–75, then, Jesus is understood as the fulfillment both of God's promise to Abraham and of his promise to David. It is this faithfulness of God to his word that elicits Zechariah's praise (cf. 2 Cor 1:18–20). Part two is a prediction concerning John the Baptist's future work. (1) He will "be called the prophet of the Most High." (2) He will "go before the Lord." (3) He will prepare the way of the Lord (cf. Mal 3:1; 4:5–6). Zechariah's prophecy agrees in its content with that of the angel of the Lord (1:16–17). These prophecies have their fulfillment in the narrative at 3:1–6; 7:26–27.

Luke 3:1–6 begins with an involved system of dating, followed by the statement, "the word of the Lord came to John the son of Zechariah in the wilderness." The style echoes the introductions to the OT prophets (cf. Jeremiah 1). This is followed by an extended quotation from Isa 40:3–5 in 3:4–6. This quotation designates John as the "voice of one crying in the wilderness" which was to precede God's great eschatological deliverance. Thereby Luke is saying that John is a prophet, but not just a prophet: he is the eschatological voice in the wilderness who prepares the way of the Lord (1:76b; 3:4b). Likewise, in 7:26–27, Jesus says the Baptist is a prophet and more: he is the one who will prepare the way.

Taken together what picture of the Baptist do these passages give? John the Baptist is portrayed as the forerunner of the Messiah, who goes in the spirit and power of Elijah, who is the epitome of the Spirit-filled prophet, mighty in word and deed. The Baptist is not Elijah—hence the description of his garments is omitted at Luke 3:16 because of their association with Elijah—but is merely endowed with the same Spirit and power as Elijah (1:17). John is a prophetic figure (1:76a; 3:1–2, 7:26), the forerunner of the Lord (1:17; 1:76b; 3:4; 7:27), who preaches repentance and forgiveness as a prelude to the coming salvation (1:77; 3:3, 6).

It has been suggested by Walter Wink (*John the Baptist in the Gospel Tradition* [Cambridge: Cambridge University Press, 1968], pp. 113–14) that John the Baptist was used typologically by the church to set forth its conception of its own role in "preparing the way of the Lord." For example, John's suffering as Elijah-incognito in Mark serves as an example to the persecuted Christians in Rome (p. 17); the Baptist in the fourth gospel is "made the normative image of the Christian preacher, apostle and missionary, the perfect prototype of the true evangelist, whose one goal is self-effacement before Christ" (p. 105). In this light it is interesting to note that the Lukan picture of John as a prophetic figure who goes before the Lord preaching repentance and forgiveness as a prelude to the coming salvation looks very much like the picture of Peter and John in Acts 3, especially vss. 19ff.

One way Luke views Christian existence is in prophetic terms. The OT prophets were those on whom the Spirit came, giving them a knowledge both of the secrets of human hearts and of the divine council's decrees. Thus empowered they spoke for God to prepare his people for the Day of the Lord. These prophets provided one category for the evangelist to use in conceptualizing the Christian experience between Pentecost and parousia. Christians were people on whom the Spirit had come. Consequently they prophesied (Acts 2:16–18). Their prophetic word sought the repentance of the people before the Lord's coming (Acts 2:38–39; 3:19–26). The Christian community, then, in Luke's view, is a prophetic community. By its very existence it prepares the way of the Lord by going before him to call people to repentance. If Mary is portrayed as a true believer, John the Baptist is drawn in terms of the true Christian evangelist: in 3:18 John is said to preach the good news to the people.

If John is portrayed as the prototype of the Spirit-filled Christian evangelist, what does he preach and for what does he hope? This model for Christian witnesses preaches Jesus and an ethical life-style. Luke

3:15–17 says the Baptist preached Jesus as the one who would baptize with the Holy Spirit and fire (cf. Acts 2:1ff.); 3:7–9 points to the necessity of bearing fruit (cf. 6:43–45; 13:6–9; 20:9–18). The meaning of this is clarified in 3:10–14: it means the refusal to hoard or to acquire more possessions than are necessary (cf. 12:13–21; 16:19–31). He witnesses so that "all flesh shall see the salvation of God" (3:6). The similarities between John's good news (3:18) and the message both of Jesus and the later church are clear. In his message as well as in the goal and source of his strength, John the Baptist in Luke-Acts functions as the prototype of the Christian evangelist.

GOOD NEWS OF A GREAT JOY

2:1–20

Luke 2:1–20 is a large unit within 2:1–52, the half of Episode Two (1:57—2:52) dealing with Jesus' birth and early life. It is composed of two parts: (a) 2:1–7 is a narrative about Jesus' birth, and (b) 2:8–20 falls into the same annunciation pattern we have encountered in 1:5–25 and 1:26–38. The two parts are joined by certain formal links. On the one hand, there is the recurrence of "the city of David" (2:4, 11) and "swaddling clothes . . . in a manger" (2:7, 12). On the other hand, each participates in a prophecy-fulfillment schema. Luke 2:1–7 speaks of the geographical site of Jesus' birth (the city of David, Bethlehem) and the family from which Jesus came (Joseph was of the house and lineage of David). Both facts are allusions to prophecy; though it is not made explicit by the evangelist, most likely to Mic 5:2:

> But you, O Bethlehem Ephrathah,
> Who are little to be among the clans of Judah,
> From you shall come forth for me
> One who is to be ruler in Israel.

Being born of the lineage of David in the city of David means Jesus is Christ the Lord (2:11). This, of course, fulfills the angelic prophecy made to Mary in 1:32–33: "the Lord God will give to him the throne of his father David." Luke 2:8–20 also is built around a prophecy-fulfillment schema. When the angel appears to the shepherds to announce the birth of a Savior, a sign is given: "You will find a babe wrapped in swaddling cloths and lying in a manger" (vs. 12). This prediction is fulfilled when the shepherds go to Bethlehem and find it as the angel had said (vss. 16, 7). Taken together, 2:1–7 and 2:8–20 function to acclaim the birth of the Davidic Messiah: a Savior, who is Christ the Lord (vs. 11). This, says the angelic messenger, is "good news of a great joy" (vs. 10).

What is good news about Jesus' birth? Why should it be regarded as a great joy? Two items of background information serve as a bridge to our answers. (1) In the Mediterranean world the birthday of a ruler was sometimes celebrated with a proclamation of the benefits of his birth. An inscription found at Priene, celebrating the birthday of Augustus in 9 B.C., reads in part,

> Providence . . . has brought into the world Augustus and filled him with a hero's soul for the benefit of mankind. A Savior for us and our descendents, he will make wars to cease and order all things well. The epiphany of Caesar has brought to fulfillment past hopes and dreams. (F. Danker, *Jesus and the New Age,* p. 24)

Here Augustus fulfills ancient hopes and brings peace. These benefits are proclaimed on his birthday. (2) In biblical literature heavenly choirs sometimes celebrate future events as though they were already fact (e.g., Rev 5:9–10; 11:17–18; 18:2–3; 19:1–2, 6–8); their song proclaims the benefits that are to ensue: 2:13–14 employs such a heavenly choir. A multitude of heavenly host sing,

> Glory to God in the highest,
> and on earth peace among men with whom he is pleased.
> (vs. 14)

The one who has fulfilled the ancient hopes expressed in the prophecies of scripture is acclaimed as one whose birth will bring glory to God and peace to people on earth. Like Augustus Jesus has on his birthday a proclamation of the benefits of his birth.

Is the peace that Jesus' birth is said to bring the same as that claimed for Augustus? In the Jewish culture from which Christianity came, peace (*shalom* in Hebrew; *eirēnē* in Greek) meant basically wholeness, the normal state of life which corresponds to the will of God. Such wholeness would characterize the basic relations of life: (a) the relation of persons and God, (b) the relation of persons with one another, (c) the relation of persons with the natural world, and (d) one's relation with oneself. This wholeness meant well-being in contrast to evil in any form. It was the gift of God. Given human sin, however, this wholeness was lost. Peace, then, became an eschatological hope (Zech 9:9–10) and the messianic figure the prince of peace (Isa 9:6).

In the NT peace reflects these Jewish roots. It refers, therefore, both to the normal state of life in line with God's will and to the eschatological salvation. As such it involves wholeness in the relation with God (e.g., Rom 5:1; Col 1:20; Eph 2:14, 17), wholeness in the relation of people with one another (e.g., Mark 9:50; 1 Cor 7:15; Eph 2:14–17; 4:3), wholeness in the relation to the physical world (e.g., Mark 5:34), and wholeness in one's relation with oneself (Rom 8:6; 15:13; Gal 5:22; Phil 4:7; Col 3:15; John 14:27).

Luke-Acts, with one exception, reflects this context. The messianic salvation is described as the way of peace (1:79). Jesus Christ is said to have preached the good news of peace (Acts 10:36). This peace associated with God's acts in Jesus involves recovered wholeness in the relation of a person with God (e.g., Luke 7:50), wholeness in the relation with the physical world (8:48), and wholeness in the relations among persons (e.g., Acts 9:31). The absence of any reference to peace with oneself is not surprising in Luke-Acts both because of the evangelist's focus on the visible and external realities of life, and because the scriptures on which Luke is so dependent have little concern with peace as an inward feeling. For Jesus' birth to be connected with the recovery of peace, therefore, was a matter of great joy, meaning the restoration of wholeness to life in every area: with God, with others, with the physical world. It is this peace about which the heavenly choir sings at 2:14.

For whom is this peace promised? Verse 14 says it is for either "men of good will" or "men of favor" (*anthrōpois eudokias*). The latter translation, which has the better support, means persons upon whom divine favor rests. The gospel mentions two occasions when recipients of divine favor are specified. In the first instance Jesus, after his baptism, is addressed as "my beloved Son, in [whom] I *take delight (eudokēsa)*: Jesus is the object of divine favor. In the second, 12:32, Jesus says to his disciples, "Fear not, little flock, for it is your Father's *good pleasure (eudokēsen)* to give you the kingdom": here Jesus' disciples are the objects of divine favor. Hence, it is among Jesus and his disciples that there is peace among humans. Here is where the wholeness of the basic relations of life is being recovered as a result of Jesus' birth and lordship. This is cause for joy.

This good news, moreover, is for "all the people" (vs. 10), outcast as well as in-group. In Luke's time shepherds were often considered outside the law. Their testimony was considered invalid because of their reputation for dishonesty (b. *Sanhedrin* 25b). Yet it was to such as these the angel announced the good news of the Savior's birth (2:8–11). This can only be regarded as a foreshadowing of the subsequent theme of God's grace shown to sinners which runs throughout Luke.

The messianic Lord is the friend of sinners (e.g., 5:29–32; 7:36–50; 10:30–37; 15:1–2; 17:11–19; 19:1–10). It is to sinners Jesus promises good news (e.g., 18:9–14; 15:11–32). The news that Jesus' birth signals the benefit of peace is intended for all the people. This is cause for great joy.

The angelic choir not only sang about the recovery of wholeness among the disciples of Jesus, a benefit available to all, it also spoke of glory to God being a benefit of Jesus' birth and rule as Lord. Psalm 85: 8–9, just as Luke 2:14, connects God's being glorified with peace among his people. How is this to be understood? Since peace is God's gift, it reflects to God's credit that wholeness is being recovered among human beings. The recovery of wholeness in human relationships, which is due to God's acts in Jesus, reflects honor to God. In other words what is good for human beings glorifies God; what glorifies God is good for human beings. Glorifying God and recovering human wholeness are not mutually exclusive: they are an indissoluble whole. When the angels sang of the benefits of Jesus' lordship, they sang both "glory to God" and "peace to men"—one song, heralding a dual benefit of Messiah's birth. That is good news of a great joy.

THE UNREDEEMED FIRSTBORN

2:21–52

Luke 2:21–52 is the second large unit in 2:1–52, the half of Episode Two (1:57—2:52) focusing on Jesus' birth and early life. The events of vss. 21–52 are joined by the theme of obedience to the Jewish law and certain pious customs of the Jews. (1) Luke 2:21 describes Jesus' circumcision on the eighth day in obedience to Lev 12:3. (2) Luke 2:22–24 telescopes at least two traditional Jewish practices prescribed by the law. Verses 22a, 24 reflect the practice of the purification of the mother after childbirth, following the directives of Lev 12:6, 8. That Jesus' mother offered birds for her purification indicates she was poor (cf. Lev 12:8): Jesus came from the poor. Verses 22b, 23, however, echo Exod 13:2, 12, 13, 15 where it is said the firstborn belongs to God and must be redeemed (cf. Mishna, *Bekhoroth*, 8). The actions of Jesus' parents at this point are "according to the custom of the law" (2:27): "And when they had performed everything according to the law of the Lord, they returned to Galilee" (2:39). (3) Luke 2:41 says Jesus' parents went to Jerusalem every year at the feast of the Passover. This was doubtless in obedience to Exod 23:14–17; 34:23; Deut 16:16, which specified that every male was to go to Jerusalem at Passover, Pentecost, and Tabernacles each year. Though the law said nothing about women, some apparently made the pilgrimage in biblical times (1 Sam 1:7; 2:19) and Hillel prescribed that they also should go to Passover. (4) Luke 2:42 indicates that Jesus' trip to Jerusalem was according to custom. This was probably in preparation for his entrance into religious responsibility which, according to *Pirke Aboth* 5:21, came at age thirteen. (5) Luke 2:51 says Jesus "went down with them and came to Nazareth, and was obedient to them." The boy Jesus fulfilled the commandment to honor one's father and mother (Exod 20:12; Deut 5:16). In 2:21–52 the evangelist depicts both Jesus' parents and the young Jesus as obedient to the prescriptions of the law: this thread ties the section together.

The thread of obedience to the law is also theologically important in

35

2:21–52. Jesus, who as a boy was obedient to the law, came from a family for whom obedience was an unargued assumption of life. In this Jesus' family fulfilled the Jewish ideal which believed the family's functions to include propagating the race, satisfying emotional needs in beneficent ways, and perpetuating religious experience. The third function was stated in a proverb: "Train up a child in the way he should go, and when he is old he will not depart from it" (Prov 22:6). It was in a family whose unargued assumption was obedience to the law that Jesus at twelve personally decided to take on himself the yoke of the kingdom of heaven (vs. 42). His subsequent obedience to his parents (vs. 51) came from a desire consciously committed to do God's will (Eph 6:2–3).

As part of the general context of the obedience by the family of Jesus to the law, we note that the model disciple, Mary, dedicates her child to God. Luke 2:22–24 falls into an AB:B'A' pattern: vss. 22a and 24 (cf. Lev 12:8), which deal with the purification of the mother after childbirth, being A and A'; vss. 22b and 23, which deal with the redemption of the firstborn, being B and B'. The prescription of Exod 13:2 concerning the first-born son was literally fulfilled in the case of Jesus, the firstborn (Luke 2:7), who was not ransomed (Exod 13:13; Num 3:47; 18:16). Contrary to normal custom, Jesus was dedicated to God and remained his property (Bo Reicke, "Jesus, Simeon, and Anna [Luke 2:21–40]," in *Saved By Hope,* ed. J. I. Cook [Grand Rapids: Eerdmans, 1978], pp. 96–108, esp. p. 100). The closest parallel to this emphasis is found in 1 Samuel 1—2, where Hannah gives Samuel, at his birth, to the Lord for as long as the child lives. Consequently, Samuel lives in the presence of Eli at the tent of meeting. If Jesus, in a similar manner, was dedicated to God and not redeemed, he belonged to God permanently. This would explain the reason Jesus would not understand why his parents did not know where to find him in Jerusalem (2:48–49): since he was God's he could be expected to be in his Father's house, as in the case of Samuel. At the plot level of the narrative, the boy Jesus had made a personal identification with the decisions his parents had made about him at his birth. In 2:21–52 family influence and personal decision combined to make the young Jesus what he was.

Luke's twelve-year-old Jesus was not only obedient to God's will, he was also possessed of spiritual discernment beyond what was normal. The story in 2:41–51 about Jesus in the temple depicts the lad as God's

Son (vs. 49) who is characterized by unusual wisdom in understanding the law. The story is enclosed within an inclusion that speaks about Jesus' wisdom (2:40 and 2:52), the centerpiece of its concentric surface structure (Henk J. de Jonge, "Sonship, Wisdom, Infancy: Luke 2:41–51a," *New Testament Studies* 24:317–54 [1978]).

A Mary, Joseph, and Jesus go to Jerusalem (41–42)
  B Jesus stays in Jerusalem, which is not noticed (43)
    C His parents seek and find him (44–46a)
      D *Jesus among the teachers* (46b–47)
    C' His parents, annoyed, reproach him (48)
  B' Jesus' reaction, which is not understood (49–50)
A' Mary, Joseph, and Jesus return to Nazareth (51a)

The centerpiece and the frame agree: Jesus is the wise one. The story portrays Jesus as God's Son who is the wise interpreter of scripture. This is a motif found elsewhere in the narrative of Luke-Acts (e.g., Luke 4:1–13; 4:16–21; 7:26–27; 10:25–28; 20:17–18; 20:37–38; 20:41–44; 24:25–27, 32; 24:44–47). Especially important is Luke 24 where the evangelist depicts the risen Christ as the one who interprets scripture for the disciples and opens their minds to understand its meaning.

Luke's portrayal of the youthful Jesus as a person of unusual discernment, within a section that emphasizes the obedience of both Jesus' family and the lad, is theologically significant. Religious understanding, insight into God's will, develops in the context of religious submission and obedience. The Johannine Jesus says, "If any man's will is to do his will, he shall know whether the teaching is from God or whether I am speaking on my own authority" (John 7:17). This statement can be expanded into a general rule of thumb: the discernment of spiritual truth—God's will—comes only after a willingness to do it, if and when it is known. In the realm of spiritual insight—including an understanding of the religious significance of scripture—one does not know God's will and then decide whether to do it. Rather one wills to be obedient to God's will first and then, and only then, does one discern what it is. Jesus, who as a youth was a precocious interpreter of scripture (God's will), was such only within the context of a conscious acceptance of the yoke of the kingdom of heaven and a personal identification with his parents' dedication of him to God as a baby: discernment followed commitment.

The way the evangelist has spoken about Jesus as a youth is only possible for one who assumes the real humanity of Jesus. (1) "And the child grew and became strong" (vs. 40a); "Jesus increased in stature" (vs 52—cf. 19:3, where the term is used of Zacchaeus who is small of stature). This is the way one talks about someone who has a human body; Heb 2:14 puts it this way: "Since therefore the children share in flesh and blood, he himself likewise partook of the same nature." In Christian history the tendency to deny the truly human body of Jesus has been called Gnosticism. (2) "And Jesus increased [made progress] in wisdom" (vs. 52). This is the way one talks about someone who has a truly human mind. Hebrews implies the same thing: "Therefore he had to be made like his brethren in every respect" (2:17); "one who in every respect has been tempted as we are, yet without sinning" (4:15). Since there is no way Jesus could have been tempted as we are unless he had limited knowledge within the confines of a human mind, as we do, Hebrews joins Luke in affirming Jesus' humanity in the mental sphere. In Christian history the tendency to deny the truly human mind of Jesus has been called Apollinarianism, after Apollinaris, bishop of Laodicea (c. A.D. 390), who held that Jesus had the body and soul of a man but that the reasoning mind in him was the eternal Logos. (3) "Jesus increased in favor with God and man" (vs. 52). This is the type of language one uses for someone who develops both religiously and socially. Hebrews speaks of the same reality: he was made "perfect through suffering" (2:10); "Although he was a Son, he learned obedience through what he suffered" (5:8). This, moreover, is something Jesus shared with Samuel: 1 Sam 2:26 reads, "Now the boy Samuel continued to grow both in stature and in favor with the Lord and with men." It was Marcion in church history who said Christ appeared in Palestine a full-grown man. For Luke Jesus grew and developed: in body, in mind, religiously, and socially: Jesus is truly human. Only thereby can he be the pioneer of salvation, a legitimate model of Christian existence.

SPIRITUAL POWER
FROM ANSWERED PRAYER

Luke 3:21-22, 15-17

L uke 3:21-22, 15-17 comes in the subsection 3:1—4:15, Episode Three in 1:5—4:15: vss. 21-22 are usually referred to as the baptism of Jesus by John; vss. 15-17 give a sample of the Baptist's preaching about the Coming One.

The distinctive Lukan perspective in vss. 21-22 can be seen more clearly if set in the context of the understanding of Jesus' baptism in the other gospels. (1) Matt 3:13-17 contains two verses (14-15) found nowhere else in the canonical tradition and which determine the first evangelist's major emphasis. It appears the evangelist is defending Jesus against the charge that he was a sinner, as evidenced by his submission to John's baptism of repentance for the remission of sins (cf. Matt 3:2, 6, 8). In this Matthew would be struggling with the same type of problem reflected in the Gospel according to the Hebrews (in Jerome, *Against Pelagius*, 3:2):

> The mother of the Lord and his brothers said to him, "John the Baptist baptizes for the forgiveness of sins; let us go and be baptized by him." But he said to them, "In what have I sinned that I should go and be baptized by him? Unless, perhaps, what I have just said is a sin of ignorance."

There is none of this in the Lukan account. (2) According to John 1:31-34 the descent of the Spirit on Jesus—presumably at his baptism—functioned to let the Baptist know Jesus' identity so John could reveal him to Israel. Again there is nothing like this in the third gospel. (3) Mark sees Jesus' baptism with the accompanying descent of the Holy Spirit as an empowering of the Son of God for his battle with Satan and the demonic powers (cf. Mark 3:22-27). The Lukan perspective is closer to Mark 1:9-11 than to either Matthew or John. But although both Luke and Mark see the Spirit's descent in terms of empowering, their perspectives are by no means identical. Luke sees Jesus' ministry in terms of the role of the Servant of the Lord in Deutero-Isaiah (cf. 4:16–21), and separates the empowering from the event of baptism while connecting it explicitly with prayer. The details of the Lukan perspective must now be examined.

Luke 3:21–22, which mentions Jesus' baptism only as a backdrop, is a prayer-scene consisting of a vision and an interpretative audition. The evangelist has turned a narrative about Jesus' baptism into an episode of prayer. Luke places great emphasis on the prayer life of Jesus (e.g., 3:21; 5:16; 6:12; 9:18, 28–29; 11:1; 22:32, 39–46; 23:34, 46). It is characteristic of the evangelist to have prayer accompanied by visions and auditions. For example, 9:28–36 mentions that while Jesus was praying, a heavenly apparition occurred—Moses and Elijah appeared—and an interpretative audition followed: "This is my Son" (cf. Acts 10; 12:5ff.; 1:14 plus 2:1ff.; Luke 22:39–46; 1:10ff.).

In 3:21–22, after his baptism and while Jesus is praying, there is a heavenly apparition: the Holy Spirit descends in bodily form as a dove upon him. To Greco-Roman hearers of Luke's narrative this would evoke echoes of the Roman use of the flight of birds of omen to discern the decrees of fate. For example, Plutarch in describing how Numa was chosen king after Romulus tells how Numa insisted that before he assumed the kingship his authority must first be ratified by heaven. So the chief of the augurs turned the veiled head of Numa toward the south, while he, standing behind him with his right hand on his head, prayed aloud and turned his eyes in all directions to observe whatever birds or other omens might be sent from the gods. When the proper birds approached, then Numa put on his royal robes and was received as the "most beloved of the gods." In such a thought-world the Lukan narrative would be viewed as an omen of Jesus' status. Exactly what that status was can be discerned from the bird involved, a dove, and the interpreting voice from heaven.

In Mediterranean antiquity the dove was symbolic of "the beneficence of divinity in love, the loving character of divine life itself" (E. R. Goodenough, *Jewish Symbols in the Greco-Roman Period* [New York: Pantheon Books, 1953—], VIII: 40–41). For the Holy Spirit to come to Jesus in the form of a dove would say to Mediterranean hearers that Jesus was beloved of God. That this is Luke's intent can be seen from the interpretation offered of the event by the voice from heaven: "You are my Son, my beloved, in you I am well pleased." This is an adaptation of Isa 42:1, in words very near to those found in Matt 12:18. This passage speaks about God's servant on whom God has put his Spirit: God's beloved is given God's Holy Spirit.

The context of 3:21–22 shows that the descent of the Spirit is not the moment at which Jesus becomes Son of God: he was that by virtue of his conception by the Holy Spirit (1:35; cf. 3:23). Rather the post-baptismal gift of the Holy Spirit is interpreted as Jesus' anointing for ministry as God's servant, an equipping of him for his task. Luke 4:16–21, the formal opening of Jesus' ministry in the third gospel, has Jesus read from Isaiah:

> The Spirit of the Lord is upon me,
> because he has anointed me to preach good news to the poor.

Then, after returning the scroll, Jesus sat down and said, "Today this scripture has been fulfilled in your hearing." The reference is, of course, to the baptism-prayer scene with its descent of the Holy Spirit on Jesus (cf. Acts 4:27; 10:38). This depiction of the descent of the Spirit on Jesus as an anointing for ministry is in line with the Lukan under-standing of the Holy Spirit generally as the empowering for ministry (cf. Luke 24:49; Acts 1:8).

A further point is that the Holy Spirit comes in response to prayer. In 3:21–22 the evangelist is interested not in what happened at the baptism but rather what happened after the baptism while Jesus was at prayer. It is a Lukan theme that the Holy Spirit is given in response to prayer (Luke 11:13; Acts 1:14 with 2:1–4; 2:21 with 2:39; 4:23–31; 8:15–17; cf. 22:16), but not necessarily in or through baptism (e.g., Acts 8:14–17; 10:44–48; 19:5–6). Here God's beloved Servant-Son is empowered for the upcoming ministry by the gift of the Spirit in re-sponse to prayer.

It is noteworthy that in the plot of the gospel Jesus found it neces-sary to receive an empowering for ministry before he embarked on his public career. He had been conceived by the Holy Spirit; he had been dedicated to God by his parents as a baby; he had personally identified with his parents' decisions about him and consciously assumed the yoke of the kingdom. Yet none of these could substitute for the nec-essary anointing-empowering given him when he prayed after his bap-tism. What is needed for adequate ministry in the Lukan understand-ing is a prior empowering by God's Spirit. This was true for Jesus and for his disciples in Acts (cf. Acts 1:8, where the promise is that the apostles will receive power after the Holy Spirit has come upon them, and then they will be witnesses). If this is what is needed, how can it be gotten?

In 3:15–17 vs. 16 points to Jesus as the one who will baptize with the Holy Spirit and with fire. Although the historical John was no Christian preacher and did not identify the Coming One with Jesus, but rather, as vs. 17 indicates, as a heavenly judge who would come at the End Time, the evangelist thinks otherwise. John the Baptist, here in 3:16, speaks of Jesus as the baptizer with the Holy Spirit and fire and understands it in terms of the event in Acts 2:1–4. The Baptist is made to anticipate an event that, from Luke's perspective, had happened and continued to happen (Acts 2:1–4; 4:31; 8:14–17; 10:44–48; 11:15–18; 19:1–7). The empowering of disciples is a gift of the exalted Christ (Acts 2:33).

The same emphasis is implicit in Luke 3:21–22. There is a remarkable correspondence in both content and sequence between the events and persons found in Luke and Acts (see C. H. Talbert, *Literary Patterns, Theological Themes and the Genre of Luke-Acts* [Missoula: Scholars Press, 1974], pp. 15–23). Among these correspondences are the baptism of Jesus followed by prayer and the descent of the Holy Spirit in a physical form, which is paralleled by the prayer of the disciples (Acts 1:14) as they await their baptism in the Holy Spirit which then occurs with accompanying physical manifestations (2:1–13). For Luke the baptism-prayer scene in Jesus' career is prototypical for his disciples' experience. Just as the Holy Spirit had come on Jesus after the baptism of repentance and in response to his prayer to empower him for his work, so the Spirit which the risen Lord has poured out (Acts 2:33) is given to his disciples, after prayer, to empower them for their mission. The one who was anointed by the Holy Spirit in 3:21–22 has become, by virtue of his exaltation, the one who pours out the Spirit, baptizing his followers with the Holy Spirit and fire. It is this baptism which empowers disciples for their ministry.

To what kind of experience is the evangelist referring when he speaks about the baptism of the Holy Spirit and fire? What are the *evidences* of this experience that Luke gives in the Acts of the Apostles? On the one hand, the gift of the Spirit is connected with power to be a witness 1:8; 2:1–42; 4:29–31; 6:10; 9:17–22; passim). It is, moreover, an indispensable power. The disciples are not to venture forth until they have received the promise (Acts 1:8; Luke 24:49). On the other hand, the presence of the Spirit is often connected with unusual phenomena like speaking in tongues and prophesying (2:4; 10:46; 19:6) when experienced initially, and with miraculous occurrences among those who have had the experience (3; 5:12–16; cf. 5:32; 8:5–7, passim). From Luke's point of view the initial experience sometimes happens before water baptism (10:44–48), sometimes in close proximity with water baptism (19:5–6), and sometimes after water baptism (8:14–17). In the Lukan community the experience could not be reduced to a predictable formula (cf. John 3:8). This is a bit different from Paul who located the experience of the Holy Spirit in its demonstrable effects in the context of proclamation (Gal 3:1–5; 1 Cor 2:1–5; 1 Thes 1:5). Since theology usually follows experience, this would be normal for the apostle who had experienced conversion, call to apostleship, and empowering for ministry as a unity. At the end of the first century people experienced the empowering of the Spirit at various times which explains the variety in Acts. It is also important to be aware that Luke–Acts focuses on the externals of religious experience, like visions, auditions, tongues, miracles. Given this general tendency, when the author speaks about the gift of the Holy Spirit in Acts, he is not talking about the secret inner work of God which convicts and converts, but rather about the moment of the Spirit's release in external manifestations. It was this release of the Spirit, in answer to prayer, sometimes accompanied by unusual phenomena, empowering people for ministry, that Luke called the baptism of the Holy Spirit. Jesus, the one who was himself anointed with the Holy Spirit to empower him for his earthly ministry, now exalted at the right hand of God, is the source of this empowering experience among his followers (Acts 2:33).

VICTORY IN SPIRITUAL WARFARE

4:1–13; 3:23–38; 4:14–15

L uke 3:23–38, 4:1–13, and 4:14–15 belong to Episode Three (3:1—
4:15) of 1:5—4:15. Together with the baptism narrative (3:21–
22), they constitute the Jesus half of the episode which corresponds
loosely to the material about John the Baptist in 3:1–20. The baptism,
the genealogy, and the temptation are linked formally by the repetition
of the expression "Son of God" (3:22; 3:38; 4:3, 9); the baptism, temptation, and concluding summary are formally connected by references
to the Holy Spirit (3:22; 4:1; 4:14). If one reads the temptation story
aright, therefore, it will be heard in the context of 3:21—4:15.

There are at least three different ways of understanding Jesus' temptations in the NT. (1) In Mark 1:12–13 the temptation functions in an
explanatory way. It is the moment at which the bearer of the Spirit
bound the strong man so his goods could be plundered (Mark 3:27).
The story explains how Jesus in his public ministry could have such
power over the demons. (2) When Heb 4:15 speaks of Jesus as "one
who in every respect has been tempted as we are, yet without sinning"
it is said in the interests of encouragement. To know our great High
Priest has been through what we are undergoing and hence is sym-
pathetic with us is a great encouragement to draw near to him with
our petitions. (3) In Luke 4:1–13 it functions in an exemplary way:
"We may be certain that the story was . . . told for its exemplary fea-
tures in order to encourage Christians facing temptations and to indicate to them how to recognize and overcome it" (I. H. Marshall, *The
Gospel of Luke*, p. 166).

One should note just who is being tempted. The context (3:22)
makes it clear that he is the Spirit-empowered Servant of God (cf. Isa
42:1). The empowering by the Holy Spirit does not keep Jesus from
being tempted: it enables him to be victorious in the midst of temptation.

The victory Jesus won was, in the first instance, by his wise use of
the scriptures (cf. 2:41–51; and 24:25–27). In each of the three temp-

44

tations, Jesus responded to the devil's approach with a quotation from Deuteronomy. In vs. 4 he used Deut 8:3, in vs. 8 he drew on Deut 6:13; and in vs. 12 Jesus employed Deut 6:16. Moreover, he knew the appropriate, as opposed to the satanic, use of scripture, rejecting the devil's interpretation in vss. 10–11 of Ps 91:11–12. The devil, in effect, said to him that the promises of God in scripture applied to anyone, at any time and place, regardless of circumstances, if that person would only claim them. Jesus refused to claim the promise. It was not appropriate for the moment. Discernment was needed to know which particular promise to claim at a given moment. In the third gospel this does not come from dialectical skill in scriptural argument.

Jesus' victory over temptation by means of his correct use of scripture was because of his heavenly resource, the Holy Spirit, the source of his discernment. At 3:21–22 Jesus had been anointed (empowered) by the Spirit for his ministry. In 4:1–2 a literal translation might read, "Jesus, full of the Holy Spirit, returned from the Jordan, and *was being led by the Spirit* in the wilderness for forty days *as he was being tempted* by the devil." This is significantly different from both Mark 1:12 ("And immediately the Spirit cast him out into the wilderness. And he was in the wilderness forty days being tempted by Satan.") and Matt 4:1 ("Then Jesus was led up into the wilderness by the Spirit to be tempted by the devil."). Unlike the other two evangelists, Luke makes certain the reader knows that during the time Jesus was being tempted, he was being led by the Spirit. Having been empowered by the Spirit, Jesus returns full of the Spirit, and in that power deals with the devil in the wilderness. From the evangelist's perspective, Jesus is victorious in temptation because the empowering of the Holy Spirit enables him to hear scripture's word addressed to his immediate needs.

Luke's point here is very similar to that made by the Pauline school, near the time of the gospel, in Ephesians 6. In the parenetic section of the epistle (chaps. 4—6), toward the end, is an exhortation to put on the whole armor of God that one may be able to stand against the wiles of the devil (6:11). The list of spiritual equipment necessary to emerge victorious from the struggle against the spiritual hosts of wickedness (6:12) is climaxed by the injunction, "And take . . . the sword of the Spirit, which is the word of God" (6:17b). The word of God (which would include the scriptures) is the weapon, but the sword is wielded by the Holy Spirit. We find, then, a similar point being made at the end of the first century by the Pauline school in epistolary form

and by the evangelist in his gospel narrative. Victory in spiritual warfare, for Christ as well as the Christian, comes from a Spirit-enabled
hearing and use of the scriptures.

The victory of Jesus over temptation, while exemplary, goes beyond
mere example. The one who won the victory was both the second Adam
and the culmination of all that God had been doing in the history of
Israel. (1) The genealogy speaks of Jesus as the culmination of Israel's
history (3:23–38). The link with Abraham (vs. 34) would speak of the
continuity of Jesus with God's ancient promises (cf. 1:55; 1:73). The
link with David (vs. 31) would serve to legitimate Jesus' claim to the
Davidic kingship (cf. 1:27; 1:32; 1:69; 2:4; 3:11). Since Luke's genealogy proceeds from David to his third son, Nathan (2 Sam 5:14; 1
Chr 3:5; 14:4), and from him, through a series of unknown names, to
Shealtiel and Zerubbabel and thence again through a series of unknown names to Joseph, it likely links Jesus with the prophets. A minority Jewish tradition erroneously held that David's son Nathan was
also the prophet and that the Messiah would descend from this non-
royal line (M. D. Johnson, "The Purpose of the Biblical Genealogies
with Special Reference to the Setting of the Genealogies of Jesus,"
Th.D. dissertation, Union Theological Seminary, New York, 1966, pp.
282–95). This descent from David through Nathan, if understood in
terms of this particular Jewish tradition, would tie Jesus to the prophetic tradition (cf. 4:24; 9:8; 7:11–17; 24:19; Acts 7:52; 3:22, for
Jesus as a prophet). The very location of the genealogy may reinforce
its links between Jesus and the prophetic tradition. Just as Moses' genealogy in Exod 6:14–25 comes after his call and just before he begins
his mission of leading the tribes out of Egypt, so Jesus' genealogy is
found after the ratification of his Sonship by God (3:21–22) and just
before the official opening of his Galilean ministry (4:16–30). This
would be an appropriate location for one who was viewed as the prophet
like Moses (Acts 3:22; 7:52). In many ways then, Jesus was the culmination of Israel's history.

(2) The genealogy also alludes to Jesus as the second Adam. Like
many Greco-Roman genealogies which traced a family back to a hero
or a god, Luke's line of descent for Jesus runs through seventy-seven
names to Adam and through him to God. The genealogy ends with the
affirmation that Adam is the Son of God. This conditions the way one
understands Jesus as Son of God in 4:3, 9. Just as Adam was Son of

God, that is, a direct creation of God, so is Jesus Son of God, because he too is a direct creation of God (1:35). Read in this way the genealogy evokes the concept of Jesus as the second Adam.

Luke 4:1–13 must be read against the background of Jesus as the culmination of all that God had been doing in the history of Israel and as the second Adam. Unlike Mark 1:12–13, this section uses a long form of Jesus' temptations. Like Matt 4:1–11, the third evangelist's story involves three specific temptations: stones to bread, worshiping the devil, and casting himself off the temple. Luke differs with Matthew, however, on the order of the temptations. Whereas Matthew gives the three temptations in the order bread, pinnacle of the temple, worship Satan, Luke reverses the order of the last two. The explanations which fit best with the immediate context are those that see Jesus' three temptations in terms either of the threefold temptation of Adam and Eve in Gen 3:6 (the tree was good for food, a delight to the eyes, and was desired to make one wise) which is echoed in 1 John 2:16 (lust of the flesh, lust of the eyes, pride of life), or of the temptations of Israel in the wilderness. Psalm 106 gives the temptation of Israel in the same order as in Luke's narrative (food, false worship, putting the Lord to the test), an order also found in 1 Cor 10:6–9. The temptations of Jesus thereby become antitypical of the experience of Israel in the wilderness and of the original pair in the garden: whereas those who came before fell, Jesus, as the second Adam and the true culmination of Israel's heritage, shows the way to victory, reversing Adam's fall and Israel's sin. Thanks to the power of God's Spirit, he has become the first of a new humanity, the leader of the faithful among the people of God. Because he has won the victory and has poured out the Spirit (Acts 2:33), his followers have the possibility of similar victory in their spiritual warfare.

The experience of temptation undergone by Jesus did not deplete his spiritual resources: he emerged with spiritual power. The narrative of the temptation, 4:1–13, is enclosed in an envelope (4:1a, 14): in 4:1a "Jesus full of the Holy Spirit returned"; language echoed in 4:14: "Jesus returned in the power of the Spirit." By means of this stylistic device the evangelist makes clear that the anointed Son, who went through his temptations while being led by the Spirit, emerged from the trials not only victorious over the enemy but also in no way depleted in his spiritual power. With a note of power (4:14) Jesus emerges from his wilderness struggles and comes into Galilee (4:14–15). The Galilean ministry (4:16—9:50), even more than the wilderness trials (4:1–13), will be the scene of the Spirit's might manifested through the one who is beloved of God.

Luke 4:16—9:50

ANOINTED WITH THE HOLY SPIRIT

INTRODUCTION

T he second large unit in the gospel is from 4:16—9:50: before it
is 1:5—4:15, the account of the prepublic career of Jesus; at
9:51 a new departure occurs, where Jesus sets his face toward Jerusalem. The material in 4:16—9:50 is held together largely by its *geographical orientation*: at 4:14 Jesus returns to Galilee and, except at
8:20 when he and his disciples cross the lake to the country of the
Gerasenes, "which is opposite Galilee," the scene is Galilee. Indications in Matthew and Mark that would otherwise locate Jesus outside
Galilee are missing (e.g., Matt 16:13 // Mark 8:27 mentions Caesarea
Philippi, but not Luke 9:18; Mark 9:30 says Jesus had passed through
Galilee, but not Luke 9:43b). The third evangelist believes the mission
to the Gentiles comes after Pentecost. He therefore treats 4:16—9:50
as Jesus' mission to Israel, with one exception. This geographical orientation of the material, however, does not prevent the evangelist from
foreshadowing in the events of Jesus' early career the things that were
to happen later in church history.

As to the theological function of 4:16—9:50, there are two main concerns in this section of the gospel. In the first place, he wants to speak
about one stage of Jesus' way. Two strands of evidence give our clue.
(1) By almost unanimous consent of scholars, the speeches of Acts
reflect the mind of the author of Luke-Acts. If so, then they should
indicate something of the way the evangelist understood Galilee in the
life of Jesus. Acts 10:34–43, of all the speeches, contains the most
detail relevant to our concerns. This speech, attributed to Peter, speaks
of (a) the time of the ministry (after the baptism which John preached—
vs. 37; before the ministry elsewhere—vs. 37); (b) the content of the
ministry (preaching good news—vs. 36; doing good, healing all who
were oppressed by the devil—vs. 38); (c) the basis for this ministry
(God anointed Jesus of Nazareth with the Holy Spirit and power—vs.
38); (d) the witnesses of this ministry ("we are witnesses to all that he
did"—vs. 39). These basic points found here in one speech are scat-

51

tered in other speeches in Acts: for example, 13:16–41, a speech attributed to Paul, mentions the time of Jesus' ministry in Galilee ("before his coming John preached a baptism of repentance"—vs. 24) and
the witnesses ("those who came up with him from Galilee are now his
witnesses"—vs. 31); the prayer of 4:24–30 refers to Jesus' anointing
(vs. 27); finally, Peter's speech in 1:15–22 speaks of the witnesses and
of the relation of Jesus' ministry to the Baptist's ("One of the men who
have accompanied us during all the time that the Lord Jesus went in
and out among us, beginning from the baptism of John"—vss. 21–
22a).

(2) A second hint as to the meaning of the Galilean ministry of Jesus is the frontispiece to the gospel (4:16–30), which is also the introduction for the Galilean section. In the Lukan version of Jesus' rejection at Nazareth we find two emphases. First, the nature of Jesus'
ministry is described. Its content is preaching good news to the poor
(vss. 18–19) and setting at liberty those that are oppressed (vs. 18). Its
basis is the anointing of Jesus with the Holy Spirit (vs. 18). This much
agrees with the picture of the Galilean ministry gained from the
speeches of Acts. Second, 4:16–30 describes the results of Jesus' ministry. There is both a rejection of Jesus by his own people and a hint
of a wider mission to all kinds of people (vss. 23–24, 25–27). Though
the speeches of Acts refer only to Jesus' rejection in connection with
Jerusalem, that the evangelist intended this rejection, as well as the
hint of a wider mission, to apply to Galilee, may be seen if we note a
similar passage, Luke 7:18–30: Jesus' ministry of healing and preaching is rejected by the Jewish leaders, but is accepted by the people and
tax collectors (vss. 29–30). Taken together, the speeches of Acts and
the frontispiece of the gospel give a reasonably clear sketch of what
the evangelist intended to say about this stage of Jesus' career.

The Galilean ministry of Jesus takes place after John the Baptist's
work has been completed (3:18–20). It is a period of preaching and
healing. Almost from the first there are Galilean witnesses present
(4:31—5:11; 6:12ff.; 8:1–3; 9:1–6), the same people who will later view
the passion events in Jerusalem. The basis for all Jesus does and says
is his anointing with the Spirit of the Lord (3:21–22; 4:16ff.). The
portrait of Jesus in this section is of one who is empowered with the
Holy Spirit. This empowering divides those Jesus meets into two
groups: those who recognize God in Jesus' work and words and those
who do not. In 4:16—9:50 the evangelist speaks about one stage of

Jesus' way. In this phase of his career, Jesus is the one who is anointed-empowered by the Holy Spirit and his activity demonstrates the kingly power of God. The accent is on power.

In the second place, Luke also wants to foreshadow in Jesus' career certain facets of the later church's life. The evangelist writes his gospel with the thought in mind of the church and the progress of its mission in Acts: in the ministry of Jesus the later ministry of the church is foreshadowed. One example should suffice. In Luke 7:1–10 is tradition also found in Matt 8:5–13. In Luke's version, vss. 3–6a are distinctive. Thereby it becomes a story of a pious centurion who sends others to secure assistance for him. The point of the tradition as it stands in Luke is the centurion's faith as contrasted with Israel's lack of faith (vs. 9). This tradition, as adapted, is remarkably like the Cornelius episode in Acts 10. It would seem the evangelist has introduced into Jesus' Galilean ministry a character like Cornelius so that Jesus' favorable attitude toward such a man and his faith foreshadows the attitude of the later church toward believing Gentiles. The Spirit-anointed Jesus in Galilee functions as a prototype of the behavior that characterizes the Spirit-empowered disciples in Acts.

The dominant emphasis on the power of Jesus and the subordinate theme of the mission of the gospel to all peoples cannot be missed by an attentive reader of 4:16—9:50. (For a detailed discussion, see C. H. Talbert, "The Lukan Presentation of Jesus' Ministry in Galilee," *Review and Expositor* 64:485–97 [1967].)

FOR THE WHOLE PERSON,
IN THE WHOLE WORLD

4:16–30

Luke 4:16–30 presents the distinctive Lukan form of the rejection of Jesus by his "own country" (Mark 6:1; Matt 13:53) or "Nazareth" (Luke 4:16); Matt 13:53–58 and Mark 6:1–6 relate the incident in much the same way, though they differ on its exact context. In the first gospel the incident ends a collection of seven parables (13:1–52); in the second gospel it completes a cycle of four miracles (4:35—5:43). In both the rejection scene happens well along in the Galilean ministry. Luke, however, tells the story in a long and very different way and places it at the beginning of Jesus' public ministry. This seems awkward in light of 4:23, which assumes 4:31–44. By so locating it, the evangelist indicates that in his story this scene does not simply relate one event among others but has programmatic significance for the whole (cf. Acts 13:13–52, a scene at the beginning of Paul's missionary work that is typical of what repeatedly happened).

The clue to the meaning of 4:16–30 is the unit's literary pattern (H. J. B. Combrink, "The Structure and Significance of Luke 4:16–30," *Neotestamentica* 7:27–47 [1973]). The unit is enclosed in an inclusion: in 4:16a,b, Jesus "came to Nazareth" and "entered into the synagogue"; in 4:30 he was "passing through" the crowd and was "going away." Within the inclusion the passage falls into an AB:A'B' pattern. In A and A', Jesus is speaking a word; in B and B' the crowd is reacting to that word. A, the initial word, deals with the form of Jesus' ministry and is found in 4:16c–21, which falls into two parts: (1) the reading (16c–20) and (2) the teaching (20–21). The reading (16c–20) is itself a symmetrically organized unit:

> A He stood up to read (16c)
>   B there was given to him (17a)
>   C opening the book (17b)
>   D Isa 61:1f., plus 58:6 (18–19)

C'   closing the book (20a)
B'   he gave it back to the attendant (20b)
A'   he sat down (20c)

(V. E. McEachern, "Dual Witness and Sabbath Motif in Luke," *Canadian Journal of Theology* 12:273 [1966]). Furthermore, the quotation (d) is a combination of Isa 61:1–2; 58:6:

> The Spirit of the Lord is upon me, because he has anointed me (Isa 61)
>> to preach (*euaggelisasthai*) good news to the poor (Isa 61)
>> to proclaim release (*aphesin*) to the captives (Isa 61)
>>> and sight to the blind (Isa 61)
>> to set at liberty (*aphesei*) the oppressed (Isa 58:6)
> to preach (*kēruxai*) the acceptable year of the Lord (Isa 61).

In the teaching (vss. 20–21) Jesus proclaims this scripture has been fulfilled by him. The anointing with the Spirit is, of course, a reference to 3:21–22. In 4:1, 14 the evangelist has taken pains to make clear that the descent of the Holy Spirit at Jesus' baptism was the basis for a continuing endowment with the Spirit. In this way the reader is prepared for the announcement of 4:18 which relates the Spirit to the whole of Jesus' ministry. The Spirit has empowered Jesus to preach the good news of God's salvation (18a, 19) and to announce the healing of the blind (18c).

What does Luke understand "proclaiming release (*aphesin*) to the captives" and "setting at liberty (*aphesei*) the oppressed" to mean? The word *aphesis* in normal Christian use means "forgiveness," and the evangelist elsewhere certainly employs the term in this way (1:77; 3:3; 24:47; Acts 2:38; 5:31; 10:43; 13:38; 26:18). It is therefore possible for the reader to hear this undertone in the word. The term is also used to mean "release from captivity." This is certainly its meaning in the context of Isaiah 61 and 58 and seems to be the dominant intent of Luke 4:18. The material which follows (4:31–41) depicts Jesus as an exorcist and healer and then in 4:43 seems to identify this activity with his preaching the good news of the kingdom. If so, then its use here would refer to Jesus' ministry of physical healing and exorcism. This would fit the general Lukan tendency to think of salvation as encompassing both physical healing and inclusion in the eschatological people of God (e.g., salvation is healing in 8:36, 48; 18:42; Acts 4:9; 14:9; it is inclusion in the eschatological family in 8:12; 13:23; 17:19; 18:26; 19:10; Acts 11:14; 15:1; 16:30). Given this, it seems correct to understand Luke's view of Jesus' mission, as set forth in 4:18–19, to include preaching, physical healing, and exorcism. This threefold activity, moreover, is portrayed as continuing in the ministry of the disciples in Acts (preaching—e.g., Acts 2:14ff.; 3:12ff.; 10:34ff.; 13:16ff.; healing—e.g., Acts 3:1ff.; 9:33ff.; 9:36ff.; 14:8ff.; exorcism— e.g., Acts 16:16ff; 19:12ff.). It is this threefold form of ministry that the empowering by the Holy Spirit produces both in Jesus and in the disciples: the ministry of Master and disciples alike focuses on the whole person.

In A (4:16c–21), Jesus' word is that the prophecies of Isaiah 61 and 58 are fulfilled in him. The peoples' response, B, is given in two parts. The first part, vs. 22a, is a statement about their reaction: "all spoke well of him, and wondered at the gracious words which proceeded out of his mouth." The second, vs. 22b, is a quotation of their words: "Is this not Joseph's son?" The basic issue is the intent of their response. Do the parts of this verse have the same intent? How are they related? The best option, given what follows, is to read 4:22 so both parts are positive responses. This is a necessity for 22a and is natural for 22b if it is taken to mean, "Is this not a hometown boy?" Such a question would contain within it an implicit demand: since he is "our boy," we can expect great things to be done for us by this Spirit-empowered servant of God. It is this inference from his family connections made by the people of Nazareth that prompts Jesus' second word.

This word, A′ (4:23–27), defines the scope of his ministry, and falls into two sections. (1) The first, vs. 23, interprets vs. 22 negatively. In effect Jesus says, "You are making a demand on me as a local boy to set up practice here in Nazareth." (2) The second section, vss. 24–27, is a multifaceted response to this implicit demand. Both proverbial wisdom ("No prophet is acceptable in his own country"—vs. 24) and scripture (vss. 25–26, the widow in the land of Sidon; vs. 27, Naaman the Syrian) argue against their demand. The implication of this response is that the local boy's mission will take him away from his hometown and that God's benefits, promised in Isaiah 61 and 58, are even for the Gentiles (vss. 25–26, 27).

Here, of course, we meet in clear-cut fashion the concern of the evangelist for the universalistic scope of God's salvation in Jesus. It is a theme already heard in the section dealing with the prepublic career of Jesus (2:31–32; 3:6, 23–38). It is found almost immediately after 4:16–30: in 4:43, after a series of exorcisms (4:31–41), Jesus resists those who would have kept him from leaving them (4:43), saying, "I must preach the good news of the kingdom of God to the other cities also; for I was sent for this purpose." The risen Lord at 24:47 tells his disciples that repentance and forgiveness of sins must be preached in his name to all nations. The commission to go to the end of the earth is repeated in Acts 1:8. The rest of Acts tells the story of the evangelistic mission from Jerusalem to Rome. In Acts 10 it is the Holy Spirit who forces Peter to move to the Gentiles. This mission, however, was already symbolized in the sending of the Seventy (or Seventy-two) by Jesus in Luke 10:1ff. If the form of Jesus' empowered ministry is preaching, healing, and exorcism, the scope of it is universal. In 4:24–27 Jesus says he must bear the good news of the kingdom beyond the confines of those to whom he is most closely related by geographical, cultural, and racial origin.

The reaction of the people to this second word of Jesus, B', is found in 4:28–29: when they heard the word they tried to kill him. "It is not so much that Jesus goes elsewhere because he is rejected as that he is rejected because he announces that it is God's will and his mission to go elsewhere" (R. C. Tannehill, "The Mission of Jesus according to Luke 4:16–30," in *Jesus in Nazareth,* ed. W. Eltester [Berlin: Walter de Gruyter, 1972], p. 62). In being rejected because of his concern for a wider mission, Jesus foreshadows the fate of his disciples in Acts (e.g., 13:44–50; 14:19; 17:4–5; 18:12; 20:3; 22:21; 28:23–29) who sometimes were abused because of a mission to the Gentiles (22:21) and sometimes turned to the Gentiles as a result of rejection by Jews (13:44–50; 28:23–29). This rejection echoes an earlier hint of the same thing in Luke 2:34b. The escape of Jesus (4:30) foreshadows the story in Acts where the gospel triumphantly survived similar acts of hostility and rejection.

To summarize: in 4:16–30 the evangelist gives a programmatic statement of Jesus' ministry—and by extension, the ministry of the church—as one empowered by the Holy Spirit, involving not only preaching but also healing and exorcism, and moving outwards to touch the whole world.

CALLED AND COMMISSIONED

4:31—5:11

T his unit falls into two parts: 4:31-44; 5:1-11. (1) The first parallels Mark 1:21-38. Both gospels give (a) an account of an exorcism in Capernaum (Mark 1:21-28; Luke 4:31-37—not in Matthew); (b) the story of the healing of Peter's mother-in-law (Mark 1:29-31; Luke 4:38-39—cf. Matt 8:14-15); (c) a generalizing paragraph about many healings and exorcisms (Mark 1:32-34; Luke 4:40-41—cf. Matt 8:16-17); and (d) a reference to Jesus' departure (Mark 1:35-38; Luke 4:42-43—not in Matthew).

The three Lukan paragraphs dealing with healing are linked together by the verb translated "rebuke" (4:35, 39, 41), thereby enabling the treatment of all three miracle stories as exorcisms or events involving exorcisms. This activity brought Jesus a tremendous following (4:37, 42; 5:1-3). In response to the desire of the people in Capernaum to keep him—as those at Nazareth had wanted to do (4:16-30)—Jesus, as at Nazareth, indicated he was under divine necessity (cf. *dei* in 4:43) to move on. Judging from the context, for Jesus to preach the good news of the kingdom must refer to his exorcisms (cf. 11:20).

(2) The second part of the larger thought unit, 5:1-11, furnishes the clue to the overall intent of 4:31—5:11. One notes first of all its location: whereas in Mark the call of Peter, James, and John comes at 1:16-20, before the exorcism and healings in Capernaum (1:21-34), in Luke the call comes after the series of miracles. This placement serves two functions in the gospel.

On the one hand, Luke's placing the call of the disciples after the series of miracles makes the point that mighty works can be the basis for discipleship. Peter, at least, must have known of Jesus' wondrous powers some time prior to his call (4:38-39). Also, when Peter in 5:5 says, "at your word I will let down the nets," Luke understands this to be based on the authority of Jesus' word already established in 4:31-36. Whereas Mark 1:22 says the people were astonished at Jesus' teaching "for he taught them as one who had authority, and not as the scribes" (Matt 7:29), Luke 4:31 states they were astonished at his teaching "for his word was with authority." There then follows an exorcism (4:33–35) to demonstrate the authority of Jesus' word to which the people respond: "What is this word? For with authority and power he commands the unclean spirits and they come out" (4:36; Mark 1:27 omits "word" and "and power"). It is this one whose word is powerful and who has healed Simon's mother-in-law by rebuking the fever (4:39) who speaks to Peter in chapter 5 and to whom Peter responds in 5:5: "Master, we toiled all night and took nothing! But at your word I will let down the nets." For the evangelist, Peter's initial response to Jesus is based on a prior knowledge of his power in Capernaum.

"Further, the story within which the call of the first disciples is placed (5:1–11) leaves little room for doubt that they followed Jesus because of his wondrous power. Only after Peter, James, and John see the miraculous catch of fish, are they summoned to follow Jesus" (P. J. Achtemeier, "The Lukan Perspective on the Miracles of Jesus: A Preliminary Sketch," in *Perspectives on Luke-Acts,* ed. C. H. Talbert [Danville, Va.: ABPR, 1978], p. 161). In Luke's schema Peter could respond to Jesus' word to let down the nets on the basis of what he had seen done for others, but his following Jesus came as a result of what he had experienced done for him by Jesus: grace was experienced in and through a miraculous deed done for him. This emphasis on miracle as a catalyst for faith is characteristic of Luke-Acts (e.g., Acts 9:35; 9:42; 13:12; 16:30, 33; 19:17; Luke 8:2; 7:18–23). Of course Luke knew that miracle was ambiguous (Luke 11:14–19) and that non-Christians could also perform mighty works (Acts 8:9–11). Nevertheless, the evangelist shows an unusually positive attitude toward miracle as a means by which faith is created. In 4:31—5:11 he makes very clear that miracle was the catalyst for Peter's response to Jesus.

In order to appreciate Luke's stance, we may compare it with that of Mark and John. The Markan view of miracle is much more negative than Luke's: he not only declares that miracles do not necessarily lead to faith (e.g., 3:19b–35; 4:35—6:6) but also asserts that to confess Jesus as Christ on the basis of his power is only partial vision and must be supplemented by the vision of his cross (e.g., 8:14–21, 22–26, 27–30; 10:46–52). The fourth evangelist has the most inclusive view of miracle in the NT: with Luke he asserts that Jesus' mighty works are sometimes instrumental in peoples' believing in him (4:53; 14:11—

i.e., signs provoke faith); with Mark he knows not everyone believes in Jesus as a result of his miracles (i.e., signs are ambiguous—6:26; 11:46ff.; 9:16, 30, 34). John shows that in order for people to see through the miracle to the sign (i.e., to Jesus' identity) some preliminary faith is sometimes present (2:11; 4:46–54; 20:30–31; 21:6–7), but at other times is not present (2:23; 3:2; 9:ff.; 11:45): when faith is already there the miracles deepen it (2:11; 4:46–54; 20:30–31); when miracles evoke faith or openness to faith, a further development is necessary if Jesus is to be understood properly (e.g., chap. 3; chap. 9). This diversity within the NT reflects the struggles to accord miracle (power) its proper place in the total scheme of things. Although power was one component in the early Christian view of God, it was not the central ingredient: Grace was. The gospels reflect the various struggles within the communities to recognize power as part of who God is and at the same time to set it within a structure in which miracle was subservient to grace and balanced by moral considerations (C. H. Talbert, "The Gospel and the Gospels," *Interpretation*, 33:351–62 [1979]).

On the other hand, Luke's placing the call of the disciples after the series of miracles allows Jesus some ministry and such success (4:37, 40, 42) that he is pressed upon by the people (5:1–3). The call of Peter, James, and John (5:10) functions, then, as Jesus' effort to get some assistance in an overly successful ministry. The same motif is found in Acts 11:19–26 where Barnabas, confronted with enormous success in Antioch, enlists Paul as a helper (cf. also Eph 4:11–12 where, if the punctuation is properly placed, the pastors and teachers function "for the equipment of the saints for the work of ministry"). Success creates the need for helpers (Luke 10:2).

If 5:1–11's location has pointed to the enlistment of the disciples, brought about by Jesus' miraculous activity, as a way for Jesus to deal with his success, the form of the passage confirms what the arrangement implied and gives clues to success for disciples involved in ministry. Confirmation comes when we note that in its present form, 5:1–11 is not so much a call story as it is a commissioning narrative. Call stories (e.g., Mark 1:16–20; 2:14; Luke 5:27–28) involve: (a) Jesus came; (b) he saw the person; (c) he called; (d) the person leaves all and follows him. A commissioning story includes: (a) an introduction describing the circumstances; (b) the confrontation between the commissioner and the one to be commissioned; (c) the commission, in which the recipient is told to undertake a specific task; (d) a protest in which the person questions in some way the word of the commissioner; (e) a reaction of fear, amazement, unworthiness to the presence of the august commissioner; (f) reassurance to the individual, providing confidence and allaying misgivings; and (g) conclusion, usually involving the beginning of the commissioned one's undertaking the assignment (B. J. Hubbard, "Commissioning Stories in Luke-Acts: A Study of Their Antecedents, Form and Content," *Semeia* 8:103–26 [1977], and "The Role of Commissioning Accounts in Acts," in *Perspectives on Luke-Acts,* pp. 187–98). Examples in Luke-Acts include Luke 24:36–53; Acts 1:1–14; 10:9–23. Luke 5:1–11 fits this form nicely: (a) introduction—5:2; (b) confrontation—5:3; (c) commission—5:4; (d) protest—5:5; (e) reaction—5:8–9; (f) reassurance—5:10b; (g) conclusion—5:11. Although there are overtones of a call story present in vs. 11, the dominant thrust is that of a commissioning of Peter for his role of catching people (i.e., mission). The disciples are commissioned to "go fishing" in order to help Jesus with an overly successful ministry. The merging of call and commissioning in 5:1–11 reflects the view that to be called to be a disciple is at the same time to be commissioned as a fisher.

The use of this commissioning form also speaks about success in a disciple's ministry. The symbolism of the story contrasts the futility of "fishing" with only human resources, with the effectiveness of "fishing" in obedience to Jesus' word. The symbolism of a great catch in response to Jesus' word after a fruitless effort prior to Jesus' command would fit the Lukan view of the church's missionary-evangelistic outreach. It was to be (a) to all nations, but (b) the disciples were to stay in Jerusalem until they were empowered (Luke 24:47; Acts 1:8). The narrative of Acts tells the working out of this principle: after being clothed with power from on high, the first fishing expedition of Peter yielded three thousand converts (Acts 2:41). "Fishing" that results in a large catch is that done in response to Jesus' initiative.

The location of the call-commissioning of Peter in time is important. Luke 5:1–11, unlike John 21:4ff., with which it has marked similarities, is located not after the resurrection but early in Jesus' Galilean ministry. This was because the Lukan view of apostleship demanded an apostle have been with Jesus from the first of his ministry to the time of his ascension (Acts 1:21–22; contrast Paul who thought what was needed was to have seen the risen Lord and received a call—1 Cor 9:1; 15:8–10; Gal 1:16). Peter, Luke was saying by his location of the episode in time, was a disciple from the first and so had the credentials for apostleship. Theologically, this view of apostleship is significant as it places the church's proclamation under the control of the career of the pre-Easter Jesus as known through his witnesses. The earthly Jesus is the criterion of the true proclamation, the primary check and balance on any ministry done in Jesus' name.

THE DIFFERENCE JESUS MAKES

5:12—6:11

Luke 5:12—6:11 falls into two parts with 5:29-32 functioning as the hinge (i.e., both as the conclusion to 5:12-32 and as the introduction to 5:29—6:11). Here as elsewhere this procedure reflects ancient rules for writing historical narrative (e.g., Lucian of Samosata). The first part tells where Jesus can be found and is a unit analogous to 4:31—5:11. (1) Just as 4:31—5:11 sets in Jesus' prior activity (miracles) the basis for his call of Peter, so 5:12-26 gives in two episodes the kind of person it was who called Levi in 5:27-28. Levi's response (vs. 28) is based on Jesus being one who restores social outcasts to community (5:12-14) and forgives sinners (5:17-26). (2) Just as Jesus' association with Peter pointed toward "catching men" (5:10b), so Jesus' call of Levi resulted in this new disciple's not only leaving everything to follow Jesus (5:28) but also his making a great feast in his house to introduce his associates to Jesus (5:29). In 5:29-32 Jesus is depicted as one who not only restores and forgives an individual but as one who also associates with the many who are in need. (3) Just as in 5:1-11 the great catch being possible only in obedience to Jesus' word foreshadowed the experience of the apostolic church, so 5:29-32 foreshadows the experience of the church after the resurrection which learned to associate with Gentiles who were believed to be unclean by strict Jews (Acts 10:1—11:18—note in 11:18, "Then to the Gentiles also God has granted repentance unto life"). Two Lukan touches in 5:32 make this clear. First, note the perfect tense (*elēlutha*) which means "I have come and my work continues" (Eduardo Arens, *The Elthon-Sayings in the Synoptic Tradition* [Göttingen: Vandenhoeck & Ruprecht, 1976], p. 62). That is, through his church Jesus continues to associate with sinners. Second, note Luke's addition of "to repentance," laying the groundwork even here for Acts 11:18. In all of this Luke's concern has been to show that Jesus is found in fellowship with sinners.

When Jesus says, "Those who are well have no need of a physician, but those who are sick; I have not come to call the righteous, but sinners to repentance" (5:31–32), he indicates not only where he is to be found but also what credentials are required for his disciples: "The church is the only fellowship in the world where the one requirement for membership is the unworthiness of the candidate" (Robert Munger). Such an understanding of Jesus and his church was strange to Greco-Roman readers. In Origen's *Against Celsus,* 3:59f., Celsus, the pagan critic of Christianity, complains that ordinarily those invited to participate in religious solemnities are the pure who live an honorable life. Christians, however, invite anyone who is a sinner, or foolish, or simple-minded. In short, any unfortunate will be accepted in the kingdom of God. By "sinner" is meant any unjust person, whether thief, or burglar, or poisoner, or sacreligious person, or robber of corpses. Why, says Celsus, if you wanted an assembly of robbers, these are just the kind of people you would call. Origen does not deny the charge but says (3:60–61) Christians extend an invitation to sinners in order to bind up their wounds (id., 7:60). Whereas Plato and the other wise ones of Greece are like physicians who confine their attention to the better classes and despise the common people, Jesus' disciples make provision for the great mass of people. If the Lukan Jesus is to be found in fellowship with sinners, the Lukan view of the church is that of a fellowship composed of social outcasts restored to community, and sinners forgiven by grace who have left all to follow Jesus.

Luke 5:12–32 is also analogous to 4:31—5:11 in focusing on how Jesus reacts to unusual success. If the former section showed him enlisting others to help, this section focuses on his withdrawal to pray. Where is Jesus to be found? He is found not only in fellowship with sinners but also in prayer with God. Jesus in Luke alternates between giving what he has and retreating to be filled, between doing what he sees needs doing and withdrawing to gain fresh vision of what should be done (3:21–22; 6:12; 9:18; 9:28f.; 11:1, passim). In this regard the evangelist depicts Jesus as a model for disciples. A disciple is not above the Lord. Disciples of Jesus will be found where he is: in prayer with God and in fellowship with sinners.

The second part of 5:12—6:11, which deals with the character and justification of a Christian style of life, is 5:29—6:11. This part is in two sections: (1) 5:29–39, a banquet scene with dialogue (cf. 7:36–50; 9:10–17; 10:38–42; 11:37–54; 14:1–24; 19:1–10; 22:4–38; 24:29–32,

41–43); and (2) 6:1–11, two sabbath controversies. The unit is joined by the repetition of key words and phrases: note "eat and drink" in 5:30, 33; "drinking" in 5:39; and three different uses of the verb "to eat" in 6:1, 4. Note also that in 6:6 the evangelist has added "on another sabbath," conforming to the wording of 6:1 ("on a sabbath"), thereby indicating he views 6:6–11 as an extension of the issue raised in 6:1–5.

The form of 5:30—6:11 is shaped by a series of charges about the life-style of Jesus and his followers raised by the Pharisees, together with Jesus' answers. (a) 5:30–32. The charge: With whom you eat and drink is problematic. You associate with the wrong kind of people. Jesus' response: The sick are those who need me (vs. 31), therefore, as host I invite sinners (vs. 32). (b) 5:33–39. The charge: Eating and drinking instead of fasting often and offering prayers is a problem; there is not enough seriousness in the style of life of your disciples. Jesus' response: 1) In 5:34–35 Jesus says fasting in the presence of the proclamation of the good news (cf. 4:18–19) makes no more sense than does fasting at a wedding feast. It is unthinkable. 2) In 5:36–38 is a double parable. A piece of cloth from a new garment is not used to patch an old one because, not having shrunken from being washed, the new cloth would tear on washing, and besides the new would not match the old (vs. 36). Also new wine is not put into old wineskins because it will burst the old, but rather into new skins (vss. 37–38). 3) In 5:39 Jesus says that after tasting something better (the old wine which is aged) no one desires an inferior product (the new wine). The difficulty in interpreting 5:39 is due to our attempt to understand "old" and "new" in the same way in vs. 39 and in vss. 36–38. In vs. 39 "old" should be paraphrased "good" and "new" by "inferior," because here "old" equals what Jesus brings—in contrast to 5:36–38—and "new" is the inferior system of the Pharisees and Baptists. (c) 6:1–11. The charge: When you eat is questionable; your style of life violates the sabbath law of Judaism (6:1–5). This flippant attitude toward the sabbath is also manifest in unnecessary healing on the holy day (6:6–11). Jesus' response: In both instances Jesus appeals to human needs taking precedence over sabbath law. His authority for acting in such a way is that he is the Son of Man (6:5) who sits (22:69) or stands (Acts 7:56) at the right hand of God. He is also an interpreter of the law whose stance is validated by the healing miracle in 6:9–10. Anyone who does not listen to him will be cut off from the people (Acts 3:22–23). Overall, the section, 5:30–6:11, shows Jesus as a "sign that is spoken against" (2:34).

The basic issue raised in this section has to do with the character and justification of the way of life of Jesus' followers. Luke's view of a disciple is one who has left all to follow Jesus. Attachment to Jesus gives an inner detachment from the world. Yet the disciples' detachment from the world did not express itself in terms of the old outer signs of what it meant to be religious, as the Jewish culture saw it. Two early second century documents tell the story clearly.

(1) The Christian *Epistle to Diognetus,* 5, says:

> For Christians are distinguished from other men neither by country, nor language, *nor the customs* which they observe. For they neither inhabit cities of their own, nor employ a peculiar form of speech, nor lead a life which is marked out by any singularity. But, inhabiting Greek as well as barbarian cities, according as the lot of each of them has been determined, and *following the customs of the natives in respect to clothing, food, and the rest of their ordinary conduct,* they display to us their wonderful and confessedly striking method of life. They dwell in their own countries, but simply as sojourners. As citizens, they share in all things with others, and yet endure all things as if foreigners. Every foreign land is to them as their native country, and every land of their birth as a land of strangers. They pass their days on earth, but they are citizens of heaven. (ANF, 1:26–27)

From this it appears that whereas Christians were detached in spirit from over-absorption in the world, in many ways their way of life was a part of the surrounding culture. This caused the problem for their closest religious kin.

(2) In Justin's *Dialogue with Trypho the Jew,* 10, Trypho is amazed at the Christian's stance in the world:

> But this is what we are most at loss about: that you professing to be pious, and supposing yourselves better than others, *are not in any particular separated from them, and do not alter your mode of living from the nations,* in that you observe no festivals or sabbaths, and do not have the rite of circumcision. (ANF, 1:199)

It appears the orthodox Jew had no problem with the Christians' spirit of detachment from the world, but with the absence of the old distin-

guishing marks that set one off from the general culture, such as observance of the sabbath laws, regular fasts and prayers, and separation
from persons who were defiled. The question inevitably would be, Why
are you Christians so lax?

The evangelist believed attachment to Jesus brought detachment
from the world (5:28—"he left everything . . . and followed him"). At
the same time, Jesus' disciples ignored many of the old outer signs of
the religiously devout. This did not mean, however, that inner attachment to Jesus and detachment from the world failed to find outer
expression in the disciples' involvement with the world. Rather Jesus
asserts that *a new inner religious reality demands a new life-style*
(5:36–39). The marks of Jesus' followers will not be sabbath observance, fasting and prayers offered, and avoidance of outcasts, but will
be joy like that at a wedding (5:33–35) and an overriding concern for
human need, spiritual (5:29–32) and physical (6:1–11). Such a way of
life has the authority of Jesus behind it.

The apostle Paul had captured this spirit when he wrote to the Romans: "The kingdom of God does not mean food and drink but righteousness and peace and joy in the Holy Spirit" (14:17).

TRANSCENDING THE TIMES

6:12–49

T his section has three major components: (1) 6:12–16, the choice of the Twelve; (2) 6:17–19, the transition from the hills where the Twelve are chosen to the plain where Jesus instructs his disciples; and (3) 6:20–49, the Sermon on the Plain.

In Luke-Acts the apostles are primarily witnesses who guarantee the historical continuity and authenticity of the church's message (Acts 1:21–22): 6:12–16, then, functions to establish an apostolic guarantee for the tradition which follows (6:20–49). In 6:20–49, Luke is saying, we have Jesus' instruction for disciples passed to us by the apostles who were with him (cf. 6:17—"he came down with them"). Note that the list of the apostles' names is repeated in Acts 1:13 and their credentials given in 1:21–22 (they have been with Jesus from the beginning to the Ascension).

Luke 6:17–19 functions in a twofold way. First, the unit delineates the audience for what follows—apostles, a crowd of disciples, and a great multitude of people. Second, it reaffirms the identity of the one who will be delivering the Sermon on the Plain, the Spirit-empowered one (4:18) who speaks of good news (4:18b) and demonstrates it in the healing of diseased bodies and spirits (cf. 4:18c,d,e). With people present to hear and those who will pass on the tradition at hand, the stage is set for the Sermon on the Plain which the evangelist says is directed to Jesus' disciples (6:20), to "those who hear" (6:27).

Although both the Sermon on the Mount in Matthew and the Sermon on the Plain in Luke are built on four blocks of similar material in the same relative order (Matt 5:2–12/Luke 6:20–23; Matt 5:38–48/Luke 6:27–36; Matt 7:1–5/Luke 6:37–38, 41–42; Matt 7:15–27/Luke 6:43–49), the Lukan sermon has a perspective of its own. This point of view can be discerned through a careful analysis of the arrangement of the material in 6:20–49. (The observations on the pattern of 6:20–49 throughout this section are influenced by Robert Morgenthaler, *Die*

Lukanische Geschichtsschreibung als Zeugnis [Zürich: Zwingli Verlag, 1948], 1:81–83.)

The Sermon on the Plain falls into three parts determined by the formulae of introduction: (1) 6:20, "And he lifted up his eyes on his disciples, and said"; (2) 6:27, "But I say to you that hear"; and (3) 6:39, "He also told them a parable." The first part, 6:20–26, contains four beatitudes balanced by four woes. This section offers congratulations and condolences to two kinds of people. The second part, 6:27–38, focuses on the life of love, in four thought units: (a) 6:27–28, a four-member unit—love, do good, bless, pray; (b) 6:29–30, a four-member unit—strikes you, takes away your cloak, begs from you, takes away your goods—followed by a summary, vs. 31; (c) 6:32–35, a four-member unit: the first three—if you love, if you do good, if you lend—are balanced by the fourth—but love, do good, lend—and followed by a summary, vs. 36; and (d) 6:37–38a, a four-member unit: two negatives—judge not, condemn not—balanced by two positives—forgive, give—followed by a summary, vs. 38b. The third part, 6:39–49, is a collection of four parables: vss. 39–40, blind man; vss. 41–42, speck and log; vss. 43–45, trees and fruit; vss. 46–49, two houses. It is concerned with principles that should govern the lives of disciples, such as the proper use of influence. The contrast between the two types of people (6:46–49) at the end of the Sermon echoes the contrast (6:20–26) at the beginning. Taken together the opening and closing contrasts serve as an inclusion around the Sermon as a whole. Any exposition of the passage (6:20–49) must follow the leads Luke has given in the pattern of his arrangement of the material.

The first part of the Sermon on the Plain, 6:20–26, contains four beatitudes and four corresponding woes. Our understanding of the Lukan intent depends first on our grasping the functions of beatitudes and woes in antiquity and second on our perception of the meaning of the key terms used here. (a) Function. The beatitude is a specific genre both in the Greek and Jewish worlds (e.g., Ps 1:1; Prov 8:34; Dan 12:12; Tob 13:14; Ps of Sol 4:23; 17:44; 18:6). Early Christians found it useful (Rom 14:22; Matt 5:3–12; John 20:29; Rev 14:13; 16:15; 22:7). Here in Luke 6 its form consists of *makarios* (blessed) followed by who is blessed and why. The beatitude does not confer a blessing; rather it extols the good fortune accruing to someone for some particular reason. It is not an exhortation to be or to do something; rather it exalts or approves a person on the basis of some good fortune. It may be paraphrased, "Congratulations to _____ because of _____." It celebrates someone's success.

The beatitudes in the NT are often eschatological: they see the present in the light of the ultimate future. They do not make their judgments on the basis of the appearance of things in the here and now, by present outward success. Instead, the one uttering the beatitude does so from a position within the councils of God and with an awareness of the ultimate outcome of history (as does a prophet, e.g., Jer 23:18, 21–22). The content of the beatitude may be in stark contrast with the painful reality of the present. Paradox is prominent. Congratulations are in order, no matter what the appearances, however, because of what will ultimately be. If the present is radically out of keeping with what will be, the beatitude may signal the reversal of all human values (1:51–53).

The woe is also a set genre in the OT (Isa 5:8–23; 33:1; Amos 5:18; 6:1; Hab 2:6–19), functioning as an expression of pity for those who stand under divine judgment. It bemoans the sad plight of the person(s) in question. Used in an eschatological context, a woe laments the plight of the person designated, whatever appearances are in the present, because of what will ultimately be.

Collections of beatitudes occur (e.g., Sir 25:7–10) and a combination of woes with blessings is not uncommon (e.g., Eccles 10:16–17; Tob 13:12; 1 Enoch 99; 2 Enoch 52). The functions of collections and combinations are the same as those of individual beatitudes and woes. In Luke 6:20–26, therefore, the evangelist is working with a form of communication characteristic of his milieu. In this context both beatitudes and woes are eschatological in cast. They offer congratulations and condolences to people in the present on the basis of what will ultimately be. They celebrate that someone's life is a success or lament that it is a failure because it conforms or does not conform to what life will be like in the New Age.

(b) Meaning of key terms. The crux of the matter is whether or not "poor," "hunger," and "weep," and their counterparts "rich," "full," and "laugh," are to be understood sociologically or religiously. It must be the latter because the gospel canonizes no sociological state. At the same time the religious meaning of the terms often derived from an earlier sociological meaning.

"Congratulations to you poor." The vocabulary of poverty which at first had merely a sociological significance, over the centuries in Israel's history took on a spiritual meaning. In the history of Israel the economically poor observed the spirit of Israel's religion more faithfully than did the affluent elite. They came to be the model of the faithful worshipers: Isa 29:18–19 links the poor and the meek; in Isa 61:1 the Massoretic text's "preach good tidings to the meek" is rendered "to preach to the poor" by the LXX; at Qumran the "poor" were the ones counting worldly goods as nothing (cf. 4QPPs37, 1:8f.; I QH 5:13f.), the devout (cf. *War Scroll*); the Ps of Sol 10:7 mention the pious and the poor in synonymous parallelism (cf. also 5:2, 11; 15:1; 18:2). By the time of Jesus, in a Jewish context, the poor person had become the type of one who is pleasing to God, that is, one who recognizes his total dependence upon God. It was this connotation Matthew aimed to make explicit by his addition of "in spirit" (5:3). That Luke also intended "poor" to carry primarily a religious connotation may be seen from 1:51–53, where in parallelism the "proud and mighty" are equated with the "rich." At the same time the evangelist recognized the "poor" religiously (the powerless who are totally dependent on God) to be oftentimes "poor" economically (cf. 1:45; 2:24). Correspondingly, Luke's lament over the plight of the rich in 6:24, "O the tragedy of you rich people," refers in the first instance to a religious situation. Religiously, the rich are those who trust in their riches (cf. 1 Enoch 94:8–9: "Woe to you, you rich, for you have trusted in your riches.") and ignore God and neighbor (cf. Luke 12:16–21; 16:19–25). Part of the good news the anointed servant preaches to the poor (Luke 4:18) is that those who are powerless and trust wholly in God are to be celebrated as the successful; those who live with the illusion they are self-sufficient are to be lamented as failures. That disciples had difficulty seeing life from this angle is evidenced by the epistle of James near the time of Luke.

"Congratulations to you that hunger now." Again, the term "hunger" has both physical and spiritual connotations in the Jewish traditions. In passages like Ps 132:15; 146:7; Ezek 34:29, the hunger is physical; in Isa 55:1–2; Amos 8:11; Sir 24:21, hunger means also a desire for spiritual satisfaction; in Ps 107:9 and Isa 49:10, the meaning may be either or both. It was the religious connotation that Matthew made explicit by adding "for righteousness" (5:6). That Luke intended the spiritual connotation to be dominant may be seen from 1:51–53 where the hungry are paralleled to the lowly as opposed to the proud. It is those who are unsatisfied spiritually, the hungry who want more than they have, who are to be celebrated. By analogy 6:25's lament over the "full" must refer to those who are spiritually satisfied, to those unaware that "man shall not live by bread alone" (4:4). The self-sufficient who are spiritually satisfied are to be pitied: "O the tragedy of you that are full."

"Congratulations to you who weep." This is a term used frequently in Luke to express mourning and sorrow of all kinds. Doubtless the fallen structures of life that oppress the defenseless ones are the implied cause of anguish (cf. Ps 126:2, 5–6; Isa 60:2; 61:3; 66:10; 65:16–19; 35:10). "O the tragedy of you that laugh now." The verb translated "laugh" in 6:25b is used in the LXX of an evil kind of laughter which looks down on the fate of enemies and is in danger of becoming boastful and self-satisfied. This nuance may be present here. If so, the lament is over those who are self-satisfied and indifferent to the needs of others (I. H. Marshall, *The Gospel of Luke*, p. 256). Those who suffer under the present structures are to be celebrated; those who revel in those structures are to be pitied.

"Congratulations to those of you who are persecuted." Persecution on account of the Son of Man is to be celebrated. Thereby one joins the goodly company of the prophets who have previously suffered the same fate. It is good company to join. "O the tragedy of you who are popular." To be well spoken of by all in a world that rejects the Son of Man and his followers is lamentable because it places one in the company of the false prophets of old. It is tragic to be in such company. Here one cannot help but hear echoes of Christian trials such as those in Acts 6—7. Note the acting out of the injunction of Luke 6:23 in Acts 5:41.

Why are the poor (powerless), whose only hope is in God, blessed? It is because, trusting only in God, they belong to the sphere of God's rule (vs. 20b). Why, when such people hunger and weep and are persecuted, are they to be congratulated? It is because in God's ultimate victory they will be favored by the structures of the New Age. The type of persons described in 6:20–23 is to be extolled because of what they have now—God himself—and because of what they will ultimately have—support from the structures of life in the kingdom of God. The type of persons described in the woes is to be pitied because, trusting only in what now is, they have nothing more for which to hope (vs. 24b). Like the bad company they keep (6:26—false prophets), they will come up short when God settles the final account (1:51–53).

The second part of the Sermon on the Plain, 6:27–38, contains four thought units (6:27–28, 29–31, 32–36, 37–38) devoted to an attempt by Jesus to break the pattern of reciprocity in human relations among his disciples. The two initial units belong together in describing love in terms of nonviolence.

The first (6:27–28) establishes a principle: do not reciprocate by returning evil for evil—"Love your enemies, do good to those who hate you, bless those who curse you, pray for those who abuse you." This is a principle also found in Rom 12:14–21 and in 1 Pet 2:18–25 as an integral part of the early church's instructions for Christian living.

The second unit (6:29–31) gives four examples of what it would mean not to return evil for evil (6:29–30) and then concludes with the Golden Rule (6:31). The four examples (strikes, takes away, begs, takes away) of nonviolence are arranged in such a way as to become illustrations of the love of the enemy mentioned in vs. 27. Here we meet Jesus' use of the "focal instance" (for what follows, see R. C. Tannehill, "Tension in Synoptic Sayings and Stories," *Interpretation* 34:142–44[1980]). In a focal instance the situation described is so specific it does not provide a very useful general rule when confined to its literal sense. The specificity is intended to shock the hearers with an extreme command, at striking variance with the way people usually behave in such a situation, to lead the hearer to think beyond the literal meaning of the words and to reflect on the whole pattern of behavior that dominates life. The specific command is not a rule of behavior which can be followed mechanically but is intended to stimulate the imagination to draw out the implications for life as a whole. If no one has struck me on the cheek or taken away my coat, what would a nonviolent response to the violence I experience mean? When the moral imagination is awakened in this way, the words have had their desired effect. Love of the enemy means not returning evil for evil but responding to violence by creative nonviolence. Although the golden rule is not distinctly Christian (Homer, *Odyssey*, 5:188–89; Isocrates, *Nicokles*, 49:1; Seneca, *On Benefits*, 2:1:1; Tobit 4:15; Philo [in Eusebius, *Preparation of the Gospel*, 8:7]; 2 Enoch 61:1; Test Naphtali 1, passim), it is used here (vs. 31) by the evangelist to say one's response to evil treatment should be motivated not by how one is treated but by how one wants to be treated. If one acts as one wants to be treated, one will not be involved in returning evil for evil.

If we are to judge from the narrative in Acts, the evangelist would regard Stephen's martyrdom (7:54–60) as an example of a situation where a disciple prayed for those who abused him; Paul's response to the Philippian jailer (16:28ff.) would be an example of a Christian's doing good to one who was, on the surface of things, an enemy. It should be noted, however, that Luke apparently had no qualms about advocating the use of legal resources for one's defense against non-Christians when these were available (16:37–39; 22:25–29; 25:10–11). He gives no indication, however, in Acts, that he approved of one Christian's using the law for redress of grievance against another Christian. In this he may have agreed with Paul (1 Cor 6:1–11).

The last two units (6:32–36, 37–38) in the second section of the Sermon on the Plain also belong together in describing love in terms of generosity. The principle is set forth: do not show good will only to reciprocate or just to those who can reciprocate.

In the Hellenistic age of the Mediterranean world the relation between a benefactor and a beneficiary consisted of reciprocal obligations composed of the gratitude of the recipient to the benefactor and a resulting obligation of the benefactor to the beneficiary who had expressed gratitude. The ground rules were as follows: A person showed some kindness to another. In doing this repayment would be expected and the benefaction would be viewed as a loan. That a response of gratitude must be forthcoming influenced one's choice of the recipient of benevolence. A benefactor would help not the poor but the well-to-do because one could expect the recompense of thanksgiving from them. The expression of gratitude that was forthcoming then placed a valid claim for further benefits on the original benefactor (S. C. Mott, "The Power of Giving and Receiving; Reciprocity in Hellenistic Benevolence," in *Current Issues in Biblical and Patristic Interpretation,* ed. G. F. Hawthorne [Grand Rapids: Eerdmans, 1974], pp. 60–72).

The unit 6:32–36 asks three questions ("If you . . . , what credit is that to you? For even sinners. . . ."), then with present imperatives says, "But habitually love your enemies, and habitually do good, and habitually lend expecting nothing in return. . . ." Such generosity transcends the reciprocity principle. The motive for one's transcending that system of doing good is found in 6:35b–36. One shows good will not to reciprocate only and not just to those who can reciprocate because one is acting as the heavenly Father acts. He is kind to the ungrateful and the selfish. One is to be merciful as he is merciful.

The last unit (6:37–38) gives four examples of showing kindness even to the undeserving and then concludes with another motivation for such behavior: "Judge not, condemn not, forgive, give." Why? "For the measure you give will be the measure you get back" (vs. 38b). If we deny mercy to another we short-circuit God's mercy to us (cf. Matt 18:23–35; 2 Cor 9:6–15).

Luke 6:27–38, then, is a two-pronged attack on reciprocity as a governing principle in human relationships. On the one hand, people should not return evil for evil but rather respond as they would want to be treated: in Luke's mind this means nonviolence in return for violence. On the other hand, people must not restrict their good deeds either to others who have been good to them or to those who can and will be good in return. God shows good will to all and gives abundantly to disciples as they give to others: for Luke this means generosity. A life lived by the principle of reciprocity is too restrictive to express the love to which Jesus has called his disciples.

The call to respond not in kind but out of kind is problematic. How is it possible to respond nonviolently to violence done to us? How is it possible to be generous with those who reject us? Granted the legitimacy of the principle—love your enemies—what resources make it possible? If there are no such resources, what good does it do to lay such a heavy burden on disciples' backs? The narrative gives a clue as to how the evangelist would answer these questions. Jesus' disciples before Pentecost tended to respond in kind (e.g., 9:52–54; 22:49–50); afterward they rejoiced "that they were counted worthy to suffer dishonor for the name" (Acts 5:41). Only God's own powerful presence can enable a person to respond other than in kind; only Pentecost makes Jesus' words anything other than an impossible ideal.

The third and final part of the Sermon on the Plain, 6:39–49, consists of four parables (6:39–40, 41–42, 43–45, 46–49). Just as in 15:3, where the evangelist says Jesus told a parable (singular) and followed the statement with three parables in the remainder of the chapter, so the singular is followed here by four stories (cf. 5:36–38). That he introduces a series with the singular indicates the unity of the parables which follow, insofar as the evangelist is concerned. In chapter 15 Luke told three stories about the lost, its recovery, and the resulting joy. Here the evangelist, in vss. 39–45, is especially concerned with the matter of Christian influence.

Influence is an issue about which Luke speaks elsewhere. In 8:16 he visualizes a Roman-style house in which the lamp is placed in the vestibule to furnish light for those who enter (contrast Matt 5:15 where a one-room Palestinian house illuminated by the lamp is assumed). The point, in the Lukan context, is that those who have made a right response to the word of God and who belong to the family of God are to be light for those who are entering God's household. The character of those who are already disciples is to illumine the way of the new converts (C. E. Carlston, *The Parables of the Triple Tradition* [Philadelphia: Fortress, 1975], p. 91). Acts reflects the same idea. In 20:17-35 Luke reports a farewell speech of Paul to the Ephesian elders in which Paul says his behavior was a guide to them about the Christian way (vss. 33–35a). In the NT period new Christians learned the meaning of the Christian way from observation of those who were already Jesus' followers. This is why Paul could speak about his converts' imitating him (1 Cor 4:15–17; 11:1; Phil 3:17; 2 Thes 3:7). Christian influence was a matter about which the third evangelist was concerned.

The place of 6:39–45 in the perspective about influence is clarified when we notice the pattern of section. It is ABA'. The central unit (B—vss. 41–42) speaks of the need for the guide to be self-critical and personally transformed before undertaking the tasks of the admonition to and transformation of a fellow disciple. This does not mean that since every disciple is a sinner "he should live and let live and be blind to moral imperfections about him. Such a stance would give the green light to evil and spell the end of mutual admonition in the community" (F. Danker, *Jesus and the New Age,* p. 89). Rather the point is that any effort at improvement of others without taking stock of oneself is ridiculous.

The other two components (A—vss. 39–40; A'—vss. 43–45) function as motivations for the central concern for personal transformation before undertaking to assist others. In vss. 39–40 the motive is that since the pupil can be no better than his teacher, the teacher must not be blind. In order to get the desired result—improvement in the life of the other—one oneself must embody the newness of the Christian way. Verses 43–45 also speak of motivation (cf., *gar,* "for" in vs. 43). Personal transformation in the selfhood of the teacher is essential because what one does and says is only an overflow from who one is. The evangelist is saying the only way those who are already disciples can function as lights in the vestibule of the household of God (8:16) is if their own personal transformation is more basic to them than their role of instructing others (cf. James 3).

The final parable (6:46–49) serves both as the end of section three (6:39–49) and as the conclusion of the entirety of the Sermon on the Plain. Its function (cf. Ezek 13:10–16; Aboth R. Nathan 24) is exhortation. Like Jas 1:21–25 it is concerned with a disciple's doing what has been heard (cf. Matt 7:21–23; John 13:17; 1 John 2:17). Those who do what they hear are stable in times of crisis (Luke 8:15; Psalm 1); not so those who are hearers only (Luke 8:14). The gospel, just as the epistle of James, is concerned that disciples not regard the essence of Christianity as a belief and a confession (you call me, "Lord, Lord") separable from a walk in the world (and not do what I tell you). When the whole self responds totally to the one Lord, the result is an indissoluble union between confession and walk.

JESUS AND OTHER
RELIGIOUS TRADITIONS

7:1–10, 11–17

Luke 7:1–10 (Matt 8:5–13) and 7:11–17 (only in Luke) belong together with 6:20ff. as a prelude to 7:18–23. This is made clear by an examination of several details in 7:18–23. (1) 7:18 (different from Matt 11:12) says the disciples of John told him of "all these things." At first reading one would think "all these things" referred to one or both of the miracles in 7:1–10, 11–17. (2) Although 7:21 (not in Matthew) says Jesus worked miracles before John's disciples, the specific works of 7:21 are not exactly those of 7:22 (same as Matt 11:5). The list of mighty works at 7:22 corresponds with those in Isa 35:5; 61:1, except the Isaiah passages do not refer to lepers being cleansed or to the dead being raised. These two items probably echo the Elijah-Elisha traditions (cf. Luke 4:25–27 with the OT parallels). It is significant that a tradition unique to Luke, 7:11–17, the raising of a dead man, precedes the story of 7:18–23, which refers in vs. 22 to raising the dead. (3) In 7:22, after the references to the mighty works, there is "the poor have good news preached to them." This, of course, was not only what Jesus had announced as his aim (4:18) but what he had explicitly done in 6:20: "Blessed are you poor, for yours is the kingdom of God." This would seem to say that "all these things" of 7:18 would have been understood by the evangelist to include 6:20ff., as well as 7:1–17; that is, what Jesus said as well as what he did.

On what basis should John the Baptist believe? From Luke's perspective the Baptist is offered miracles and the proclamation of good news to the poor which are prophesied in scripture as events of the last days. The data by which John's response is evoked consist of what his disciples had seen and heard (7:22; cf. 1 John 1:3).

This pattern (an eschatological message accompanied by signs and wonders which evoke a response to Jesus) is that which characterizes the Acts of the Apostles (cf. 2; 3—4; 8; 10; 13; 16). From the evangelist's point of view, it is the confrontation with both things seen and things heard that truly raises the issue of Jesus' identity.

Within the larger context the evangelist is especially interested in the story in Luke 7:1–10 where the centurion stands as a type of a believing Gentile. Two strands of evidence combine to make this clear. First, although 7:1–10 recounts the same basic tradition found in Matt 8:5–13 (cf. John 4:46–54), the Lukan form of the healing is expanded by vss. 3–6. Luke's centurion deals with Jesus, not directly as in Matt 8:5–7, but indirectly through two embassies, the first consisting of elders of the Jews and the second of friends. The Jewish embassy speaks to Jesus of the centurion's meritoriousness: "He is worthy to have you do this for him, for he loves our nation, and he built us our synagogue" (7:4–5). Second, this distinctively Lukan section is echoed in Acts 10:1–2: "At Caesarea there was a man named Cornelius, a centurion . . . , a devout man who feared God with all his household, gave alms liberally to the people, and prayed constantly to God." In the overall architectonic scheme of Luke-Acts, in which the events of Acts parallel those in the gospel in content and sequence, these two passages correspond. The evangelist has thereby tied these two episodes together so 7:1–10 functions as a foreshadowing of the conversion of the Gentiles. In other words, the story of the centurion in 7:1–10 gives dominical precedent for the mission to the Gentiles in the narrative of Acts. More precisely, 7:1–10 gives dominical precedent for Peter's actions in Acts 10, just as Luke 8:26–39 gives a warrant for Paul's move outside the bounds of Jewish territory in Acts 13—28. The centurion in 7:1–10 is a type of the believing Gentile in Jewish territory.

The centurion is, moreover, an example of one who has faith in Jesus without having seen him: he deals with Jesus not directly but through two embassies. He represents the Gentiles who "without having seen him . . . love him" (1 Pet 1:8). John reflects the same concern, both in the story of the Greeks who approach Jesus only through the disciples (12:20ff.) and in the beatitude near the end of the gospel: "Blessed are those who have not seen and yet believe" (20:29).

When the elders of the Jews cite the centurion's religious credentials to Jesus and proclaim him worthy (vss. 4–5), we meet another Lukan theme: attitudes toward other religious traditions. At least three points on a spectrum need to be noted. (1) Luke believes Jesus fulfills Judaism. (2) He thinks Jesus judges much of pagan religion. (a) Christianity is entirely opposed to magic; that is, the use of spiritual power for personal gain (Acts 8:9ff.; 13:6ff.; 19:19). (b) Christianity undermines pagan religion motivated by financial greed (Acts 19:23ff.). (c) Christianity calls for repentance from those who worship the creation rather than the Creator (Acts 17:22ff.; 14:8ff.). (3) The evangelist also believes Jesus completes pagan piety that follows the light it has, worshiping the Creator instead of the creation and engaging in ethical behavior. This posture is stated most explicitly in the speech attributed to Peter in Acts 10:34–35: "Truly I perceive that God shows no partiality, but in every nation any one who fears him and does what is right is acceptable to him." It is this third point that is foreshadowed in Luke 7:1–10. It raises the question of whether or not Luke had either a natural theology (that is, whether one could infer from either the world or from human nature that God is) or a belief in a general revelation (that is, God is at work in all times and places disclosing himself through the world and in every person's depths).

Clarification of Lukan thought on this point depends on a comparison with that of Hellenistic Judaism, Paul, and Justin Martyr. (1) Ancient Judaism had a natural theology of sorts. The Wisdom of Solomon asserts (13:1–9) there is a possibility of an inference being made from the greatness and beauty of created things to God as their Creator (vs. 5); however, the Gentiles have not made this inference (vs. 1). Josephus (*Antiquities* 1:7:1 §154–57) gives another tradition (e.g., Genesis Rabbah 38:13) about Abraham's theistic inference from nature, succeeding where the Gentiles had failed. Philo's *The Migration of Abraham,* 35, also refers to the possibility of a theistic inference being made from the order or rule seen within the human being. In certain circles of ancient Judaism there was a natural theology which held that any human being could, by inference, reason from either nature or the human self to God—though, in fact, some did and some did not.

The author of Luke-Acts has something in common with Hellenistic Judaism. In Acts 14:17, in a speech attributed to Paul and Barnabas in Lystra, we hear that God "did not leave himself without witness, for he did good and gave you from heaven rains and fruitful seasons, satisfying your hearts with food and gladness." There are signs in the natural order which witness to God. Whether or not they have been seen and acknowledged is not mentioned explicitly. The context of the speech, however, vss. 12, 13, 18, seems to indicate that these Gentiles have not attained a knowledge of God. Acts 17:22–31, a speech attributed to Paul, says God the creator made human beings "that they should seek God, in the hope that they might feel after him and find him" (17:27). Verses 29, 30a, 23, however, seem to indicate that, rather than finding the Creator, the Gentiles have worshiped the creation instead. They did not attain a knowledge of God. These two passages seem very much like Wis 13:1–9. The possibility of a natural knowledge of God is there but it has not been actualized.

The distinctiveness of Acts 10 (and possibly Luke 7:1–10) is that here we find a Gentile who feared God (vs. 2). Cornelius had apparently realized the possibility. It is of those Gentiles who had made the correct inference that Peter speaks in Acts 10:34–35.

This emphasis, however, must be set alongside Acts 4:12 if we are to understand the evangelist correctly. In 4:12 Peter says, "And there is salvation in no one else, for there is no other name under heaven given among men by which we must be saved." So in the Cornelius episode of Acts 10, the Gentile's correct inference via natural theology must be completed by Peter's preaching of Jesus and by the Holy Spirit's falling on Cornelius and his household as a sign of their response in faith. In the theology of Luke-Acts, Jesus is the completion of a correct response made to the witness of God given in the natural order. When in Luke 7:1–10 the centurion is pronounced worthy by the Jews, he is, as noted above, a foreshadowing of the worthy centurion Cornelius of Acts 10 who, in turn, symbolizes a whole class of people in Luke's own time. The evangelist is thinking of virtuous and godly pagans whose following of the light they have has been the preparation for Christ. For such people Christ is the completion of their developing relation to God.

(2) A comparison of Lukan thought with that of Paul is also helpful in clarifying the perspective of Luke-Acts on this matter. In Rom 1:19 the second part of the verse clarifies the first: "For God has manifested it to them" (vs. 19b) shows that the apostle is thinking in terms of a general revelation rather than a natural theology. The media of the revelation are "the things made"; the time of the revelation is "from the creation of the world"; and the content of the revelation is "his eternal power and deity" (1:20). In Rom 1:21 Paul indicates the revelation was actualized, at least to the degree that made humans responsible: "although they knew God they did not honor him as God or give thanks to him." There are some significant differences, then, between the views of Paul and the third evangelist on the matter of the Gentiles' knowledge of God. Luke, like Hellenistic Judaism, talks about a

natural theology instead of a general revelation, about Gentiles who do not worship the creation but acknowledge the Creator.

(3) Justin Martyr forms a final point of comparison. This church father of the first half of the second century believed in a general revelation. He identified the preexistent Son of God with the reason (of the Stoics) of whom the whole human race partakes. There is, then, in Justin's thought, a general revelation to all people, though some distort or pervert it. If anyone lives according to reason, however, that person is a Christian, even if usually thought to be an atheist, as for example, Socrates (*Apology I,* 46:1–4). Yet the general revelation is imperfect and needs to be completed by the special revelation in the incarnation (*Apology II,* 13). Here, as in Paul, the emphasis is on a general revelation. Unlike Paul, Justin thinks the revelation comes not by means of the created order but through the cosmic Christ who enlightens every person. Like the author of Luke-Acts and Paul, Justin thinks God's act in Jesus is necessary to do something left undone without it (cf. also Clement of Alexandria, *Stromateis,* 6).

In their estimation of the religious potential of pagans, Paul is the most pessimistic. There is just enough actualization of general revelation to make all people responsible for their sin. Justin is the most optimistic. Some follow the general revelation, live according to reason, and, like Socrates, can be regarded as Christians even though they live apart from special revelation. Luke stands between these two, in league with Hellenistic Judaism, assessing the possibilities of the pagan religious response to God neither totally positively nor totally negatively, but nuanced. For some pagan religion Jesus is exclusively judge; for other pagan piety Jesus is the completion of the path already taken on the basis of natural theology. Luke 7 and Acts 10 give the evangelist's estimate of the latter position.

How does the evangelist understand the centurion's piety to be completed by Jesus? Though the Jewish elders deem the centurion "worthy" (vs. 4), the second embassy composed of friends of the Gentile makes clear that the man considered himself unworthy (vs. 6). After the confession of his unworthiness, he expresses his absolute trust in Jesus' authoritative word: "Look," he says, "I know from personal experience what the word of a person in authority will do. A word from my superiors makes me act, just as a word from me causes my subordinates to obey. So you just say the word and my servant will be healed" (7:7–8). That Jesus does in fact have authority over the created order comes clear in Luke's narrative in 8:22–25. Here Jesus' response is, "I tell you, not even in Israel have I found such faith" (7:9). Whereas the elders of the Jews had pointed to the good works of the centurion, Jesus praised his faith. The story, thereby, presents the centurion as a type of pious Gentile whose relation to God is completed by a confession of his unworthiness before Jesus and by placing his faith in Jesus' authority.

Comparison of 7:1–10 and 5:1–11 shows that Peter, a Jew, and this Gentile come to Jesus in the same way: (a) confession of sin or unworthiness (5:8; 7:6), and (b) trust in Jesus' authority (5:5, 11; 7:7–8). The same theme is put into the mouth of Peter in his speech at the Jerusalem Council (Acts 15), where he says God "made no distinction between us and them, but cleansed their hearts by faith" (Acts 15:9). Also he says, "We believe we shall be saved through the grace of the Lord Jesus, just as they will" (15:11). Paul had made the point earlier in Gal 2:15–16. Whether it is a Jew whose tradition is fulfilled or a pagan whose appropriate response to the light available is completed, the way to Jesus involves some discontinuity with the past (hence the sense of unworthiness or sin) and a submission to a new authority (the lordship of Jesus).

For Luke, Jesus is the ultimate revelation toward which all others point. Whether Jesus is related to other religious traditions primarily as judge or primarily as the fulfillment or completion depends upon the degree of discontinuity or continuity between the other traditions and the revelation in Jesus. Even those religious traditions with the greatest continuity to Jesus still stand before him "unworthy" and in need of submission to his ultimate authority.

CONFIRMED FORGIVENESS

7:36–50, 18–35

Luke 7:36–50 is a story with similarities to that of Jesus' anointing by a woman in Bethany found in Matt 26:6–13 // Mark 14:3–9 // John 12:1–8. In Matthew and Mark it is an unnamed woman, at Bethany, in the house of Simon the leper, who anoints Jesus' head, during the last week of Jesus' life. In the fourth gospel, it is Mary, at Bethany, in the house of Mary, Martha, and Lazarus, who anoints Jesus' feet and wipes them with her hair, at the beginning of the last week ·of Jesus' life. Here it is an unnamed woman, in Galilee, in the house of Simon the Pharisee, who washes Jesus' feet with her tears and dries them with her hair, who kisses his feet and anoints them, early in the public ministry. The meaning of this distinctive Lukan form of the tradition may be grasped if we concentrate on the context and on the inner organization of the unit.

The context shows that the story in 7:36–50 functions as an illustration of certain issues delineated in vss. 29–35. Immediately preceding 7:36–50 is a large unit of material held together by the focus on John the Baptist in its several parts (7:18–23, 24–28, 29–30, 31–35), the last two parts being linked by a further affinity, a reference to people justifying God: "all the people and the tax collectors justified God" (vs. 29); "wisdom is justified by all her children" (vs. 35—"Wisdom" is a periphrasis for God or for the *boulē tou theou* [purpose of God]. At first sight this use of the verb "to justify" seems strange but Jewish usage shows it is not. In the Psalms of Solomon, *dikaioun* (to justify) does not refer to a human's justification but rather refers to God. God's people justify him; that is, they vindicate the sentence, judgments, and name of God, accepting and acknowledging them to be righteous (2:16; 3:3; 4:9; 8:7, 27). The same usage is found in Ps 51:4: "thou art justified in thy sentence and blameless in thy judgment" (cf. also 2 Esdr 10:16; b. Berakoth 19a). It is this same usage we encounter in Rom 3:4 which cites Ps 51:4, and in 1 Tim 3:16. Both Luke 7:29 (cf. Matt 21:32) and 7:35 (// Matt 11:19) use the verb *dikaioun* in this way.

Here the verb "justified" should be paraphrased "demonstrated or acknowledged to be righteous" (G. Schrenk, *TDNT*, 2:213–15).

In both 7:29 and 7:35, for God to be justified means for him to be acknowledged to be right in the positions taken in the ministries of John and Jesus. It amounts to the acknowledgment of the divine authority of the careers of the Baptist and Mary's son and the acceptance of God's will for one's life as stated by those two (cf. vs. 30). Luke 7:29 says the tax collectors justified God, that is, they accepted the will of God set forth by his servant John, but the Pharisees did not. Luke 7:35 says God's children are those who justify him, that is, accept God's purpose for their lives. Since the will of God set forth in John's ministry was summed up in his "baptism of repentance for the forgiveness of sins" (3:3), for the evangelist to say the Pharisees rejected God's purpose for them is to say they did not repent and did not receive God's forgiveness. Since Jesus came to call sinners to repentance (5:32), to reject him was to miss the acceptance of God that Jesus' presence mediated (5:17–26, 27–32). To justify God was to acknowledge the rightness of his call in John and Jesus and to repent and be forgiven: This the people and the tax collectors did; this the Pharisees and the lawyers did not.

The Pharisee in 7:36 is to be understood as partaking of the character of the Pharisees in 7:29–30. The woman in vss. 37ff., like the tax collectors, had acknowledged God's verdict on her and had received her forgiveness from God. The Pharisee did not accept God's verdict on him and had not received forgiveness in any significant way. The story in 7:36–50, then, is an illustration of those who justified God and of those who did not. In the context it is the overt sinners (the people and tax collectors) who acknowledge the rightness of God's verdict about them stated in the preaching of John and Jesus, repent, and receive forgiveness. The covert sinners (Pharisees and lawyers) do not accept God's will for them, do not repent, and do not receive divine forgiveness. In the illustrative story, "it was a sin of the flesh [Jesus] forgave, a sin of the spirit he reproved" (*Luther's Meditations on the Gospels*, trans. and arranged by R. H. Bainton [Philadelphia: Westminster Press, 1962], p. 49). In Luke's view, everyone, those with covert sins of the spirit as well as those with overt sins of the flesh, stands in need of forgiveness. Luke 7:36–50 tells a story of one who received divine pardon and one who did not.

There are at least two crucial patterns of organization in 7:36–50.

Overall the unit falls into a chiastic pattern. After the introductory statement in 7:36 which serves to locate the events at mealtime in a Pharisee's house, the story has an AB:B'A' pattern.

A The woman's actions toward Jesus: a display of unusual affection (7:37–38)
B The Pharisee's negative judgment of Jesus (7:39)
B' Jesus' response to Simon's appraisal (7:40–47)
A' Jesus' response to the woman (7:48, 50)

A and A' are action oriented. They focus on the woman's display of affection toward Jesus and on Jesus' confirmation of her forgiveness (vs. 48). B and B' involve explanations to two questions: first, why is the woman known to be forgiven by her display of affection and second, how can Jesus pronounce the confirmation of her forgiveness? These questions will shape the discussion of the passage which follows.

In the East the door of the dining room was left open so the uninvited could pass in and out during the festivities. They were allowed to take seats by the wall, listening to the conversation between the host and guests. When Jesus sat at table with Simon the Pharisee, a woman of the city entered. Instead of sitting by the wall and listening, she lavished her affection on Jesus: (a) she wet his feet with her tears and wiped them with the hair of her head; (b) she kissed his feet; and (c) she anointed his feet with ointment (vss. 37–38). That Jesus permitted the act evoked a negative response from his host (vs. 39).

Verses 39–47 (B and B') comprise what has been called a "Socratic interrogation" and consist of four component parts: (a) question by the opponent (vs. 39); (b) counter-question (vs. 42b); (c) forced answer from the opponent (vs. 43); and (d) refutation of the opponent on the basis of his forced answer (vs. 47). Originating in Hellenistic rhetoric, this form was used by both Jews and Christians in organizing their materials (E. E. Ellis, *The Gospel of Luke* [rev. ed., Greenwood, S.C.: Attic Press, 1974], p. 121).

(a) The Pharisee's unspoken question in 7:39 is cast in the form of an unreal condition in present time; that is, both clauses are regarded as untrue. Jesus, it is assumed, does not know the woman. He, therefore, cannot be a prophet. Note that the story uses this denial by Simon to affirm that Jesus is indeed a prophet; he discerns what the Pharisee is thinking and tells a parable (vss. 41–42a) which ends with

(b) a counter-question: "Now which of them will love him more?" (vs. 42b). (c) Simon's answer is forced: "The one, I suppose, to whom he forgave more" (vs. 43a). (d) Jesus agrees (vs. 43b) and draws an inference (vss. 44–47): "Although, Simon, you did not act discourteously but were correct enough as a host, you did not perform any special acts of hospitality. This woman, however, has lavished affection on me. Why would she do that?" Jesus answers his own question in vs. 47.

There are two possible ways of reading vs. 47. (1) "Because of her conduct her many sins have been forgiven." Here the sinful woman's love is understood as the cause of her forgiveness. (2) "Her many sins have been forgiven, as is evidenced by her conduct." Here the woman's love is viewed as the evidence of her forgiveness. The second reading is linguistically possible (e.g., 1:22; 6:21) and is demanded by the context. The New English Bible's reading is to the point: "And so, I tell you, her great love proves that her many sins have been forgiven; where little has been forgiven, little love is shown." Why is the woman known to be forgiven? The answer is that her display of affection is evidence of it.

After the evangelist tells of Jesus' acts on behalf of needy people, whether physical or spiritual, he often relates the responses he deems appropriate. Sometimes the response is horizontal, an ethical one (e.g., 19:8—"Behold, Lord, the half of my goods I give to the poor; and if I have defrauded anyone of anything, I restore it fourfold."). At other times, the response is vertical, directed not toward other human beings but toward God (e.g., glorified God—5:25–26; 7:16; praised God, 17:18) or, as in the story here, toward Jesus. The evangelist sees the appropriateness of both horizontal (ethical) and vertical (worship) responses to God's forgiveness and healing. In 7:36–50 the emphasis is on lavish affection shown to Jesus as a sign of one's prior salvation (vs. 50), and the absence of that display is regarded as evidence of the lack of an appropriation of forgiveness. Affection and praise lavished on Jesus is an authentic and appropriate evidence of divine forgiveness. Their absence is evidence of unappropriated redemption. Seeing the woman's outburst of love, Jesus said to her, "Your sins are forgiven" (vs. 48).

The question of those at table with Jesus shapes the next phase of the discussion: "Who is this, who even forgives sins?" (vs. 49) How is it that Jesus can pronounce confirmation of the woman's forgiveness? The clue is given in vs. 39, Simon's unspoken negative judgment of Jesus: "If this man were a prophet, he would have known who and

what sort of woman this is who is touching him, for she is a sinner."
Jesus knows the thoughts of Simon's heart and responds to them: the
inference must be that Jesus is a prophet. A prophet is one who knows
not only the minds and hearts of human beings but also the mind of
God (cf. 1 Kgs 22:19ff.).

The third evangelist presents Jesus in prophetic terms on many occasions. In 4:16–30 the motif begins: Jesus is the anointed prophet
who is not accepted in his own country; Luke 7:16 reports the peoples'
response to the raising of the widow's son at Nain was to exclaim, "A
great prophet has arisen among us" (cf. also 13:33; 24:19; Acts 3:22–
23). Here the mark of a prophet is his spiritual discernment and ability
to see beneath the surface of events. Jesus certainly fits this category:
he knows the ultimate outcome of history (6:20–26); he discerns the
thoughts of Simon (7:39ff.); he knows the mind of God about the
woman's sins (7:48). To pronounce the forgiveness of sins because
one knows the mind of God on the matter is a prophetic act (2 Sam
12:13; Isa 40:2; cf. 4QPrNab 1–3:2–4, a fragmentary Aramaic text from
Qumran, where a Jewish exorcist remits the sins of the Babylonian
king, Nabonidus). This is doubtless how the evangelist understood a
similar act of Jesus in 5:17–26. The possibility of Jesus' acting this
way lies in his having been anointed with the Holy Spirit (4:18–19) so
he can "proclaim release to the captives." The fourth gospel depicts
Jesus in the same way: Jesus, on whom the Spirit has descended and
remained (1:32), possesses a knowledge of human hearts (e.g., 1:48;
2:25; 4:17–19, 39). It is of interest to note that Jesus' discernment of
the Samaritan woman's situation elicits the response, "Sir, I perceive
you are a prophet" (4:19). The Johannine Jesus also knows the mind
of the Father (e.g., 5:19–20; 8:28–29).

The spiritual discernment of the anointed Jesus is also a part of the
equipment of the Spirit-baptized disciples in Acts (e.g., 5:3–4; 8:23).
The same is true in the fourth gospel: after the risen Lord has breathed
the Holy Spirit on the disciples (20:22), he can say, "If you forgive the
sins of any, they are forgiven; if you retain the sins of any, they are
retained" (20:23). This is best understood as prophetic confirmation of
what God has done because, being filled with the Spirit, one, like the
prophets of old, knows the mind of God. A similar point is made in
Paul: in 1 Cor 2:10–12, in another connection, the apostle says Christians know the mind of God by means of the Holy Spirit; in 1 Cor 12:8,
speaking of some gifts of the Spirit, he refers to "the utterance of

knowledge." This is almost certainly referring to the type of spiritual discernment that comes from the presence of the Holy Spirit in the life of a prophet, be he Jesus or a Christian. To use Paul's categories, in Luke 7:39–47, 48, we find two words of knowledge uttered by Jesus. By means of the Spirit Jesus discerns both the hearts of people and the mind of God. In exercising this prophetic capacity of spiritual discernment, Luke regards Jesus as prototypical for his disciples (knowledge of the mind of God—Acts 2:14ff.; 13:1–3; 16:9–10; knowledge of the hearts of men and women—Acts 5:1–11; 20:29–30). The empowering presence of God imparts spiritual discernment to the prophetic community of Jesus' disciples, the same discernment manifest in Luke 7:36–50 by Jesus.

THE MINISTRIES OF WOMEN

8:1–21

Luke 8:1–21 is a thought unit consisting of a parable (8:4–8), a request for an explanation of the story by the disciples (8:9–10), and the explanation of the parable (8:11–15), to which have been added an introduction (8:1–3) and two small units which further elucidate the theme of the parable (8:16–18, 19–21). The key terms "hear" (8:8b, 10, 12, 13, 14, 15, 18, 21) and "word" (8:11, 13, 15, 21) act as glue to join the pieces.

The introduction (vss. 1–3) serves to validate the authority of the preaching of the church (which is referred to in the parable and its interpretation (vss. 4–8, 11–15), by showing it was based on the testimony of witnesses who were with Jesus when the kingdom of God was being disclosed (W. C. Robinson, Jr., "On Preaching the Word of God [Luke 8:4–21]," in *Studies in Luke-Acts*, ed. L. E. Keck and J. L. Martyn [Nashville: Abingdon, 1966], p. 136). Those who were "with him" (vss. 1b–2) belong to two groups: (1) the Twelve, and (2) the women. Both groups are designated by the evangelist elsewhere as those who came with him from Galilee (23:49; 23:55; 24:10; Acts 1:11; 13:31). It appears to be Luke's intention to set the Twelve and the women alongside one another as guarantors of the facts of the Christ event.

The evangelist pays special attention to women in his narrative of Jesus and the early church: Luke 1:24ff., Elizabeth (only in Luke); 1:26ff., Mary (only in Luke); 2:36ff., Anna (only in Luke); 4:38ff., Simon's mother-in-law; 7:11ff., the widow at Nain (only in Luke); 7:36ff., the sinful woman (only in Luke); 8:2–3, women who ministered to Jesus and his disciples (only in Luke); 8:43ff., woman with a hemorrhage; 10:38ff., Martha and Mary (only in Luke); 13:10ff., the crippled woman (only in Luke); 15:8–10, the parable of the woman with a lost coin (only in Luke); 18:1–8, parable of the widow (only in Luke); 21:1ff., the widow who gave her all; 23:49, 55, the women at the crucifixion; 24:10–11, 22–23, the women at the tomb; Acts 1:14, the women and Mary at prayer; 5:1ff., Sapphira; 6:1ff., the widows; 9:36ff., Dorcas; 12:12ff., Mary the mother of Mark and Rhoda; 16:14ff., Lydia; 16:16ff., the slave girl who is healed; 17:12, Greek women of high standing believed; 17:34, Damaris; 18:2, 18, 26, Priscilla; 21:9, Philip's four daughters; 23:16, Paul's sister; 25:13, Bernice.

It is interesting to note how the evangelist frequently sets women alongside men in various ministries. We have already noted the Galilean women alongside the Galilean men as guarantors of the facts of Jesus' career. There are other instances. (1) The women of Luke 8:3 "serve" (*diēkonoun*) just as the men in Acts 6:2 "serve" (*diakonein*) tables. In this matter Luke manifests continuity with early Christianity generally. In Rom 16:1 Phoebe is a deaconness (*diakonon*). 1 Tim 3:8–12 probably refers to deaconnesses, not to wives of deacons. Pliny's letter to Trajan early in the second century also mentions deaconnesses. (2) In Luke-Acts women prophesy alongside men (Anna in Luke 2:36–38, adjacent to Simeon in 2:25–35; Acts 2:17–18 says the Spirit has been poured out on all flesh so that "your sons and daughters shall prophesy"; Philip's four daughters who prophesied are mentioned alongside Agabus in Acts 21:9–11). Again Luke possesses continuity with the early church in its practice: e.g., 1 Cor 11:5, from the first century, and Tertullian, *Against Marcion*, 5:8, near A.D. 200. (3) Women are listed alongside the Twelve in prayer before Pentecost in Acts 1:12–14. In the ancient church generally, women engaged in public prayer (e.g., 1 Cor 11:4–5; 1 Tim 2:8–9; *Didascalia Apostolorum* 15:124). (4) Women sometimes have church services in their houses (Acts 12:5, 12; 16:15) just as men do (Acts 18:7). This is a practice also found in Rom 16:3–5 and Philm 1–2. The Cemetery of Priscilla on the Via Salaria in Rome shows that a Christian woman of means could use her house and lands for the service of the church. Again Luke reflects common Christian practice. (5) At least one woman teaches, together with her husband, who is the second named, and the one taught is a male preacher. So Priscilla and Aquila teach Apollos in Acts 18:26. This is a singular reference in the NT. It is in striking discontinuity with 1 Tim 2:12 ("I permit no woman to teach or to have authority over men; she is to keep silent") and possibly with 1 Cor 14:34–35 ("the women should keep silence in the churches. For they are not permitted to speak, but should be subordinate. . . . If there is anything they desire to know, let them ask their husbands at home. For it is shameful for a woman to speak in church"). This may

be a post-Pauline interpolation from the hand of a Paulinist who reflected the same point of view as 1 Tim 2:12. It may just as easily be
an integral part of 1 Corinthians and be a reference to Maenadism
(ecstatic behavior on the part of women under the influence of an
orgiastic deity, like Dionysius), or perhaps to some other type of clamor
which was disruptive. This disruptive noise would be prohibited (Richard and Catherine Kroeger, "An Inquiry into Evidence of Maenadism
in the Corinthian Congregation," in *SBL 1978 Seminar Papers,* ed.
P. J. Achtemeier [Missoula: Scholars Press, 1978], 2:331–38). If 1 Cor
14:34–35 is an interpolation reflecting the posture of 1 Tim 2:12, it is
in discontinuity with Luke-Acts. If, however, the passage refers not to
women teaching but to disruptive noises of whatever kind, the Corinthian passage is irrelevant to a discussion of women teachers. The difference in Luke's attitude in Acts 18:26 and that of the author of 1
Tim 2:12 is very likely that Priscilla in Acts represents the orthodox
Pauline line (cf. Acts 18:1ff.) in Luke's story, whereas women in the
Pastorals were the special prey of the heretics (e.g., 2 Tim 3:6–7). A
special circumstance dictated the stance taken in the Pastorals. In later
Christianity, however, it was the stance of the Pastorals rather than of
Luke-Acts that dominated Christian practice. In the Lukan scheme of
things, women often functioned side by side with men in Christian
ministry, including the ministry of teaching.

The ministry of women in the narrative of Luke-Acts did not cancel
their traditional roles in society, though on occasion it did stretch them
a bit. They reflect a variety of roles in society. (1) There are single
women living with their parents (e.g., Acts 21:8–9, Philip's four unmarried daughters). (2) There is a businesswoman who is apparently
without a husband (e.g., Lydia, Acts 16:14–15), though with a household. (3) There is a wife who works with her husband in the family
business (e.g., Priscilla who with Aquila was a tentmaker, Acts 18:
2–3). (4) There are married women involved in motherhood (e.g., Mary,
the model disciple, Luke 2:1ff., 41ff.). In each case, the women disciples used whatever role they occupied as a vehicle for the furtherance
of God's will. Their ministries varied just as their roles in society did,
but each had a ministry within the context of her particular role.

In some cases the roles defined by society were stretched by the
women's ministry. Luke 8:1–3 is a perfect example of this: It was not
uncommon for women to support rabbis and their disciples with their
own money, property, or foodstuffs (j. Horayot 48a, 1.44; Esther Rab-

bah II, 3; b. Shabbath 62a; b. Berakoth 10b; b. Rabba Kamma 119a), but for a woman to leave home and travel with a rabbi was not only unknown, it was scandalous (Ben Witherington, III, "On the Road with Mary Magdalene, Joanna, Susanna, and Other Disciples—Luke 8: 1–3," *Zeitschrift für neutestamentliche Wissenschaft* 70:243–47 [1979]). Yet the women of 8:1–3, including Joanna, the wife of Chuza, Herod's steward, not only provided for Jesus and his disciples but also accompanied them. Here the social roles were stretched but not shattered. A generation earlier Paul had stood against the shattering of a woman's social role (e.g., 1 Corinthians 7 argues against separating from one's spouse because of one's religious experience, and 11:2–16 speaks against a woman's casting off the symbols of her sexuality in the name of her Christian faith). In Luke's own time the household codes (Col 3:18ff.; Eph 5:21ff.; 1 Pet 3:1ff.) stood for the stability of social roles, though with modifications produced by the leaven of Christian grace, lest Christianity be identified with the disreputable Oriental cults that catered to women and undermined the stability of family life. It would appear that the third evangelist is as positive toward the ministry of women in the church as his social structure would allow. He did not, however, want to undermine the church's chances in Greco-Roman culture by advocating "customs which it is not lawful for us Romans to accept and practice" (Acts 16:21).

In the ancient church there were three ways of ordering the ministry of women: lay ministry (e.g., evangelism, praying and prophesying in church, opening one's home to the church); clerical ministry (e.g., the institution of widow and of deaconness in the third century); and the ministry of the religious (e.g., in the Byzantine world and in the middle ages in the West, it is the nuns who inherit the chief privileges of the earlier widows and deaconnesses: cf. Jean Daniélou, *The Ministry of Women in the Early Church* [London: Faith Press, 1961]). In terms of this threefold structure, one would have to say that Luke viewed the ministry of women as a lay ministry. This, however, is a position determined by the social structures of the world in which the evangelist lived.

Luke 8:4–21 focuses on the matter of responses to the church's proclamation. The unit begins with the parable of the sower (vss. 4–8). In vs. 9 the disciples ask Jesus the meaning of this particular parable, not the parables in general as in Mark 4:10. The interpretation (vss. 11–15) explains that the point has to do with responses to the "word of God" (Acts 6:7; 12:24; 13:49; 19:20). The question is: why did the gospel find a lasting response in so few? Wrong responses are due to the devil (cf. Luke 22:3), to lack of roots which makes one vulnerable in time of temptation (cf. Luke 22:40, 46; 2 Pet 3:17), and to the cares, riches, and pleasures of life (cf. Acts 5:1–11).

The right response on hearing the word is to "hold it fast in an honest and good heart, and bring forth fruit with patience" (vs. 15; cf. Rom 5:3–4; Heb 6:11–12; 12:1–3, etc.). The distinctive Lukan *en hypomonē*, "with patience," gives the opposite of all wrong responses. It is this "hearing the word of God and doing it" (vs. 21) which characterizes the family of Jesus in Luke-Acts (Luke 1:38, 45; Acts 1:14) and will characterize all Jesus' disciples (Luke 6:47; 10:37; 11:28; cf. Jas 1:22–25).

Those who have made a right response to the word of God, as Jesus' family has done in Luke's narrative, are to be light for those who enter the household of God (vs. 16). As mentioned above, the house assumed is a Roman-style one in which the lamp is placed in the vestibule to furnish light for those who enter. The perseverance of those who are already disciples will illumine the way of new converts.

UNIVERSAL POWER
AND VESTED INTERESTS

8:22—9:6

This section is a single thought unit in the evangelist's scheme, beginning with a distinctive Lukan time reference: "one day" (cf. Mark 4:35; Matt 8:23). This was apparently intended to set all that follows, through 9:6, within the framework of a day. Within these temporal boundaries the material is held together by several interlocking devices. (1) Four miracle stories (8:22–25; 8:26–39; 8:40–42, 49–56; 8:43–48) demonstrate Jesus' power and are followed by 9:1–6, a pericope in which Jesus gives power and authority to the Twelve. (2) The four miracle stories are further linked with 9:1–6 by Jesus leaving a place he is not welcomed (8:37), and telling his disciples about departure from a town that does not receive them (9:5). (3) Key words play a role in joining the four miracle stories. (a) 8:22–25, 26–39 refer to the lake (8:22, 33) and to the boat (8:22, 37). (b) In 8:25, 35, 37, 47 (?), 50, we encounter references to fear. (c) There is a focus on "salvation/being saved" in 8:36, 48, 50. (d) Whereas 8:42, 43 have "twelve years" in common, 8:48, 49 both contain "daughter," 8:48, 50 refer to "faith." Taking our clue from the time reference in 8:22 and the various interlocking devices mentioned, we may regard 8:22—9:6 as a single unit. If so, what point is the evangelist making?

The evangelist focuses on Jesus' gift of his own power to disciples prior to his sending them out to minister. A comparison of the organization of the material in Luke with its arrangement in Matthew and Mark clarifies this intent. (1) In Mark the four miracles in 4:35—5:43 (storm at sea; demoniac healed; hemorrhaging woman; raising of Jairus' daughter) are followed by the rejection of Jesus at Nazareth (6:1–6). The point of this arrangement is that miracles do not necessarily lead to faith. (2) In Matthew the four miracle stories are separated, though they all come in the collection of ten miracle stories to be found in 8—9 (Matt 8:23–27, the storm at sea; 8:28–34, two demoniacs; 9:18–

95

19, 23–26, the raising of Jairus' daughter; 9:20–22, the woman with a hemorrhage) and in the same relative order as in Mark and Luke. To understand Matthew's intention we must reflect on the way his gospel is organized. The core of the gospel falls into five cycles of material: chapters (a) 3—7; (b) 8—10; (c) 11—13; (d) 14—18; (e) 19—25. Each cycle is divided into what Jesus did, followed by what he said, with a verbal or thematic link in each cycle. In terms of this overall scheme, chapters 8—10 constitute Cycle Two; chapter 10 is what Jesus says (instructions for missionaries) and begins with the statement that Jesus gave the Twelve "authority over unclean spirits, to cast them out, and to heal every disease and every infirmity" (vs. 1). In 10:8 the charge is given to the Twelve: "Heal the sick, raise the dead, cleanse lepers, cast out demons." This teaching follows a narrative section (chaps. 8—9) in which Jesus performs ten miracles including the cleansing of a leper (8:2–4), the healing of all who were sick (8:16), the casting out of demons (8:24–34), and the raising of the dead (9:18–19, 23–25). Also, as Jesus preached the gospel of the kingdom (9:35) so the disciples are charged to do (10:7). The point of this material in the arrangement of the gospel is that Jesus' miracles show he has authority to give to his disciples. Just as in Cycle One (Matthew 3—7) Jesus did not ask his disciples for a righteousness (chaps. 5—7) he had not performed (3:14–15), so in Cycle Two Jesus does not give his missionaries an authority he does not possess.

Luke's arrangement has similarities with both Mark and Matthew. On the one hand, in 8:22–56 the four miracles come together as in Mark 4:35—5:43. On the other hand, Luke's unit of four miracle stories is not followed by the rejection at Nazareth, as in Mark 6:1–6. Rather, like Matthew 10, Luke has the miracles followed by the sending of the Twelve: 9:1–2 says Jesus called the Twelve together and gave them "power and authority over all demons and to cure diseases, and he sent them out to preach the kingdom of God and to heal." The location of the four miracles just prior to the sending of the Twelve seems to say that, like Matthew, the third evangelist aimed to demonstrate the authority Jesus possessed before telling us he gave this power and authority to the Twelve.

This makes an interesting pattern in Luke's picture of the Galilean ministry. In 4:31—5:11 we found four miracles climaxed by the call and commissioning of Peter: the miracles functioned as a catalyst for Peter's response of faith. Now at the end of the Galilean section is another series of four miracles followed by the sending of the Twelve: the mighty works that precede the commissioning demonstrate the authority of the one who gives power and authority to his emissaries.

Given the nature of Luke-Acts, one would expect to find in the narrative of Acts events corresponding to the miracles in Luke 8:22–56. This we do find: (a) with 8:22–25 compare Acts 27; (b) with 8:26–39 compare Acts 16:16ff.; (c) with 8:40–42, 49–56 compare Acts 9:36–43; and (d) with 8:43–48 compare Acts 5:15; 19:12. In other words, in 8:22—9:6 the evangelist is foreshadowing the experience of the power of the risen Christ in the ministries of his apostles ("sent ones"). The power they have is not theirs but is the power of Jesus (Luke 24:49; Acts 1:8; 3:12, 16; 4:7–12): disciples of Jesus do not minister in their own strength but in the strength of their Lord.

Note also that Jesus called the Twelve together and gave them power and authority (9:1) *before* he sent them to preach and heal (9:2). This also foreshadows the experience of the church in Acts, which was to stay in Jerusalem until clothed with power from on high (Luke 24:49), to witness after the Holy Spirit had come upon it (Acts 1:8): Jesus does not assign a task until he has first equipped those who are to perform it.

Within 8:22—9:6 we focus on one of the miracle stories, 8:26–39, because of its special contribution to the overall emphasis in the larger unit. This story tells of the man who had a legion of demons. The first dimension of meaning in this exorcism story is connected with the textual problem in 8:26. Does Jesus come to the country of the Gerasenes, Gadarenes, or Gergesenes? The best reading is "Gerasenes" (so also for Mark 5:1, though in Matt 8:28 Gadarenes seems the best reading). The difficulty with this is that Gerasenes refers to the inhabitants of Gerasa, modern Jerash, some thirty miles southeast of the Sea of Galilee. Though geographically difficult the reading is theologically important: Gerasa was Gentile territory, as is confirmed by the reference to the herd of swine (8:32). Here for the only time in the gospel Jesus journeys beyond the boundaries of Jewish territory onto pagan soil; his mission reaches to the Gentiles. Here the evangelist sees foreshadowed the future missionary activity of the church that reaches pagans. Salvation is for all people (cf. Luke 2:32; 3:6; 4:25–27; Acts 26:18; note that Luke 9:1–6, like Mark 6:7–13 but unlike Matt 10:5, does not restrict the apostles to Israel). But Luke's point here is more than just the universality of Jesus' concern: it is rather the universal scope of

Jesus' power. That is why a miracle story is used. Jesus has power
over demons even in Gentile territory. Furthermore, if the unclean
spirits (8:29) which had entered the unclean animals (8:32–33) thought
that by driving the herd of swine into the lake they could escape Jesus'
power or damage his mission, they were mistaken. The one who cast
them out is he who controls the sea also (8:22–25). Again the emphasis is on Jesus' universal power. This is important in the section, 8:22—
9:6, because the power of Jesus is given to his "sent ones." The Christian missionaries, then, need fear neither the sea (Acts 27—28) nor
the power of the demonic in foreign lands (Acts 16:16ff.; 19:13ff.):
Jesus' power is universal.

A second dimension of the story's meaning has to do with the types
of response Jesus' universal power evokes. On the one hand, the power
of Jesus to heal produces discipleship. This theme is met again in this
pericope. Luke alone of the synoptists notes that the cured man was
"sitting at the feet of Jesus" (8:35), the posture of a disciple (cf. 10:39;
7:38; 17:16), reinforced by the man's desire to be "with him" (8:38).
In some, Jesus' power evokes faith.

On the other hand, there is also present in 8:26–39 the theme of the
rejection of Jesus (cf. 2:34–35; 4:28–29; 6:11). When the swine are
destroyed by drowning, the herdsmen go into the city and tell what
had happened. When the people come and find not only the man well
but also the herd gone, they ask Jesus to depart from them (8:37; note
9:5, the rejection of the Twelve). Although the theme that Jesus' rejection is tied to economic motives is not explicitly present in the use
of the story by Matthew and Mark, the larger context of Luke-Acts
makes it certain this was the third evangelist's intent.

Two stories from Acts illustrate Luke's belief that rejection of Jesus
and his representatives often comes from economic motivation. (a) Acts
19:23ff. tells of a certain Demetrius who appealed to the economic
motive in stirring up antagonisms against Paul in Ephesus. The author
takes pains to emphasize the economic dimensions of the rejection.
Verse 24 says the idol-making enterprise "brought no little business to
the craftsmen"; vs. 25 has Demetrius say, "Men, you know that from
this business we have our wealth"; in vs. 27 Demetrius warns, "There
is danger . . . that this trade of ours may come into disrepute." After
the uproar ceased Paul departed (20:1). (b) The story in Acts that corresponds most closely to Luke 8:26–39 is found at 16:16ff. Here Paul
casts out a spirit of divination from a slave girl who had "brought her

owners much gain by soothsaying" (16:16). The author tells us in vs.
19 that "when her owners saw that their hope of gain was gone, they
seized Paul and Silas and dragged them into the market place before
the rulers." The result was a beating (vs. 22), imprisonment (vs. 23),
and ultimately a request that they leave the city (vs. 39). The language
of the request to leave is the same as in Luke 8:37 (Acts 16:39—*ērōtōn
apelthein;* Luke 8:37—*ērōtēsen . . . apelthein*). Given the theme of
the rejection of Jesus and his gospel because of economic motivations
found elsewhere in Luke-Acts, and given the Lukan tendency to foreshadow in the gospel what is treated explicitly in Acts, it is virtually
impossible to read 8:26–39 without hearing the evangelist saying the
troubles experienced by Christian missionaries because of the economic vested interests threatened by their ministry were already a part
of Jesus' career. The one who has universal power is also the one whose
rejection is sometimes tied to the threat he poses to economic vested
interests. This is both warning and consolation to his followers.

A third dimension of meaning in the exorcism story is linked to the
conclusion of the narrative. Matthew ends his exorcism story (8:28–
34) with the request for Jesus to leave the neighborhood. Both Mark
5:1–20 and Luke 8:26–39 follow the request for Jesus to depart with
a dialogue between Jesus and the healed man. Mark 5:18 suggests the
man asked to accompany Jesus as he was getting into the boat. Luke
8:37–39, however, has Jesus leave ("he got into the boat and returned"). Apparently after Jesus' departure in Luke, the healed man
who had accompanied him asked "that he might be with him." Jesus,
however, sent him away, saying, "Return to your home, and declare
how much God has done for you" (vs. 39). Several things emerge from
this ending.

(1) The evangelist uses the story as "a paradigm of what conversion
involves: the responsibility to evangelize" (I. H. Marshall, *The Gospel
of Luke,* p. 341).

(2) The place of the man's witness was in his own home country
(vs. 39).

(3) The means of evangelization to be employed by the man was his
personal testimony; the content of his witness was his healing by Jesus. The significance of this can be understood only if we recognize
the Lukan distinction between two types of disciples or witnesses: those
who were "with him" (cf. 8:1) and those who were not (8:38–39).

On the one hand, the evangelist is concerned to emphasize that certain disciples (the Twelve and the Galilean women) were "with Jesus" from the baptism of John until the time when Jesus was taken into heaven (Acts 1:21–22). In Galilee the witnesses are assembled (Luke 5:1–11; 6:12–16; 8:1–3) and are present with Jesus throughout his ministry, with one exception, 9:1–6. During the absence of the Twelve, however, Luke records nothing about Jesus' deeds or words. The Galileans accompany Jesus to Jerusalem and there see and hear everything: in 23:49 that circle observe the crucifixion and death of Jesus; in 23:55 the burial of Jesus' body was witnessed; in 24:1–11 the same women come to the tomb and do not find the body; in 24:33ff. Jesus appears to the Eleven; and in Acts 1:11 the men witness Jesus' ascension. These Galileans, primarily the Twelve, are those who bear witness to Jesus' resurrection (Acts 1:21–22). In Luke-Acts, then, the Twelve are those who accompanied Jesus from the beginning of his ministry to the ascension. They are the Galileans, the eyewitnesses who have sufficient knowledge of the gospel history and its meaning because they have been with Jesus and heard and seen all things.

In Luke's mind these eyewitnesses control the destiny of the church. This is seen in the theological geography of Acts where Jerusalem controls Christian missions. (a) It is from Jerusalem the universal preaching of the gospel is to begin (Luke 24:47; Acts 1:4, 8). (b) Every new expansion of the church in apostolic times had to receive the approval of Jerusalem (e.g., Acts 8:12, 14–15; 11:1–2, 18, 19–21, 22; 15:2, 12ff.). (c) Paul's entire ministry is given a Jerusalem frame of reference: his conversion is authenticated by the apostles in Jerusalem (9:27ff.); his work at Antioch is undertaken at Barnabas' initiative (11:25f.); his missionary commission is given by a church which was Jerusalem approved (13:1–3); each of his missionary journeys ends at Jerusalem (15:2; 18:22; 21:17); he recognizes the validity of and appeals to the witness of the Twelve (13:31); he refers difficult questions to Jerusalem (15:2), accepts Jerusalem decisions (21:23–26), and appeals to Jerusalem authority (16:5). In sum, Jerusalem controls the mission enterprise in Acts. The meaning of this dominance is closely connected with Jerusalem being, for Luke, the place where the Twelve reside (Acts 1:4; 8:1b; 9:27; 11:1–2; 15:2, 4; 16:4). Jerusalem control is control by the Twelve, which is control by the true facts of gospel history. This is the significance of being "with him." Those who were "with him" guarantee the tradition of Jesus' work and words. It is this true tradition about Jesus which the evangelist sees as controlling the church's life.

On the other hand, Luke speaks of disciples and witnesses who are not of the Twelve. In Acts Paul represents such people. The Lukan scheme regards Paul as an apostle (Acts 14:14) and teacher of the church, but like the *Epistle of the Apostles* 31, subordinates him to the Twelve. He is a witness to the things in which he has seen the risen Christ (Acts 26:16). In the overall scheme of Luke-Acts, Paul, like the Gerasene man delivered from demons, is a witness to what Jesus Christ had done in his experience but he is not one who was "with him" in the days of his flesh. The Gerasene man was instructed to go home and declare how much God had done for him. He was to bear witness to God's activity in his experience among the Gentiles, a valid missionary enterprise because commissioned by Jesus. Because a person was not with Jesus and the Twelve by no means allows rejection of his ministry (cf. Luke 9:49–50)—both types were commissioned by Jesus, so both are legitimate. Yet those who were "with him" function as a control on those who were not.

The theological issue has to do with the relation between religious experience and tradition. The Gerasene man, like Paul in Acts, symbolizes those Christian witnesses who evangelize from their own experiential religion. Something has happened to them: it is due to Jesus; they invite others to let it happen to them. Luke regards this as authentic evangelistic activity, but at the same time, the criterion by which one may know that a given religious experience is Christian is the authority of the tradition about the earthly career of Jesus. Those who were "with him" are the source of and symbolize that tradition. In Lukan thought there is no cleavage between experience and tradition, between theology and devotion. The two belong together.

THE DARK NIGHT
OF THE "NOT YET"

9:7–50

Luke 9:7–50 marks a crucial turning point in the plot of the gospel and functions to conclude the Galilean ministry which began with 4:16; it also sets in motion a new departure in the unfolding of God's plan in the narrative of Luke-Acts. Two questions about Jesus' identity give focus to the passage as a whole. (1) The first is raised by Herod. Luke, like Mark but unlike Matthew, follows the pericope of the sending of the Twelve with that of Herod's reaction (Matt 14:1–2; Mark 6:14–16; Luke 9:7–9). In both Matt 14:2 and Mark 6:16 Herod states, in effect, that Jesus must be John the Baptist raised from the dead. Luke 9:9, however, is different: Herod says, "John I beheaded; but who is this?" The Galilean ministry of Jesus as depicted in Luke raises a christological question: Who is Jesus? (2) The second question about his identity is raised by Jesus himself. In order to have this question adjacent to the first, Luke has omitted a major unit of material found in Mark 6:45—8:26/Matt 14:22—16:12. At the end of his association with the disciples in Galilee, Jesus asks, "Who do you say that I am?" (9:20). The material that follows these two questions about Jesus' identity gives the answer.

In 9:20ff. and 9:28ff. there is an exposition of who Jesus is. He is the one who, through prayer, moves into a new stage of the spiritual process, a stage that involves rejection, suffering, and death. He is also the one who calls his disciples to participation in the same developmental process. The discussion which follows will explore the various dimensions of this picture.

It is a Lukan concern "to show that prayer is the instrument by which God has directed the course of holy history, both in the life of the Son of Man and in the development of the Christian Church" (A. A. Trites, "The Prayer Motif in Luke-Acts," in *Perspectives on Luke-Acts*, p. 169). In Acts the narrative begins with the Twelve and others

102

at prayer (1:14) just prior to the empowering at Pentecost (2:1ff.). The motif of prayer followed by empowering for witness in Jerusalem recurs in 4:31. In Acts 10—11 the prayers of Cornelius and Peter are used by God to include a Gentile household in the eschatological people of God. Acts 13:1–3, moreover, tells how the Gentile mission of Paul grew from a context of prayer: God communicates his will for new departures in his plan to servants while they are at prayer. The same emphasis is found also in the gospel. It is in the context of prayer that Zechariah learns he and Elizabeth will have a son who will go before the Lord "in the spirit and power of Elijah" (1:10, 13, 17). In 3:21–22 Jesus at prayer receives his anointing for ministry and is acknowledged by a heavenly voice as God's beloved. As a result, he begins his Galilean ministry (4:16ff.). Luke 6:12–16 portrays Jesus at prayer before his choice of the Twelve. Given this motif in Luke-Acts it is no surprise to find the evangelist in Luke 9 signaling a new development in Jesus' career by showing Jesus at prayer (9:18ff., 28ff.).

Both references to prayer in 9:18 and 9:28–29 are distinctively Lukan (cf. Matt 16:13 // Mark 8:27; Matt 17:1 // Mark 9:2). Both link Jesus' prayer with his coming suffering. (1) On the one hand, 9:18 says it was "as he was praying alone" that he asked his disciples about his identity. Peter's reply, "You are the Christ of God" (9:18–20), is not followed either by Jesus' praise of Peter (as in Matt 16:17–19) or by Mark's "And he began to teach them" (8:31). Luke joins the command to silence with the prediction of the passion so the command loses importance. He also omits the rebuke of Peter (Matt 16:22–23 and Mark 8:32–33). This concentrates all the attention on Jesus' prediction of the passion (9:22), the fate of Jesus. Implicit within 9:18–22 is that Jesus, while at prayer, came to the realization he must suffer, die, and rise (cf. 24:26, 46; Acts 2:23–24). The anointed one, endued with the power of the Holy Spirit, will enter into his final glory only after rejection, suffering, and death. Furthermore, by putting the passion prediction (9:22) in direct discourse (contra Matt 16:21 // Mark 8:31), Luke makes it a part of the preceding dialogue. It becomes Jesus' prayerful response to Peter's confession.

(2) On the other hand, the transfiguration narrative in 9:28ff. has also been turned into a prayer scene. Typically the evangelist depicts prayer as associated with a heavenly apparition and a divine communication (e.g., 3:21–22; Acts 10—11). In prayer Jesus enters the heavenly world and there is a conversation with two heavenly residents

about his departure (*exodon;* cf. *eisodou* in Acts 13:24). Jesus' exodus
is his departure from this world, his ascension, but this transpires
through the cross and resurrection. This narrative, like the previous
one, makes it explicit that Luke understands Jesus to be convinced
through prayer he would die in Jerusalem.

If prayer was the medium through which Jesus came to an awareness of God's will for a new departure in his life, the content of that
will involved not immediate exaltation but rather rejection, suffering,
death: the one who was anointed with the Spirit would be rejected and
killed. There are several significant implications of this picture of Jesus.

In the first place, Luke depicts Jesus' career in developmental terms.
This has already been noted at 2:40, 52, in physical, mental, social,
and spiritual areas. The focus here is on one who develops in stages of
a spiritual process. In the gospel Jesus, in his adult life, passes through
three stages: (a) empowering (3:21–22; 4:16ff.); (b) suffering-death
(chap. 9ff.); and (c) resurrection-glory (Luke 24). In Luke 9 there is a
movement from stage (a) to stage (b), a movement made possible by
prayerful discernment.

In the second place, Jesus is one who calls his disciples to participate in the same developmental process through which he lived. Here
it is not empowering or glory about which he speaks, but suffering-
death. Luke 9:23a ("and he was saying—imperfect tense—to all") continues the dialogue begun at 9:18. After telling of his fate (9:22), as
discerned in prayer (9:18), Jesus speaks of the disciples' style of life.
For Luke discipleship is a continuing experience, so in 9:23 ("If any
man would come after me") the evangelist uses a present infinitive
(*erchesthai*—to come) instead of the aorist (*elthein*—v. Matt 16:24;
Mark 8:34), the emphasis being on the continuing nature of the relationship. Also Luke adds "daily" to the "take up his cross" of Matt
16:24/Mark 8:34. Whereas Matthew and Mark have in mind the initial
act, Luke stresses that the disciple takes up the cross daily, that is,
continually. Just as the disciples had been given a share in Jesus' power
(Luke 9:1–6), so now they are called to share his death: "If any man
would come after me, let him deny himself and take up his cross daily
and follow me" (9:23).

How can it be that the Spirit-empowered Jesus must suffer? How
can it be that his empowered disciples must share the same experience? The answer lies in the eschatology of main-line first century

Christianity, which combined a "now" and a "not yet" (cf. Paul in 1 Corinthians 4; 15; Philippians 3). The New Age had broken in with the resurrection of Jesus, but the Old Age continues until the parousia. We live in the overlap. To hold these two realities (now—not yet) has always been among the most difficult tasks for Christian life and thought. There is perennially the temptation to allow one to swallow the other: either the emphasis is so focused on the powers of the New Age at work in believers that an eschatological reservation is lost, or the focus is so directed to believers' involvement in the structures and limitations of this life that the power of the Holy Spirit in the midst of weakness is overlooked.

The evangelist, having presented Jesus in his Galilean ministry as a Spirit-empowered conqueror of evil, now is concerned to show that even such a figure is subject to the limitations of this age. He is not immediately and automatically triumphant because of the power of the Spirit unleashed in his life in healing, exorcism, and teaching, but he will be rejected and killed. Only on the other side of this subjection to the limitations of this age will he enter into his final glory. The same limitations apply also to the disciples. Theologically it is necessary to juxtapose "anointed with the Spirit" and "destined to die" because to say less would be to break the delicate balance between the "now" and the "not yet" of Christian existence.

What purpose could such suffering serve for Jesus and for his disciples? In order to answer this question, two items of information are necessary: one from the NT at large and one from Luke. (1) The third evangelist frames Jesus' earthly career within two temptation scenes (4:1–13; 23:35, 36–37, 39). As we have previously seen, the first, 4:1–13, must be read against the background of Jesus both as the culmination of all God had been doing in the history of Israel and as the second Adam, as shown in the genealogy of 3:23–38. The order of the temptations in 4:1–13 echoes not only the threefold temptation of Adam and Eve in Gen 3:6 but also the temptation of Israel in the wilderness as given by Psalm 106: the temptations of Jesus thereby become antitypical of the experience of Israel in the wilderness and of the original pair in the garden. Whereas those who came before were disobedient, Jesus, as the second Adam and as the true culmination of Israel's heritage, is obedient and thereby has reversed Adam's and Israel's sin. This temptation narrative thus understood has the effect of setting all that follows in Jesus' earthly career under the sign of his obedience.

As will be seen later, a second temptation sequence comes at 23:35, 36–37, 39. It is also a threefold temptation. Jesus spoke of the divine necessity of his death (9:22, 44; 18:31–33); in the garden he surrendered to the divine will even though it meant death (23:39–46); now on the cross he faces the temptation to use divine power for self-preservation (a power he still has—22:51). Three times he is confronted with the demand: "Save yourself" (23:35, 37, 39). That he does not is his obedience unto death, the perfection of his obedience to the Father (cf. 13:32). The Lukan frame around the public ministry of Jesus defines Jesus' career as the way of obedience, even unto death.

(2) In the NT one stream of early Christian thought regarded Jesus' death not only as an atonement for sin and as a defeat of the powers of evil but also as Jesus' ultimate act of obedience or faithfulness to God (e.g., Phil 2:8; Rom 5:18–19): Jesus died rather than sin. In this context Jesus' suffering and death were the arena in which his obedience to God was perfected. Heb 2:10 says God made "the pioneer of their suffering perfect through suffering"; "Although he was a Son, he learned obedience through what he suffered; and being made perfect he became the source of eternal salvation to all who obey him" (5:8–9). Corresponding to this view of Christ's suffering and death was the belief that suffering, and death if necessary, was the arena in which Christians wrestled with sin and, therefore, where they also had their obedience to God developed. 1 Pet 4:1–2 says, "Since therefore Christ suffered in the flesh, arm yourselves with the same thought, for whoever has suffered in the flesh has ceased from sin, so as to live for the rest of the time in the flesh no longer by human passions but by the will of God." Hence the emphasis is on suffering as discipline (Heb 12:7ff.), as a proof (1 Pet 4:12), or a testing (1 Pet 1:6–7) of Christian faith. The NT speaks of a suffering endured by Christ and Christians alike which is the arena in which obedience to God is perfected.

It is in the context of a view of suffering that is integral to the process of spiritual growth that Luke 9 should be understood. Jesus, through prayer, has come to see he is about to enter a new phase of God's plan for him. He is moving beyond the initial stage of empowering-illumination into a dimension of life which, though still empowered, is characterized by rejection (9:22). In this phase he will learn obedience through what he suffers (Heb 5:8–9). His obedience to God in the face of rejection, persecution, suffering, and finally death will signal his victory over sin (1 Pet 4:1–2).

The importance of rejection, persecution, suffering, and the threat of death in the process of spiritual growth is that each entails the possibility of the loss of something which the self either holds dear or is tempted to grasp: one is threatened with the loss of economic security, of status, reputation, or of life itself. Circumstances remove the possibility of one's holding to any of these finite treasures as security, and the suffering of rejection detaches one from these real or potential false gods. That is why the stage of suffering is called purification. One learns obedience to God alone through what is suffered. Rejection or persecution shatters real or potential idols and allows God to draw one to himself alone. This redemptive dimension of suffering would not be possible without the prior stage of empowering or illumination. From the evangelist's perspective only as God lives within is there the potential for suffering to be experienced as purification. The way of Jesus, therefore, was from empowering through suffering to glory.

The Jesus who walked this way also called his disciples to participate in the same developmental process, saying a disciple should "deny himself and take up his cross daily" (9:23). Bearing the burdens of life is an unlikely interpretation because the cross was not a burden but an instrument of death. A condemned person carried it on the way to execution. So to "take up [one's] cross daily" means to live daily as a condemned person, to "deny [one]self." If so, then self-denial means to live the life of a condemned person, one who has been stripped of every form of worldly security, even physical existence. For such a one, there is nothing and no one to whom there can be permanent attachment except the one who goes before carrying his cross. All other attachments have been terminated by the sentence of death, a sentence passed upon oneself.

Luke 9:24–26 consists of three sayings beginning in a similar way: vs. 24—For whoever; vs. 25—For what; vs. 26—For whoever. These verses illumine two benefits of denying oneself, taking up one's cross, and following Jesus. The benefits are given in negative form, as dangers to be avoided. In vss. 24–25 Jesus speaks of a present danger to be avoided by denial of self. One will, by holding to the old self, lose the true self or life (cf. 4:5–8). Self-denial in a Lukan context does not mean the annihilation of one's created individuality and worth, as in some Eastern religions, but it means rather the repudiation of the personality structure that absolutizes the self rather than the Creator, so the good created self (Gen 1:31) can emerge free from the perversions that have covered it over. It is only when one's idolatrous attachments to the created order are stripped away and the Creator exists as one's ultimate concern that the created self is saved.

In vs. 26 Jesus speaks of a future danger to be avoided by denial of self. The one who responds wrongly to Jesus now will face the eschatological judge whose coming will vindicate Jesus' earthly life and mission. Only a life lived here and now without idolatrous attachments to the created order will be vindicated in the New Age where God is all in all. Both in the present and ultimately, only a life lived as a condemned person yields the meaning the Creator intended. Upon such a way of life the empowered Jesus was now embarking (9:22, 44, 31) and to such a way he called his empowered disciples. Regardless of whether or not a disciple's way involved the physical martyrdom to which Jesus' path led, it was to be lived as a condemned person, as one stripped of all attachments other than to God. Only thereby could the self be purified in the way God desired; only thereby could one's obedience to God be perfected.

Jesus closes his teaching about "rejection-suffering-death-purification" with a reassuring promise: "But I tell you truly, there are some standing here who will not taste death before they see the kingdom of God" (vs. 27). The form of vs. 27 is distinctively Lukan: Matt 16:28 reads, "see the Son of Man coming in his kingdom"; Mark 9:1 says, "see the kingdom of God come with power." Both refer to the parousia. But here Jesus says simply, "see the kingdom of God." In this form the reference must be to the presence of the kingdom seen or experienced within history. Since 17:21 speaks of the kingdom being present in Jesus' ministry, this seems the likely meaning. That context presents Jesus' words about an absolute allegience to him in which every other attachment is stripped away. Now this same Jesus says some who hear his words will indeed experience this kingly rule of God in their lives. This is a word of assurance.

Luke 9:51–19:44

GUIDANCE ON THE WAY

INTRODUCTION

The third major section in this gospel is 9:51—19:44. The first, 1:5—4:15, was an account of the prepublic career of Jesus; the second, 4:16—9:50, a narrative of Jesus' Galilean ministry. This section is within the framework of a journey to Jerusalem (9:51, 53; 13:22, 33; 17:11; 18:31; 19:11, 28, 41, 45), though the geography cannot be satisfactorily traced: in 9:51–53 Jesus passes through Samaria; in 10:38–42 (cf. John 12:1–3) he appears to be on the outskirts of Jerusalem; 13:31–33 locates him either in Galilee or in Perea; 17:11 places him between Samaria and Galilee; he is at Jericho in 18:35—19:10; 19:11 locâtes him near Jerusalem. Today it is widely recognized that this travel section is an editorial framework created by the evangelist.

The arrangement of the journey to Jerusalem is determined by two factors. First, there is an inclusion that holds the entire unit together. The travel section both begins (9:51ff.) and ends (19:28ff.) with a rejection of Jesus (by a village of the Samaritans, 9:52; by Jerusalem, 19:39–44). Second, a chiastic pattern determines the overall arrangement of the material.

A To Jerusalem: rejection in Samaria (9:51ff.)
  B Following Jesus (9:57ff.)
    C How to inherit eternal life (10:25ff.)
      D Prayer (11:1ff.)
        E Signs of the Kingdom (11:14ff.)
          F Conflict with the Pharisees (11:37ff.)
            G Present faithfulness and the future kingdom (12:35ff.)
              H Healing followed by accusation (13:10ff.)
                I Exclusion from messianic banquet/Inclusion (13:18ff.)
                  J Prophets perish in Jerusalem (13:31–33)
                  J' Jerusalem kills the prophets (13:34–35)
                I' Exclusion from messianic banquet/Inclusion (14:7ff.)

H' Healing followed by an accusation (14:1ff.)
G' Present faithfulness and the future kingdom
(16:1ff.)
F' Conflict with the Pharisees (16:14ff.)
E' Signs of the kingdom (17:11ff.)
D' Prayer (18:1ff.)
C'+ How to inherit eternal life (18:18ff.)
B' Following Jesus (18:35ff.)
A' To Jerusalem: rejection by Jerusalem (19:11ff.)

(K. E. Bailey, *Poet and Peasant: A Literary-Cultural Approach to the Parables in Luke* [Grand Rapids: Eerdmans, 1976], pp. 79–82; C. H. Talbert, *Literary Patterns, Theological Themes and the Genre of Luke-Acts* [Missoula: Scholars Press, 1974], pp. 51–56.)

Luke 9:18–50 functions as a prelude to the journey to Jerusalem. Just as the Galilean ministry began (4:16ff.) after Jesus in prayer received his anointing and the attestation of a heavenly voice (3:21–22; cf. 4:18), so the journey to Jerusalem begins (9:51ff.) after Jesus in two sessions of prayer (9:18; 9:28–29) receives his perception of the necessity of suffering (9:22, 31, 44) and the attestation of a heavenly voice (9:35). Since the journey to Jerusalem contains two motifs—(a) Jesus goes to his death, and (b) Jesus instructs the disciples—the material in 9:18ff. supplies the bases for what follows: (a) the necessity of suffering perceived in prayer, and (b) the authority for Jesus' subsequent instruction.

The authority for the instruction of Jesus' disciples is set forth in two paragraphs (9:28–36; 9:37–43a). Apparently in the Lukan account of the Transfiguration the conversation between Jesus, Elijah, and Moses was not overheard by the three who were asleep. In 9:32 *diagrēgorēsantes* could mean either the disciples "kept awake" or "when they came awake," the latter being the more probable. In either case it is to be inferred they were ignorant of the conversation but saw only Jesus' glory (9:32) and were distressed to see the heavenly visitors slipping away from Jesus (*diachōrizesthai* gives the sense "while they were beginning to go away"). Peter's response was an attempt to hold the glory by delaying the departure of Moses and Elijah (9:33). As though in response to the disciples' desire to hold this glory, a cloud overshadows them and a voice comes from the cloud: "This is my Son, my Chosen; listen to him" (9:35; cf. Ps 2:7; Isa 42:1; Deut 18:15): God himself in audible voice declares Jesus' teaching to be authoritative (cf. Acts 3:22–23).

Luke omits the discussion about the coming of Elijah found in Matt 17:9–13; Mark 9:9–13 and places immediately after the Transfiguration the exorcism story of 9:37–43. In so doing he makes the exorcism an integral part of the Transfiguration rather than a postlude. Furthermore, Luke's form of the exorcism story makes it a demonstration of Jesus' authority rather than, as in Matt 17:14–21; Mark 9:14–29, a teaching about the disciples' ministry of healing. In Luke all the stress falls on the authority of Jesus, so 9:37–43 goes together with the voice from heaven (9:35) to reaffirm Jesus' authority prior to his telling his disciples he must be delivered into the hands of men (19:44), before he delivers his *didache* on the way to Jerusalem (9:51—19:44). In this way 9:18ff. functions as a basis for the travel section.

Luke 9:51—19:44 functions theologically in a number of ways. (1) The didactic material given in the context of a journey fits Luke's conception of the life of faith as a pilgrimage, always on the move (cf. Acts 9:2; 19:9, 23; 22:4; 24:14, 22 where the Christian faith is designated "the Way"). This is true for Jesus and for his followers. (2) The journey is to Jerusalem and to Jesus' death. It is in respect of his sufferings that Jesus is described as "going on ahead" of the disciples (19:28). Since it is "through many tribulations that we must enter the kingdom of God" (Acts 14:22), Jesus goes before his disciples as *archēgos* (Acts 3:15; 5:31; Heb 2:10; 12:2), that is, pioneer or leader. (3) Some of the material prefigures the wider mission to be narrated in Acts (e.g., the mission of the Seventy [or Seventy-two] in Luke 10 prefigures the mission of Philip, Barnabas, and Paul in Acts). (4) The presence of the Galileans throughout the travel section furnishes a guarantee for the preservation and continuity of the tradition of Jesus after his ascension. What we are told in 9:51—19:44 has been delivered to us by those who from the beginning were eyewitnesses and ministers of the word (1:1–4).

THE COSTS OF DISCIPLESHIP

9:51—10:24

The first major thought unit in the travel section (9:51—10:24) is linked together by a variety of devices. In 9:52 and 10:1 Jesus sends someone before his face prior to his arrival. This joins 9:51-62 with 10:1ff. The rejection of Jesus by Samaritans (9:52–56) is followed by a threefold dialogue on discipleship (9:57–62), the first of which echoes the Samaritan rejection. In the second and third dialogues (vss. 60, 62), the references to the kingdom of God are Lukan and tie this section together with 10:1ff. where vss. 9, 11 repeat distinctive Lukan references to the kingdom. The unit 10:1–24 is joined by several interlocking devices: vss. 1, 3–4, 16 are linked by the verb "send forth"; vss. 5–7, 8–9, 10–11 by "into whatever [house or city] you enter"; vss. 12, 13–15 by "it will be more tolerable" (on that day or in the judgment); vss. 17–20 are linked by the reference to the return of the Seventy (esp. by the reference to joy in vs. 17 and the twofold "to rejoice" in vs. 20); vss. 21, 22 are joined by their common use of "Father" and "reveal." As a unit, vss. 21–22 are linked to vss. 17–20 by the time reference, "in that same hour," and the mention of Jesus' rejoicing (a different word but the same idea as in vss. 17–20). The concluding unit, vss. 23–24, is tied to what precedes by the introduction in vs. 23 (his disciples) and by the key word "hear" which ties into 10:16. In these ways the evangelist has woven 9:51–10:24 into a unified whole.

The basic pattern of the unit is ABA': 9:52–56 constitutes A; 10:1–24 is A': in both Jesus sends out disciples to prepare for his coming; in both the motif of rejection is present. Luke 9:57–62 constitutes B: here the focus is on the costs of following Jesus. Any discussion of the thought of 9:51–10:24 must take account of the Lukan patterning of the material. Luke 9:52–56 and 10:1–24, therefore, will be treated together and 9:57–62 separately.

A (9:52–56) and A' (10:1–24) point to the Lukan theology of world mission (2:32; 3:6; 4:25–27; 8:26ff.). On the one hand, in 9:52–56 Jesus moves into Samaritan territory. Though he is rejected the story

114

gives a warrant from the life of Jesus for the Christian mission into Samaria in Acts 8. On the other hand, 10:1–24 foreshadows the Gentile mission in Acts 13—28. (a) Luke 10:1, a verse peculiar to this gospel, mentions the Seventy or the Seventy-two others (i.e., besides the Twelve) who are sent two by two. This seems to be Lukan because 22:35, which is addressed to the Twelve, echoes 10:4, seeming to imply that the material in chapter 10 was originally addressed to the Twelve. The textual evidence is very evenly divided between Seventy and Seventy-two. This vacillation of the manuscripts is best explained by Genesis 10 in the Massoretic Text in which the number of the nations of the world is seventy, whereas in the LXX the number is seventy-two. Whatever the original reading, then, the point is the same. The number seventy or seventy-two symbolizes all the nations of the world: the mission is a universal one. (b) Luke 10 includes in its first twenty-four verses much of the material found in Matthew's instructions to the Twelve regarding missionary activity in chapter 10. Luke, however, does not have the saying found in Matt 10:5–6: "Go nowhere among the Gentiles, and enter no town of the Samaritans, but go rather to the lost sheep of the house of Israel." Although the Lukan geography does indicate the mission of the Seventy was within Jewish territory, the omission of the saying allows the number, with its symbolism of all nations, to foreshadow the later Gentile mission. (c) The basic architectural pattern controlling Luke-Acts is the series of correspondences in content and sequence between events in the gospel and those in Acts (C. H. Talbert, *Literary Patterns, Theological Themes and the Genre of Luke-Acts* pp. 15–23). In this parallelism between the two volumes of Luke's work, 10:1ff. comes at just the point to make it correspond with the missionary journeys of Paul to the Gentiles in Acts 13ff. These three strands of evidence, taken together, indicate that Luke intended 10:1ff. to foreshadow the Gentile mission of the church and gives a warrant from the career of Jesus for the Gentile mission of Paul, just as 9:52–56 gives such a warrant for the Samaritan mission of Acts 8. Luke 9:52–56 and 10:1–24 (A and A'), like 4:16–30 at the beginning of the Galilean ministry, focus on the Lukan universalism at the start of the travel narrative: the gospel must be carried to all peoples.

There is a sense in which 9:1–6, 52–56; 10:1ff. belong together as part of a pattern in the gospel. All three speak of Jesus "sending out" disciples. Luke 9:1–6 specifies it was the Twelve who were sent, while

9:52–56 is ambiguous: vs. 52 says he sent out messengers, while vs. 54's reference to James and John would seem to imply the Twelve are involved. In 10:1 the reference is to seventy (or seventy-two) others, the "others" being important. More than just the Twelve are involved in mission; indeed the mission that symbolizes universality is not carried out by the Twelve as such. Here again we see intimations of the narrative in Acts with its distinction between the work of the Twelve and that of others, like Paul. Taken together, 9:1–6, 52–56; 10:1ff. lay the foundation in the earthly life of Jesus for the commission of the risen Christ in Acts 1:8: "You shall be my witnesses in Jerusalem and in all Judea and Samaria and to the end of the earth."

Luke 9:52–56 (A) and 10:1–24 (A') not only present the theology of world mission, they also offer guidelines to govern missionary behavior. On the one hand, both A and A' contain a note of rejection following the theme of universality. Two different responses to this rejection are mentioned. (1) In the Samaritan episode (9:52–56), James and John ask Jesus about the possibility of calling down fire from heaven on those who rejected him, reminiscent of an Elijah episode in 2 Kgs 1:10 (cf. Sir 48:3). Jesus rejects any retaliation against his rejecters. Here is one guideline for dealing with rejection. It is in line with early Christian instruction about disciples' response to offending non-Christians (cf. Rom 12:18–21; 1 Pet 2:20–25; 3:16–17). (2) In the section of the mission of the Seventy (or Seventy-two), the response to rejection is very much that of 9:5. Luke 10:10 instructs the disciples to remove the dust from their feet as an acted parable against those rejecting them (cf. Acts 13:51 where Paul and Barnabas "shook off the dust from their feet" against those in Antioch of Pisidia who responded negatively). This symbolic act declared those who rejected the message had no part in the eschatological people of God. This judgment was to be made, but retaliation was to be foregone.

On the other hand, 10:1–24 contains a number of other guidelines for missionaries, as may be seen when the train of thought is traced. After a universalistic note (10:1) there is a call for prayer that God will supply laborers for the missionary work (vs. 2; cf. Acts 13:1–3). The missionaries are totally dependent on God for their protection (vs. 3) and sustenance (vs. 4a). Their mission is urgent and must not be delayed (vs. 4b; cf. 2 Kgs 4:29). The missionaries are not to have any qualms about subsisting off the generosity of others (cf. 1 Cor 9:4ff.), but are not to beg from house to house, accepting the hospitality of one house (vss. 5–7; Acts 16:15; cf. 1 Kgs 17:15; 2 Kgs 4:8). They are not to worry about the restrictions of the Jewish food laws but are to eat what is set before them (vs. 8: cf. 1 Cor 10:27). Proclamation of the kingdom is to be by deed and word (vs. 9; cf. 11:20). Rejection of the missionaries makes one liable at the judgment (vss. 12, 13–15) because Jesus is identified with them: rejection of a messenger equals rejection of Jesus. Furthermore, the closeness of Jesus and the Father means that rejection of Jesus equals rejection of God (vs. 16: Acts 9:5; 22:7–8; 26:9–11, 14–15). The manifestation of Jesus' power in the work of the missionaries is testimony to the power of Satan being broken (vs. 18; with 10:19 cf. Acts 28:1–6; 18:9–10; 27:23–24). The demonstration of power over the demonic, however, is not to be a disciple's major desire, because an emissary of the Lord can perform mighty works in his name and still miss the kingdom (cf. Matt 7:22; 1 Cor 9:27). One's primary concern must be for personal salvation (vs. 20; cf. Exodus 32:32; Ps 69:28; 87:4–6; 139:16; Dan 10:21; 12:1). This is a warning to the disciples to place less importance on the miraculous. It is to those who are unlikely candidates that both the divine power of Jesus's name and the greater importance of having one's name in the book of life are revealed (vs. 21). It is God who knows who his Son is and to him the Father has given this authority which the missionaries experience (vs. 22; cf. 3:21–22). Moreover, since it is the Son who knows the Father, he is the one to make God and his will known (vs. 22b; cf. 9:35). Finally, Jesus' disciples are to be congratulated because of what they have seen (experienced), namely, the indications in the missionaries' power over Satan that the time of fulfillment has come—a time which people of the past were unable to see (experience [vss. 23–24; cf. 1 Pet 1:10–12]). From such a survey we can see the evangelist has used this section not only to foreshadow the Gentile mission of the church, but also to give certain instructions and guidance that would be needed at the time the gospel was written (e.g., payment of missionaries; eating of any food set before them; balance in one's concern for power in ministry and for one's own relationship with God).

In 9:57–62 (B) the focus is upon the costs of discipleship and consists of a threefold dialogue: a—I will follow you (vss. 57–58); b—follow me (vss. 59–60); a'—I will follow you (vss. 61–62). Here three would-be disciples misunderstand the nature of the commitment called for by Jesus. To each Jesus states the stringent demands he places on those who would follow him.

In *a* (vss. 57–58) Jesus responds to a man's expression of willing-ness to follow him wherever he went. Having just been refused hos-pitality by a Samaritan village (9:53), Jesus tells the man of the con-sequences of following him: Jesus is homeless; he does not belong to a settled family (cf. Sir 36:24–26 where one who "lodges wherever night finds him" is the unmarried man with no home of his own); to follow Jesus wherever he goes would mean to share the homeless lot of the Son of Man (cf. 18:28–30). To ponder the consequences of dis-cipleship thusly is to raise the question of the man's resolve.

In *b* Jesus takes the initiative and says, "Follow me" (vs. 59a). The response was "Lord, let me first go and bury my father" (vs. 59b). Burial of the dead was a religious duty among the Jews taking prece-dence over all others. Even priests, who were not normally allowed to touch dead bodies, could do so in the case of close relatives (Lev 21:1–3), so the burial of a father was, to a Jew, the primary duty of filial piety (Tob 4:3; 6:15). An unburied relative apparently was equivalent to the presence of a corpse in the room (b. Berakoth 18a). Since the presence of a corpse defiled a person, it precluded the performance of any other religious rite. Sir 38:16 is intelligible in this context: "My son, let your tears fall for the dead. . . . Lay out his body with the honor due him, and do not neglect his burial." That business, Jesus replied, must look after itself: a disciple must go and proclaim the kingdom of God, because discipleship comes above the highest claims of family and one's duty to it. (Cf. 1 Tim 5:8 where the other side of abandonment to Jesus is spelled out: one is called upon to care for his family.)

In *a'* (vss. 61–62) another says he will follow Jesus, but, like Elisha, only after he has said farewell to those at home (cf. 1 Kgs 19:19–21). Jesus' response is in the form of a proverb (Hesiod, *Works and Days,* 443; Pliny, *Natural History,* 18:19:49): only those who can plow a straight furrow by moving toward a mark without looking away for a moment, no matter what the distraction, are single-minded enough for a disciple's role which calls for perseverance to the end (cf. Phil 3:13; Heb 12:1ff.; Matt 5:8; 13:44–46).

These three dialogues dealing with the costs of discipleship call for an absolute detachment from property and family and for a single-minded devotion to Jesus that perseveres to the end: "Following him is not a task which is added to others like working a second job. . . . It is everything. It is a solemn commitment which forces the disciples-to-be to reorder all their other duties" (Robert Karris, *Invitation to Luke* [Garden City, New York: Image Books, 1977], p. 130). When disciples go out as missionaries, it is to this type of relationship with Jesus they are calling their hearers. It is, moreover, to this type of relationship the missionaries themselves are called.

ON LOVING GOD
AND THE NEIGHBOR

10:25-42

For the evangelist the whole of 10:29–42 is an exposition, in haggadic form and in reverse order, of the two great love commandments of 10:27. The story of the Good Samaritan, vss. 29–37, deals with the meaning of the commandment to love one's neighbor as oneself (vs. 27b); the story of Martha and Mary, vss. 38–42, interprets the injunction to love God with one's whole self (vs. 27a). A discussion of 10:25–42 must deal with both parts of Luke's exposition.

At the level of Lukan theology, the Good Samaritan pericope functions as an interpretation of the command to love one's neighbor. The form of 10:25–37 is that of a *controversy dialogue* with two parallel parts (J. D. Crossan, "Parable and Example in the Teaching of Jesus," *New Testament Studies* 18:285–307 [1972]). Part One, vss. 25–28, has four components: (1) the lawyer's question (vs. 25); (2) Jesus' counterquestion (vs. 26); (3) the lawyer's own answer (vs. 27); and (4) Jesus' command (vs. 28). Part Two, vss. 29–37, has the same four components: (1) the lawyer's question (vs. 29); (2) Jesus' counter-question (vss. 30–36); (3) the lawyer's own answer (vs. 37a); and (4) Jesus' command (vs. 37b). The two parts are held together by the key words "neighbor" (vss. 27, 36) and "do" (vss. 25, 28, 37). This form appears distinctly Lukan when a comparison is made with the other synoptics.

On the one hand, 10:25–28 has parallels in Matt 22:34–40 and Mark 12:28–31. (a) Like Matthew, Luke says Jesus' opponent was a lawyer, that he came to test Jesus, and that he addressed him as Teacher. (b) Unlike Matthew or Mark, however, the question put to Jesus (vs. 25) was not about the greatest or first commandment but about how to inherit eternal life (cf. 18:18). (c) More important, in Luke alone Jesus asks the lawyer, "What is written in the law? How do you read?": that is, the counter-question. (d) Also Luke alone has the lawyer, not Jesus, give the answer (vs. 27). (e) Finally, only in Luke does Jesus respond with an appraisal and a command: "You have answered right; do this and you will live" (vs. 28). Part One of the controversy dialogue depends upon the Lukan distinctions.

On the other hand, 10:29-37 is unique to the gospel. It is generally recognized that the parable of the Good Samaritan is confined to vss. 30-35 and that vss. 29, 36-37 are redactional, due either to Luke or to a pre-Lukan hand that formed the two-part controversy dialogue. It is this redactional material that makes vss. 29-37 fit the controversy dialogue model. Either the evangelist shaped the material in this way or chose this form in preference to another. (Note that Luke omits the Matthew-Mark version of the lawyer's question at the end of his gospel.)

The thrust of the double controversy dialogue can be discerned if we examine first of all the two questions with which its two parts begin and, secondly, the commands with which each part ends. (1) The lawyer asks Jesus, "What shall I do to inherit eternal life?" (vs. 26). Since it is two Jews talking and since it was assumed by Jews that the people of God would inherit the New Age, the import of the question is clear. The lawyer is asking what he as an individual should do to guarantee his place in the people of God who would inherit eternal life: "What do I do to belong to God's people?" Moreover, when the lawyer asks, "Who is my neighbor?" he is wanting to know how he can spot others who belong to God's covenant people. The Jews interpreted "neighbor" in terms of members of the same people or religious community, that is, fellow Jews (cf. Matt 5:43). Even within the Jewish people there was a tendency to exclude certain others from the sphere of neighbor. For example, the Pharisees sometimes excluded the ordinary people of the land and the Qumran Covenanters excluded the "sons of darkness" (1 QS 1:10; 9:21f.). Jews generally excluded Samaritans and foreigners from the category of neighbor. Hence the lawyer's question was basically, "Who belongs to the category of God's people?"

(2) Note that both parts of the controversy dialogue end on the same theme: "do." Verse 29 reads, "do this [present infinitive], and you will live." Verse 37b says, "Go and do likewise" [present infinitive]. The language indicates that the concern is with a certain type of continuing behavior. If the two parts of the dialogue open with questions about who belongs to God's people, they end with commands to behave in a certain way. What is the prescribed way of acting?

Part One has the lawyer give his view about the orientation that characterized the covenant people of God: Deut 6:5, love God, and Lev 19:18, love your neighbor, are joined in the lawyer's response. Assuming that the Testaments of the Twelve Patriarchs represent pre-Christian Judaism, the two great commandments had already been linked in Jewish thought (T. Issacher 5:2; 7:5; T. Dan 5:3). "You have answered right" (vs. 28a)—Jesus approves of this interpretation of the law—"Do this, and you will live" (vs. 28b; cf. Lev 18:5; Gal 3:12). This accent on doing is in line with the Lukan emphasis on "hearing the word of God and doing it" (cf. 8:21; 6:47; 3:10–14; 1:38). Loving God and loving the neighbor are the signs of covenant loyalty which will guarantee one will live in the New Age with the people of God.

The Lukan transition in vs. 29 (cf. 16:15; 18:19–21) indicates that what follows flows from the need to deal with the lawyer's self-justification: "How can I spot others who belong to God's people so that I can love them?" In response to this question the story of the Good Samaritan is told. After the story Jesus asks, "Which of these three, do you think, proved neighbor to the man who fell among robbers?" (vs. 36); that is, which man acted like one who belonged to the covenant people of God? Which one loved? The answer from the lawyer was inevitable: "The one who showed mercy on him" (vs. 37a). The command of Jesus is the unit's conclusion: "Go and *do* likewise" (vs. 37b).

The Good Samaritan narrative functions at the level of Lukan redaction as an exemplary story. The point is that we should go and do likewise, a commentary on what "loving the neighbor as oneself" really means. It means to act like the Samaritan. The focus Luke gives the parable of the Good Samaritan is not on how Jesus acted but on what Christians of the evangelist's own day should do (Jan Lambrecht, "The Message of the Good Samaritan [Luke 10:25–37]," *Louvain Studies* 5:121–35 [1974]). In the Lukan context this means that people who belong to God's covenant community show love (a) that is not limited by the clean-unclean laws (cf. Acts 10, 15); (b) that does not limit itself to friends but has a universal scope (cf. Luke 2:32; 3:6; 4:25–27; 10:1ff.); and (c) that does not look for recompense (cf. Luke 6:32–36). This, of course, was the way Jesus loved.

In order to deal adequately with 10:25–37, it will be necessary to depart from the procedure normally followed in this commentary. Whereas usually the explanation of a unit is concerned exclusively with what the material meant for Luke, at this point we will treat also the function of the parable of the Good Samaritan in Jesus' *Sitz im*

Leben. Before this can be done a word is necessary about the recent interpretation of parables. (The best summary can be found in Norman Perrin, *Jesus and the Language of the Kingdom* [Philadelphia: Fortress Press, 1976], pp. 89–193.)

The modern study of the parables has shown (1) that the way a parable is used in a gospel is not necessarily the way it originally functioned (so Jeremias), and (2) that a parable may function either to instruct or to provoke: that is, it may be a simile in which the lesser known is clarified by the better known ("the kingdom of God is like") or a metaphor in which two not entirely comparable elements are juxtaposed resulting in a shock to the imagination. The shock forces the listener to make a judgment on the situation in the parable (so Funk, Crossan). It has been on the provocative function of the parables that the most recent interpreters have placed greatest emphasis. The parable of the Good Samaritan makes a fine example.

Detached from its redactional setting in the controversy dialogue, the parable consists of 10:30–35. The dissimilarity of its contents to Judaism and of its form with early Christianity argues for its origins in Jesus' ministry. In order to hear the parable as the original Jewish hearers did, one must recognize: First, Jews despised Samaritans, the descendents of the mixed population which followed Assyria's conquest of Samaria in 722 B.C. (2 Kings 17). Possessors also of a syncretistic religion, the Samaritans opposed the efforts of Ezra and Nehemiah to rebuild Jerusalem and reestablish the sanctuary of Yahweh (Ezra 4:2ff.: Neh 2:19; 4:2ff.), building a rival temple on Mount Gerazim. Josephus (*Antiquities* 11:8:4 §324) says this was during the reign of the last king of Persia (335–30 B.C.) but his story is suspect. This Samaritan temple was razed by John Hyrcanus in 128 B.C. (Josephus, *Antiquities* 13:9:1 §256; *War* 1:2:6 §63)—Josephus says it was in exasperation over the Samaritans' prolonged apostasy and treachery. Pompey liberated them from the Jewish yoke in 63 B.C. Enmity existed between Jews and Samaritans at the time of Christian origins (e.g., John 4:9; Luke 9:52–53), some rabbis even saying acceptance of alms by a Jew from a Samaritan delayed the redemption of Israel. Also a maxim emerged that no Jew need trouble himself to save a Samaritan's life (b. Sanhedrin 57a). In light of the existing tensions, Jewish hearers could be expected to respond negatively to any references to Samaritans.

Second, Jews who were loyal to the scriptures would be concerned about the laws of cleanness and uncleanness. Among these laws were those which dealt with the uncleanness contracted from touching a dead body (Num 19:11–13, 14–19; Mishna, *Eduyoth*, 8:4). As noted above, priests were exempted from burying even their relatives, except for the nearest of kin—mother, father, son, daughter, brother, virgin sister (Lev 21:1–3). This was because as priests they must avoid uncleanness. The chief priest was not to defile himself even to bury his father and mother (Lev 21:10–11). When, therefore, Jesus' hearers were told the priest and Levite avoided any contact with the man who was half-dead (vs. 30), they would know these religious figures did exactly as they were instructed to do by scripture (G. B. Caird, *The Gospel of St. Luke* [Baltimore: Penguin Books, 1963], p. 148).

The parable makes the despised Samaritan the hero and the Bible-believing-and-obeying priest and Levite the villains. This demands the hearers say what, for them, cannot be said, what is a contradiction in terms: bad (Samaritan) cannot be good; and good (priest and Levite) cannot be bad. If as a hearer one accepts the judgment of the parable, then one's whole world of values is shattered. In this way, the original parable in its setting in Jesus' career aimed not to instruct but rather to challenge, to provoke, to shatter stereotypes. The stereotyper is challenged in his judgments; the usual criteria for evaluating a person's worth are replaced by that of unselfish attention to human need wherever one encounters it. This is provocative. It raises questions about one's caricatures of others and the norms used to identify the good and the bad. It also raises questions about this Jesus who confronts hearers with standards of judgment that are so different from their own. Who is he to overthrow my evaluations of others?

What functioned in Jesus' original setting as a provocation and challenge became in the gospel an exemplary story which teaches disciples how to love their neighbor. This difference in function should not be seen as discontinuity, as though the evangelist were distorting the original material. The same parable which in its address to people commited to other values involved the hearers in such a way they were led to a judgment that was an abrupt reversal of their old world could, on the other side of conversion, function in quite a different way. If one's old world is shattered, a new one must be constructed around one's discipleship to Jesus. "The way the world comes together again through the parables matters just as much as the way its idolatrous security is shattered" (W. A. Beardslee, "Parable Interpretation and the

World Disclosed by the Parable," *Perspectives in Religious Studies* 3:123–39 [1976]). To use the parable of the Good Samaritan as an exemplary story is to allow it to function in the constitution of a new world for those who have already been converted from the old way. To use it as a provocation that shatters the old world of a person is to allow it to function as a catalyst for conversion. It "may turn out to be the case that an alternation between these two types of speech—confirmation and unsettling—is required for communicating the Christian vision" (W. A. Beardslee, "Narrative Form in the New Testament and Process Theology," *Encounter* 36:301–15 [1975]). The parable of the Good Samaritan, then, functions in two ways depending upon whether it is addressed to those whose world and values need shattering or to those whose world needs solidifying. Both are legitimate functions carried out by means of the same form of speech.

The second part of the thought unit, 10:38–42, tells the story of Martha and Mary. If the parable of the Good Samaritan, at the level of Lukan theology, dealt primarily with the meaning of the commandment to love one's neighbor, this episode deals with the meaning of the first commandment. The clue to understanding the role of 10:38–42 in relation to 10:25–28 is the interpretative principle voiced by R. Akiba: "Every section in scripture is explained by the one that stands next to it" (Sifre on Numbers §131). This is reinforced in that 18:18–30 corresponds to 10:25–42 in the chiastic pattern of the travel narrative. Both sections follow the same arrangement: (a) dialogue on the law; (b) love of neighbor; and (c) love of the Lord (Bastian Van Elderen, "Another Look at the Parable of the Good Samaritan," in *Saved by Hope*, pp. 109–19).

Luke 10:38–42 asserts that to love the Lord with all your heart, soul, strength, and mind means to sit at the Lord's (Jesus') feet. To sit at a person's feet was the equivalent of "to study under someone" or "to be a disciple of someone" (cf. Acts 22:3—Paul was raised "at the feet of Gamaliel"). To love God with your whole being, Luke says, is to be a disciple of Jesus. Busyness guarantees nothing; listening to Jesus' words is the crucial point (cf. 5:5). Jesus' response to Martha's agitated request (vs. 40; cf. 12:13; 6:41–42) is plagued by textual problems. The two with the best manuscript support are: (1) "Martha, you are anxious and troubled about many things; one thing is needful"; and (2) "Martha, you are anxious and troubled about many things; few things are needful or one." A final decision is difficult, given the evidence. If

(1) were chosen, the meaning would be that Mary has chosen the one thing that is needful, discipleship, receiving from Jesus rather than trying to be the hostess of the one who came to serve (cf. 22:27). In this case, Mary would be living "by everything that proceeds out of the mouth of the Lord" (Deut 8:3; cf. Luke 4:4; John 6:27). If (2) were chosen, the meaning would be something like, "A couple of olives, or even one, will suffice at present. Mary has the main course already" (F. Danker, *Jesus and the New Age*, p. 133). The good portion would be the "food which endures to eternal life" (John 6:27), which is Jesus' gift to his disciples. With either reading, the point is that loving God means submission to Jesus and receiving from him.

Mary and Martha in this story are a study in contrasts. Mary is characterized by an undivided attention to Jesus himself. She is also one who receives from the Lord. Martha was distracted, not wholly focused on Jesus himself. The reason was her "much serving" (vs. 40). Her desire to work for Jesus distracted her focus on Jesus and prevented her receiving from him what she needed. This study in contrasts holds up Mary as the embodiment of what it means to love God wholly, just as the parable of the Good Samaritan held up the Samaritan as the embodiment of what it means to love one's neighbor.

The thought unit, 10:25–42, consists of an exposition of the two great commandments for disciples. To love one's neighbor means to act like the Samaritan. To love God means to act like Mary. These are the two characteristics of those who belong to the covenant people of God: to receive from the Lord and to give to others. Without the former the latter is either not desired or becomes a burden that produces anger at those who are not doing their part.

PRAYER: FOR WHAT AND WHY?

11:1–13

L uke 11:1–13 is composed of a number of independent traditions:
(a) vss. 1–4 (cf. Matt 6:9–13); (b) vss. 5–8 (only in Luke); (c)
vss. 9–10 (cf. Matt 7:7–8); and (d) vss. 11–13 (cf. Matt 7:9–11). These
traditions are held together not only by the common theme of prayer,
but also by a complex series of interlocking devices. (1) Verses 1–4 are
linked to what follows in several ways: (a) "And he said to them" (vss.
2, 5), both only in Luke; (b) Father (vss. 2, 11), heavenly Father (vs.
13); (c) bread (vs. 3), loaves (vs. 5), the latter only in Luke. (2) Verses
5–8 are linked to what follows by "I tell you" (vs. 8), "And I tell you"
(vs. 9), the latter not being in Matt 7:7. (3) Verses 9–10 are linked
with vss. 11–13 by "ask" in vss. 9–10, 11, 12, 13. Clearly the evangelist intended to tie these diverse materials into a single unit dealing
with prayer.

In their present form, these verses consist of a request for instruction by a disciple (vs. 1) followed by Jesus' *didache* (vss. 2–13), the
content of which deals first of all with what to pray for (vss. 2–4) and
then with why one should make a habit of praying (vss. 5–13).

For what should a disciple of Jesus pray? The distinctive Lukan perspective may be grasped only if 11:2–4 is compared with the original
form of the Lord's Prayer. Three versions of the prayer are found in
early Christianity: Matt 6:9–13; Luke 11:2–4; and *Didache* 8:2. The
form in the *Didache* is indebted to that in Matthew, so there are only
two basic forms of the prayer preserved by the early church. That in
Matthew represents the shape of the prayer as it circulated in Jewish
Christianity, that in Luke the shape used by Gentile Christians at the
end of the first century. The original form of the prayer appears to
have contained the number of petitions in Luke with the language of
Matthew being generally more original (Joachim Jeremias, "The Lord's
Prayer in Modern Research," *Expository Times* 71:141–46 [1960], and
R. E. Brown, "The Pater Noster as an Eschatological Prayer," *New*

Testament Essays [Milwaukee: Bruce, 1965], pp. 217–53). This rule of thumb yields the following result:

> Father:
> Hallowed be thy name;
> Thy kingdom come.
> Give us this day our bread for the morrow;
> And forgive us our debts, as we forgive our debtors;
> And lead us not into temptation, but deliver us from
>   the Evil One.

There is an address followed by two "Thou-petitions" and three "us-petitions."

The two "Thou-petitions" are synonymous parallelism. Since it is disciples who already stand within the kingdom who are praying, to say "Thy kingdom come," would be to ask for the final consumation. The two initial petitions, then, ask God to intervene to bring the New Age to pass. What this would mean for God is that his name would be reverenced and his rule acknowledged.

The first two "us-petitions" view the eschatological victory from the perspective of what it would mean for disciples. The term *epiousion* is difficult because it is so rare. In the third century Origen (*De Oratione* 27:7) said he could find no example of it in other Greek writers. Etymology yields two possible translations: either "daily" (from *epi einai*) or "for the future" (from *epi* plus *ienai*). Jerome said that the Gospel of the Hebrews read it in the latter way, as a reference to the eschatological bread, the manna from heaven, or the food of the messianic banquet. Since the first two petitions are eschatological, it seems preferable to read it in an eschatological manner. Parallel to the petition for the heavenly bread is the prayer for forgiveness, that is, the eschatological forgiveness of sin. The coming of the New Age would mean that God's name would be reverenced and his rule accepted; that disciples would participate in the messianic banquet and their sin be ultimately blotted out.

The last "us-petition" is concerned with the idea of eschatological temptation which is the work of the devil. In the final encounter between God and the Evil One which ushers in God's kingdom, the disciples ask to be sheltered: preserve us from temptation and its source.

The prayer as a whole is the prayer of a community ("Give *us*"; "*our* bread"; "forgive *us*"; "*we* forgive"; "lead *us*"; "deliver *us*") which believes it has a unique relation to God. The simple *"Abba*-Father" is without analogy in Jewish prayers of the first millennium A.D. This is the way small Jewish children addressed their earthly parents, and to a Jewish mind it would have been irreverent and unthinkable to call God by this familiar word (Joachim Jeremias, *The Central Message of the New Testament* [London: SCM, 1965], pp. 19–21). This unique relation could be described as informal intimacy. In the prayer the community asks for two things: (1) the speedy (cf. "this day") coming of the eschatological kingdom of God with all of its benefits both for God and for the disciples; and (2) protection in the eschatological crisis which precedes the shift of the ages. The historical Jesus taught his disciples to pray for the immediate shift of the ages and for the protection that would guarantee their participation in the New Age. It assumes a single-mindedness that is jarring. The disciples are to pray for one thing essentially: the realization of the ultimate ideal, God's kingdom, the New Age. They are to ask for it to appear immediately. Such a prayer functions provocatively, asking about the ones addressed, why do they not desire this one thing? Why cannot they desire this one thing? What does it say about them that they cannot pray this way? In this sense the prayer calls for a change in the hearers, for the purification of their desires.

The Lukan form of the Lord's Prayer differs from the original not in the number of petitions but in the wording. The place to begin in noting the differences is with the "us-petitions" in vss. 3–4: "Go on giving us day by day our daily bread" (vs. 3). Luke's present tense "go on giving" (Matthew uses the aorist—give today) and the uniquely Lukan "day by day" (cf. 9:23; 19:17; Acts 17:11) control the understanding of this petition. Whatever the qualifying *ton epiousion* may mean elsewhere, here the translation "daily" seems appropriate. The evangelist sees the petition as the disciples' request for God to go on supplying their physical needs day by day. It is not specifically an eschatological prayer in this context. Jesus is telling the disciples, some of whom had been sent out without extra provisions (9:3; 10:4) and had found their needs supplied (22:35), to pray for the provisions they need for the day. Given the Lukan hostility to the accumulation of unneeded possessions (e.g., 12:16–21), one should perhaps understand the evangelist to mean "pray for what you need for the day and for no more."

In vs. 4 the Lukan differences may be a clue to the evangelist's intention. Whereas Matthew uses "debts" as a term for violations of both the relation to God and the relations of others to us, Luke uses "sins" for our offenses against God. He leaves, however, the debtor language in the second part of the petition. He specifies that we ourselves are continually forgiving all who are indebted to us. If one's understanding of this sentence is determined not by evidence outside the gospel but only by the context, this too may be a part of the Lukan concern with possessions (cf. 6:27–38, especially vss. 34–35, 30). The evangelist may aim for his readers to hear that they should expect God to forgive their sins against him as they continually forgive all of their debtors (understood in terms of "things"). If so, then passing God's forgiveness along to others within the community means something broader than Matthew's context would indicate. In any case, here again the prayer is asking for something within history.

If the petitions in vss. 3, 4a are concerned with the daily life of disciples in this world, it is unlikely that the final petition of vs. 4b should be read as referring to the tribulation just before the eschaton: "Lead us not into temptation" should almost certainly refer to the ordinary temptations of daily life (cf. 4:13; 22:38; Acts 20:19). This would include not only the inward seductions of the devil but also the outward trials which test faith (cf. Sir 2:1ff.; Rom 5:3–5; Jas 1:13). If so, this petition would parallel the Jewish prayer, "Bring me not into the power of sin, nor into the power of guilt, nor into the power of temptation" (b. Berakoth 60b). If the idiom "to enter temptation" means not "to be tempted" but rather "to yield to temptation" and if the negative qualifies the idea of entry, then the petition would be understood as "cause us not to succumb to temptation" (J. Carmignac, *Recherches sur le 'Notre Pere'* [Paris: Letouzey & Ane, 1969], pp. 236–304, 437–45). This would fit the Lukan mind: both Jesus (4:13; 22:28) and his disciples (22:28; Acts 20:19; 14:22) undergo temptations but, empowered by the Holy Spirit, they overcome and do not succumb.

Most likely the first two Lukan petitions should be read in a similar way. While a request for the eschaton should certainly not be excluded, the scope is broad enough to include the disciples' present also. The ancient textual variant in vs. 2b which replaced "hallowed be thy name. Thy kingdom come" with "Let thy Holy Spirit come upon us" (Tertullian, *Against Marcion,* 4:26) reflects the way these two "Thou-petitions" were understood by some. Given 11:13's "the heavenly Father will give the Holy Spirit to those who ask him," the petition calling for the coming of the kingdom was apparently understood in terms of the gift of the Holy Spirit. Though the textual variant is not original, its reading of the passage's intent may be correct. This can only be decided after an exploration of the relation between the Spirit and the kingdom in Luke-Acts. (Cf. J. D. G. Dunn, "Spirit and Kingdom," *Expository Times* 82:36–40 [1970–71]; S. S. Smalley, "Spirit, Kingdom and Prayer in Luke-Acts," *Novum Testamentum* 15:59–71 [1973]; G. W. H. Lampe, "The Holy Spirit in the Writings of St. Luke," in *Studies in the Gospels,* ed. D. E. Nineham [Oxford: Blackwell, 1955], pp. 171–72.)

In Paul the Spirit is the present-ness of the coming kingdom. Where the Spirit is the kingdom is, so to have the Spirit is to have part in the kingdom here and now (cf. 1 Cor 4:20; 2 Cor 5:5; Rom 8:23; 14:17). The same thrust is found in Luke-Acts where the ideas of the power of the kingdom and the working of the Spirit of God are brought into a very close relationship. They are in fact virtually identical. In Acts 1:4 the risen Christ speaks with the apostles about the kingdom of God during his forty days of appearances. At least part of this talk deals with the baptism in the Holy Spirit (Acts 1:4–5). When the apostles ask the risen Lord about the kingdom (Acts 1:6), he responds with words about the Holy Spirit (1:7–8). Luke 12:32 says it is the Father's good pleasure to give the disciples the kingdom, which parallels 11:13: the Father will give the Holy Spirit to those who ask him. So when 17:21 says "the kingdom of God is in your midst," Luke means that the kingdom is present because Jesus is the unique bearer of the Spirit (1:35; 3:22; 4:18). The kingdom is present in Jesus insofar as he has the Spirit. In Luke-Acts the presence of the Spirit is the "already" of the kingdom. Where the Spirit is, there is the kingdom. God's eschatological reign is both mediated and characterized by the Spirit, of whom Jesus is the carrier *par excellence.* So in the gospel the disciples who pray, "Thy kingdom come," realize in the pentecostal gift of the Holy Spirit a partial fulfillment of their prayer. In such an experience they "see the kingdom of God" before they taste death (9:27). Given this close identification of the present dimension of the kingdom and the gift of the Holy Spirit, 11:2, "Thy kingdom come," may be a petition for the eschaton, but it is also a plea for the gift of the Holy Spirit. The early variants on the text were, then, at least partially accurate perceptions of the Lukan mind.

For what should a disciple pray? In a *Sitz im Leben Jesu* the Lord's Prayer functions as a call to petition God for an immediate shift of the ages. The assumptions within the prayer are provocative and shatter all of the hearers' illusions about their devotion to God and his rule. In the context of the third gospel, the model prayer serves a didactic purpose. It gives instruction to disciples about what to pray for in the midst of the on-going historical process: daily bread, forgiveness, victory over temptation, the gift of the Holy Spirit, and the ultimate victory of God. The shift in function in the gospel arises from the lived experience of the church which had continued to exist for fifty or so years. In that time the disciples had found the power unleashed at the resurrection of Jesus—the power that would bring the eschaton to the cosmos—was already at work among the believers. This power was sufficient for all their needs. Out of this experienced reality, they prayed not only for God to bring history to its fulfillment but also for his continued provision of their needs.

Why should a disciple pray? Luke 11:1–13 answers this question not only with the teaching of Jesus (vss. 5–13) but also with his example (vs. 1). On the one hand, it was the example of Jesus that evoked one of his disciples' request, "Lord, teach *us* to pray." A disciple prays because Jesus' example points in that direction. Jesus was a praying activist; from prayer he derived his spiritual power.

On the other hand, Jesus' teaching in 11:5–13 gives a twofold reason for praying. (1) In vss. 5–10 a parable found only in Luke (vss. 5–8) is followed by what amounts to an interpretation (vss. 9–10). The parable's story of a neighbor, who when confronted with a midnight traveler for whom he had no food, shamelessly persisted in his requests to a friend until the friend got up and supplied his needs, has been understood in two very different ways. Some take it to advocate a stormy, unrelenting insistence that persists until God grants the request. Just as the neighbor refused to take "no" for an answer and so had his request met, so also the disciples should persist with God who will eventually respond to shamelessness ("importunity" in the RSV should be "shamelessness" as in NEB). Others, however, take the parable to be a "how much more" story (cf. 18:1–8). If a reluctant friend who does not want to answer a neighbor's request will do so simply because of his neighbor's shamelessness in persisting, how much more will God who is eager and willing answer your prayers. The disciples should pray because God wants to answer. The second interpretation is the more probable because (a) 18:1–8, which is a parallel passage, seems to support this second reading; (b) 11:9–10 makes the point that one should make a habit of asking, seeking, and knocking because God is certain to answer prayer; (c) 11:11–13 is cast into a "how much more" form; and (d) the first interpretation runs counter to the spirit of Matt 6:7. Viewed in this way, vss. 5–10 function to answer why pray: a disciple prays in the first instance because God will answer.

(2) Luke 11:11–13 gives a second reason why disciples should pray—here again the mode of thought is "how much more." Verses 11–13 differ from their Matthean parallel (7:9–11) in two respects, one important and one insignificant. (a) Luke's two comparisons involve first the fish-serpent and then the egg-scorpion parallels, while Matthew's are first the loaf-stone and then the fish-serpent correspondences. The difference has no major bearing on the meaning. Background information offers the most assistance in understanding the parallels. On the one hand, the fish-serpent parallel is illuminated by there being a type of unclean fish in the Sea of Galilee that can reach five feet in length, crawl on land, and has the appearance of a snake. This eel-like creature is most probably the serpent mentioned here. On the other hand, the egg-scorpion correspondence is clarified when we see that when a scorpion's limbs are closed around it, it is egg-shaped. The point is that even sinful parents will not be cruel enough to give their offspring something positively harmful. If an evil parent will not give hurtful gifts but rather good gifts when asked, how much more will God? (b) Whereas Matt 7:11 says, "how much more will your Father who is in heaven give *good things* to those who ask him," Luke 11:13 reads, "how much more will the heavenly Father give the *Holy Spirit* to those who ask him." Here the difference is major. For the third evangelist the good gift of the heavenly Father is not primarily things, even good things, but the Holy Spirit. After his baptism while Jesus was praying the Holy Spirit descended upon him (3:21–22). In Acts 1:14 the disciples are praying before the pentecostal gift of the Spirit in Acts 2. Indeed, the evangelist would see this promise of Jesus in 11:13 as the basis for Pentecost. What happened there was not only a fulfillment of the promise of the risen Lord (Luke 24:49; Acts 1:4–5, 8) but also of the earthly Jesus. These verses, 11:11–13, furnish a second reason why disciples should make a habit of praying. God will not give anything harmful to those who ask. Above all, he will give himself to those who ask him. If the point in vss. 5–10 is the certainty of God's answer, in vss. 11–13 it is the goodness of the gifts bestowed

by God. With the reference to the gift of the Holy Spirit in vs. 13 to those who ask, the reader returns to the idea with which the larger unit began: "Thy kingdom come" (vs. 2). In the gift of the Spirit the rule of God is present. Furthermore, it is the Father's desire to give the kingdom (12:32).

HEALING IN
BIBLICAL PERSPECTIVE

11:14–36

Much of the material in 11:14–36 has parallels in the other synoptics but this disparate material has been cast into a unifying pattern: an action of Jesus (vs. 14) leads to a double assault on Jesus (a—vs. 15; b—vs. 16) which is followed by a double reply by Jesus (a'—vss. 17–28; b'—vss. 29–36). Such a pattern of "action-assault-reply" is characteristic of the Lukan narrative (e.g., 5:17–26, where vs. 20 is the action, vs. 21 is the assault, and vss. 22–24 are the reply; 7:36–50, where vss. 37–38 are the action, vs. 39 is the assault, and vss. 40–48 are the reply in two parts; 13:10–17, where vss. 10–13 are the action, vs. 14 is the assault, and vss. 15–16 are the reply; 15:1–32, where vs. 1 is the action, vs. 2 is the assault, and vss. 3–32 are the triple reply; Acts 11:1–17, where vs. 1 is the action, vss. 2–3 are the assault, and vss. 4–17 are the reply). As it stands this unit consists largely of answers to two reactions to Jesus' miracle (vs. 14, only in Luke): (1) the charge that Jesus was a magician (vs. 15), and (2) the demand for a sign to authenticate Jesus' authority (vs. 16, only in Luke).

Luke 11:14, the action of Jesus, reads very much like a summary of a miracle story. As elsewhere (4:39; 6:18; 8:2; 9:6, 1; 10:9, 17; 13:11, 14, 16; Acts 5:16; 10:38; cf. Matt 12:22), the evangelist understands the healing as an exorcism: the man's inability to speak was due to a speechless demon. It is interesting to note that in the gospels the same problem, inability to speak, can be attributed to three different causes: (1) Luke 1:20—Zechariah's inability to speak is due to a divine judgment on his unbelief; (2) Luke 11:14—the man's inability to speak is due to a demon that was dumb; and (3) Mark 7:32—the man's speech impediment is attributed to neither demonic nor divine causation but is apparently assumed to be due to natural causes. This raises the question of the larger biblical perspective on the causes of sickness.

Apparently all three factors mentioned as a cause of dumbness are considered in the Bible as causes of disease generally. (1) There are certainly instances where sickness is directly due to God's punishment of sin (e.g., 2 Sam 12:14–23, esp. vs. 15; 2 Kgs 15:4–5; 1 Cor 11:29–32). (2) In other places sickness is due to Satan (e.g., Job 2:6–7; Luke 13:16; 2 Cor 12:7), though used by God for his purposes. (3) In still other places sickness seems to be due neither to a person's sin nor to Satan's harassment but to the imperfections of the created order (Gen 3:14–19 where the roots are to be found for this view; John 9:2–3; Rom 8:19–23; 1 Cor 15:50; Gal 4:13–14) in which human beings participate. Even godly people, because they are flesh (mortal), get sick (2 Kgs 13:14; Dan 8:27; Gal 4:13; Phil 2:25–30; 2 Tim 4:20).

The cause of the man's distress in 11:14 was having a demon that was dumb. He was not being punished by God for his sinfulness, nor was he the unfortunate victim of a flawed universe: he was in bondage to demonic evil.

If there are multiple causes of sickness in the biblical perspective, there are also multiple avenues to healing. (1) If sickness is due to one's sin, the proper response is repentance, confession, forgiveness (cf. Jas 5:14–16, which seems to be dealing with sickness caused by sin, especially vs. 16a; cf. 1 Cor 11:30–31). (2) If sickness is due to oppression or attack by Satan and his hosts, then two options are offered. In the first place, the demon can be cast out in the name of Jesus Christ (e.g., Acts 16:18; 19:11ff.). Given sin and demonic oppression as possible causes of human illness, one can see why the NT writers regard signs and wonders as following the gospel (e.g., 2 Cor 12:12; Rom 15:18–19). Wherever sin and spiritual oppression are conquered by Jesus, there will inevitably be accompanying healings and deliverances. Often physical and psychological relief are inevitable by-products of Jesus' conquest of evil. They are to be expected. In the second place, ultimately only God can lift Satan's oppression, and sometimes he does not see fit to do so either at once (cf. Job) or ever in this life (cf. 2 Cor 12:7ff.). When this is the case God uses the trouble for some good purpose (2 Cor 12:9; cf. Rom 8:28). (3) If sickness is due to the imperfections in the natural world, then again two options are offered. On the one hand, in both the OT (e.g., 1 Kgs 17:17–24; 2 Kgs 4:32–37; 5:1ff.) and the NT (e.g., the gospels) healing sometimes takes place via a miraculous intervention of God. On the other hand, there is also an understanding of healing through medicine (e.g., Isa 38:1–5, 21; 1 Tim 5:23; cf. Tobit where medical knowledge comes from God via revelation—e.g., 6:7–8). These two options are rooted in the Bible's understanding of God as both Creator, who has given human beings the capacity to understand the world, and Redeemer, who intervenes, accepts responsibility for both sin and the flaws in his world, and does for us what is beyond the limits of our ability. If God is both Creator and Redeemer, then these two options cannot be played off against one another, as both are a part of who God is and how God acts (cf. Sir 38:1–15). Given the multiple causes of sickness attested to by scripture, it takes discernment to know what is the cause in any given situation, what is the proper avenue of cure, and whether God wishes to heal at spiritual, emotional, and physical levels, all in the here and now, or whether he wishes to save the physical healing until the resurrection.

The means of healing the man's distress in 11:14 was deliverance, the casting out of the unclean spirit by the authoritative word of Jesus. The man was not called upon to repent of his sin, nor was he sent to a doctor for a prescription. He was in bondage to demonic evil, so by power of the Holy Spirit (4:14) Jesus delivered him.

God's miraculous intervention through Jesus to deliver a dumb demoniac leads to a double assault on Jesus. Some said, "He casts out demons by Beelzebul, the prince of demons" (vs. 15). This is the charge that Jesus is a magician: that is, Jesus is accused of using demonic power to achieve his ends. No matter that someone was made well; how Jesus did it is questionable. Jesus' exorcism caused others to test him, seeking from him a sign from heaven (vs. 16): that is, some demanded objective verification of his credentials. No matter that a man was made well; proof is required that this was God's doing. With these two unbelieving reactions to the healing the evangelist demonstrates that Jesus' miraculous deeds do not always evoke faith.

The response to the charge that Jesus' exorcism was due to demonic power is twofold. (1) Verses 17–19 say what the miracle does not mean. It does not mean Jesus is a magician because (a) that would be illogical (vss. 17–18), and (b) it would be inconsistent (vs. 19). It would be illogical because division leads to destruction. Satan, therefore, would not permit rebellion in his own ranks. Furthermore, to accuse Jesus of magic because of his exorcism would be inconsistent since other Jews perform exorcisms without being labeled "servants of Beelzebul" (Acts 19:13ff.; Josephus, *Antiquities* 8:2:5 §45–48; 2:13:3 §286; Tob 6:1–7;

8:1–3). If Jesus' critics are not willing to ascribe other exorcists' work to magic, they cannot so label Jesus.

(2) Verses 20–23 say what Jesus' miracle does mean. If it is ascribed to the "finger of God" (a direct, unmediated act of God, cf. Exod 8:19; 31:18; Deut 9:10; Ps 8:3), it means the kingdom of God has come upon you (vs. 20). This fits with 11:1–13 where kingdom of God and Holy Spirit are virtually synonymous. It means the stronger one (cf. 3:16) has overcome Satan (vss. 21–22). Possession of the defeated one's armor was evidence of the victor's triumph (cf. 2 Sam 2:21 LXX). It is not adequate, however, to cast out a demon if there is no acceptance of the kingdom of God whose power is attested by its expulsion (vss. 24–26). Only God's rule of human life prevents the return of demonic activity, hence those are blessed who "hear the word of God and keep it!" (vss. 27–28). Exorcism, then, is not evidence for Jesus' being a magician but rather for the inbreaking of God's rule in his ministry. In order to benefit permanently from this divine power, however, one must respond properly.

The response of Jesus to the demand for proof that his actions are by God's authority falls into three parts. (1) No sign shall be given to this generation "except the sign of Jonah" (vss. 29–30). Mark 8:11–12 has a similar tradition which says simply, "No sign shall be given to this generation." Matt 12:38–40 more closely parallels Luke: "no sign . . . except the sign of the prophet Jonah (12:39). In Matt 12:40, however, the evangelist inserts a statement peculiar to his gospel explaining his understanding of the sign of the prophet Jonah: "For as Jonah was three days and three nights in the belly of the whale, so will the Son of Man be three days and three nights in the heart of the earth." For Matthew the sign of Jonah is Jesus' crucifixion and resurrection. Luke's view of Jesus' response to the demand for a sign is not that of either Matthew or Mark. He understands the sign of Jonah to be Jonah's call to repentance: "For as Jonah became a sign to the men of Nineveh, so will the Son of Man be to this generation" (vs. 30); for the men of Nineveh "repented at the preaching of Jonah" (vs. 32). The first part of Jesus' reaction to the demand for a sign is to say that the only sign to be given is the prophetic call to repentance.

(2) The second part of the response is found in vss. 31–32: Gentiles will condemn Israel at the judgment because they (the queen of the South and the men of Nineveh) made the appropriate response to the wisdom of Solomon and the preaching of Jonah; Israel, however, fails

to respond properly to something greater than either Solomon or Jonah, namely, the presence of the Holy Spirit in the ministry of Jesus. The notion that the Gentiles would witness against Jews at the judgment was exactly the opposite of Jewish belief (cf. the Christian adaptation of the Jewish belief in 1 Cor 6:2). The second part of Jesus' response to a demand for a sign is to say that Gentiles respond to the call to repentance better than Israel (cf. Acts 13:44–52; 20:23–29; Luke 7:1–10).

(3) The third part of Jesus' response, vss. 33–36, joins three originally unconnected sayings (vss. 33, 34–35, 36) with the catchword "lamp." In this context the unit likens Jesus' ministry to a light that illuminates those who enter a house. There is nothing hidden about the light. Any lack of illumination is due to the recipient. If he or she has a sound eye, light will flood one's whole being. The eye is thought of as a funnel through which light can enter if it is not stoppered. If the eye is not sound (i.e., stoppered), then the self will be dark, unilluminated by the light which shines without (cf. Prov 4:19). Luke's point is that those whose spiritual sight has not been damaged have no need for a sign from heaven (the Gentiles!); the light of God's rule manifest in Jesus' ministry is seen by them clearly. Jesus' ministry is a public light to those entering the kingdom of God (vs. 33). The failure to respond properly is a spiritual analogue to the person whose body is full of darkness because of a diseased or blind eye (vss. 34–35). Hence the call for a sign is a symptom of spiritual blindness.

Rightly understood the power at work in Jesus' healing is God's and is evidence of his rule's presence. Since only one who has experienced God's rule is able to see his kingdom at work (cf. the Greco-Roman principle that it takes like to know like), one who wishes to know whether God is at work in Jesus needs first of all to hear his call to repentance and to respond properly. Unless one has experienced, through repentance, the rule of God in one's life, it will be impossible to recognize its presence in the ministry of Jesus. The presence of God in miracle cannot be recognized by one without God's rule in the individual heart.

POSSESSIONS, PREPAREDNESS, AND REPENTANCE

12:1—13:21

Much of the material in 12:1—13:21 has parallels elsewhere in the synoptic tradition. Sometimes this material is used quite differently from the way the third evangelist employs it. For example, Matt 10:27 gives a reason for missionaries not to be afraid of opposition, but in Luke 12:3 it is a warning against hypocrisy. Or in Luke 12:57–59 the point is to escape the adversary, not to be reconciled with him as in Matt 5:25–26. The third evangelist has taken these diverse materials and has organized them into a two-part unit. Part One is addressed to Jesus' disciples (12:1–53). Jesus speaks first to them (12:1), issuing a call for a Christian response in three areas of life: with regard to persecution (12:1–12), to possessions (12:13–34), and to preparation for the parousia (12:35–48). This charge is climaxed by a paragraph on the divisive effects of Jesus' ministry (12:49–53). Part Two is addressed to the multitudes (12:54—13:21). Jesus, in speaking to them, issues a call for conversion. We find in 12:1—13:21, then, a collection of diverse traditions joined in a framework which may be ascribed to the evangelist. One might think of this large unit as a Christian homily directed first to the disciples (12:1–53) and then to the unbelievers present (12:54—13:21). That non-Christians attended early Christian worship services is clear from 1 Cor 14:23–25.

Part One (12:1–53), which is addressed to the disciples, gives teaching in three areas: (1) on persecution; (2) on possessions; and (3) on being prepared for the parousia. Luke 12:1–12, on persecution, will be discussed in this commentary in connection with 21:12–19. Luke 12:13–34 focuses on a disciple's attitude toward possessions: vss. 13–21 speak to the problem of covetousness, vss. 22–32 to that of anxiety, and vss. 33–34 serve as a general conclusion to the section as a whole. This section is joined to 12:1–12 by the repetition of "multitude" (vss.

1, 13), "do not be anxious" (vss. 11, 22), and birds (sparrows in vs. 6, ravens in vs. 24). Verses 13–21, which deal with covetousness, are tied to vss. 22–34, which focus on anxiety, by means of "treasure" (vss. 21, 33, 34), "barns" (vss. 18, 24), and similar statements in vss. 15b and 23.

Luke 12:13–21, which addresses the problem of covetousness, is peculiar to this gospel. This subsection consists of a pronouncement story climaxed with a rebuke of covetousness (vss. 13–15), followed by a parable about the rich fool (vss. 16–21) which expounds the folly of such a covetous attitude. Covetousness was prohibited in the Decalogue (Exod 20:17; Deut 6:21) and was spoken against by the prophets (e.g., Mic 2:2). It was a problem in the church before Luke (e.g., Rom 1:29; Mark 7:22) and at the time of Luke-Acts (e.g., Col 3:5; Eph 5:5; 1 Tim 6:10). In vs. 15a Jesus warns, "Beware of all covetousness." The reason why is set forth in the form of a principle in vs. 15b: "for a man's life does not consist in the abundance of his possessions." Jesus says that what a person is cannot be confused with what a person has.

The parable of the rich fool in vss. 16–21 functions as an exposition of what covetousness is and why such an attitude is folly. Covetousness here is depicted as the accumulation of additional goods by those who already have enough for their needs. It is a craving for more, not because it is needed, but from a desire to hoard. Such striving acts as a means of security and reflects disregard for God and neighbor. That is why both Col 3:5 and Eph 5:5 regard covetousness as idolatry. To trust in one's accumulated wealth as a means of security is folly: "For what does it profit a man if he gains the whole world and loses or forfeits himself?" (Luke 9:25; cf. Sir 11:18–19; Ps 39:6). The accumulation of additional goods when one has enough guarantees not one's security but one's status as idolater. In Luke-Acts the purpose of wealth is found in its being shared.

Luke 12:22–32, which focuses on the problem of anxiety about possessions, falls into two parts (vss. 22–28; vss. 29–32), each with a balanced structure. (1) Verses 22–28, the first part, begin with an injunction: "Do not be anxious about your life, what you shall eat, nor about your body, what you shall put on" (vs. 22). The reason given is, "For life is more than food and the body more than clothing" (vs. 23). An exposition of "food" and "clothing" follows. Verses 24–26 are an exposition of "food." If God feeds the birds, since you are of much greater value than they, God will feed you too (vs. 24). Besides, anxiety is as ineffective in the area of what you will eat as it is in wanting to add eighteen inches to your height (vss. 25–26). Verses 27–28 are an exposition of "clothing." If God clothes the grass—witness the splendor of the lilies in bloom—since you are more significant, will he not clothe you? (vss. 27–28).

(2) Verses 29–32, the second part of the subsection dealing with anxiety, fall into two balanced units: one telling what to avoid, the other what to seek. In vs. 29 the disciples are told, "Do not seek . . . nor be of anxious mind." Verse 30 gives the reason: "For (*gar*) all the nations of the world seek these things; and your Father knows that you have need of them." In vss. 31–32a the disciples are told, "Instead, seek. . . . Fear not, little flock." Verse 32b gives the reason: "for (*hoti*) it is your Father's good pleasure to give you the kingdom."

In 12:22–32 the disciples are enjoined not to be anxious about food and clothing, the necessities of life, because those who seek God's kingdom (in Luke this includes not only the present experience of the Holy Spirit but also the dwelling with Jesus after death and the ultimate rule of God in the New Age) will find God trustworthy to meet all such needs. Do not be anxious. Trust God. He will provide (Ps 23:1).

Life is God's gift, as are those things that sustain and protect life. For those who trust the power and the goodness of the giver of life, anxiety may abate, the grasping hand may relax, and covetousness be replaced by generosity. Hence the section on possessions is climaxed by 12:33–34, a specific injunction to almsgiving (cf. 11:41; 16:9; 18:22; 19:8; Acts 2:44–45; 4:32–37; 9:36; 10:2, 4, 31; 20:35; 21:24[?]; 24:17). The Jewish practice of almsgiving is echoed in passages like Tob 4:7–11 ("Give alms from your possessions to all who live uprightly," vs. 7) and Sir 3:30 ("almsgiving atones for sin," cf. 29:12). In the Lukan community those with possessions were expected to provide for the poor (vs. 33—cf. Acts 2:44–45; 4:32; 4:34–37; 11:27–30): this was a sign that their treasure was in heaven and their hearts as well (vss. 33–34). The Lukan stance is echoed in 1 Tim 6:17–19. In contrast, covetousness is an indication that God's kingdom is not one's prime pursuit, and anxiety about food and drink an indication that one is unable to trust in God's power and goodness (cf. Gen 3:1–6 where sin is identified with anxious distrust of God's goodness and provision).

Although Jesus believed no one can serve God and money, he called his disciples, in vss. 33–34, to serve God with money.

In 12:35–48 the evangelist turns to the matter of being prepared for the parousia. The sayings in this subsection have a post-Easter perspective. They envisage a situation in which the disciples are awaiting their absent master's return and in which some of the disciples occupy positions of leadership and pastoral responsibility. Within this framework the evangelist first addresses all Christians and then the pastoral leadership. (1) Verses 35–40 enjoin readiness on all Christians. Two parables make the point (vss. 35–38, 39). The first parable tells of servants who are ready for their master's return from a marriage feast and who, upon his return, receive an unheard-of reward: the master serves the servants. What kind of servants receive the reward? Two striking images convey the meaning. "Girded loins" means that the long outer garment is gathered around one's waist so it will not interfere with the most strenuous activity. The verb is a perfect imperative which commands one to be already in a certain state: "Let your loins be already girded"—that is, "Be the kind of servant who never needs to be told to gird them because you always live in this condition." If one is to live with perpetually girded loins, one's lamp is to be continually burning (present imperative). This type of readiness is that which the master rewards. The second parable, the householder and the thief (vs. 39), posits a perpetual watchfulness: though the householder could not stay awake all the time watching for the thief, this never-ending alertness is expected from Jesus' disciples. Verse 40 gives Luke's point: "You also must be ready; for the Son of Man is coming at an hour you do not expect." The readiness enjoined is that which desires to be open to the Master at any moment (vs. 36). All Christians are called to this ready openness.

(2) Verses 41–48 call for faithfulness on the part of those with leadership roles in the Christian community. Peter's question in vs. 41 (only in Luke) provides the opportunity for warnings about the abuse of their positions by church leaders (cf. Acts 20:28ff.; 1 Cor 3:10ff.; 11:21; 1 Tim 4:12–16; 2 Pet 2:1–2, 13). Jesus' parabolic saying is concerned with the situation of a servant who is placed in charge over other servants (vss. 42–43). If he is doing his job when the master comes, he will be blessed (vss. 43–44). If, however, he is irresponsible in his duties he will be punished by the master. A gradation of punish-

ments is given: (a) for active tyranny, death (*dichotomēsei* in vs. 46 means "to cut in two," that is, the dismemberment of a condemned person); (b) for deliberate neglect, a severe beating; and (c) for unintentional neglect, a light beating. This reflects Jewish thought about sins which were unconscious and less culpable than those that were deliberate (cf. Num 15:27–31; Deut 17:12; Ps 19:12–13; b. Baba Bathra 60b). Furthermore, those in positions of leadership, to whom much has been entrusted, will have more expected of them (vs. 48b; cf. Jas 3:1). Christian leaders, then, even more than disciples generally, need to be prepared for the parousia-judgment (cf. 21:34–36; 1 Cor 4:1–5). Readiness for them means their faithfulness in doing the commission given them by the master.

The section addressed to disciples (12:1–53) is climaxed by a paragraph dealing with the divisive effects of Jesus' ministry (12:49–53). The unit is comprised of three originally independent sayings (vss. 49; 50; 51–53), each with a similar form: "I came"; "I have"; "I have come." Taken together, the train of thought is as follows. In vs. 49 Jesus, whom John the Baptist had said would baptize with the Holy Spirit and fire (3:16), looks forward to and longs for that moment. In that time the Spirit, like a burning fire, will accomplish the work of judgment in the hearts of people. But (*de*) Jesus' "baptism" is the precondition for that to happen (vs. 50). The variant in Mark 10:38 shows Jesus' baptism to be his suffering and death. So after his death, the fire will come. This corresponds with the Lukan chronology: Pentecost follows passion. The result of Jesus' coming, the outpouring of the Spirit and fire, and the proclamation of the gospel will be *division*. This theme was anticipated in the birth narratives (2:34–35): "The call for decision is a call for 'division' " (E. E. Ellis, *The Gospel of Luke*, p. 182). From Luke's point of view, the presence of the Holy Spirit in the life and proclamation of the church produces division before it produces unity. Jesus is the great divider.

The second of the two major sections of 12:1—13:21 is addressed to the multitudes (12:54—13:21). This part of the discourse is tied to the first (12:1–53) by the use of "hypocrites" (12:56; 13:15; cf. hypocrisy in 12:1) and the threefold "I tell you" (*legō soi* in 12:59; *legō humin* in 13:3, 5; cf. 12:51, 44, 37, 27, 22, 8, 4) as well as the reference to the multitudes (12:54; 13:17; cf. 12:1, 13). The address to the multitudes is a call for conversion in two parts (12:54–59 and 13:1–21).

The first part, 12:54–59, is a twofold exhortation to interpret the signs of the times properly (vss. 54–56) and to respond rightly to the challenge of the moment (vss. 57–59). In vss. 54–56 Jesus says the crowds need to be as discerning in their interpretation of the time (that is, the meaning of Jesus' mission) as they are in discerning the weather. To fail to do so will spell disaster (cf. 19:41–44). In vss. 57–59 Jesus says the people need to be as discerning about the realities of God's judgment as they are about settling accounts with a bill collector. In everyday life people wisely settle accounts before they become liable to the jurisdiction of the judge and are thrown into debtor's prison. The same wisdom is called for in the face of the approaching judgment of God (cf. Acts 10:42–43; 17:30–31).

The second part, 13:1–21, gives two significant signs together with their proper interpretation. Luke 13:1–9 raises the question of the meaning of the absence of tragedy in a person's life. "Our lives are going smoothly. As any good Jew knows, trouble is God's punishment for sin, while tranquility is a sign of God's blessing. Our lives are tranquil; there is no disaster. Why then should we repent?" Luke 13:1–9 is a response in three sections to such a position. (1) The first two sections are based upon some recent occurrences in Jerusalem (vss. 1–3, 4–5): the massacre of some Galileans by Pilate (tragedy due to a human cause) and the death of some caused by the fall of the tower of Siloam (tragedy due to a natural cause). Tragedy, says Jesus, is not the measure of one's sinfulness and one's need to repent. Those whose lives are tranquil likewise need to repent. (2) The third section, 13:6–9, is a parable about a fig tree that after three years bore no fruit. Since a fig tree supposedly reached maturity after three years, the probability was that it would not ever bear fruit. The owner wanted it cut down and replaced, but the vinedresser asked for one more year to see if it would bear. The point is that the absence of judgment here and now cannot be construed as a sign of one's righteousness. Rather, if judgment does not strike immediately, it is a sign of God's mercy, not his approval (cf. Acts 14:15–17; 17:30; Rom 2:4ff.; 2 Pet 3:9ff.). One is being given a last chance. Taken together, 13:1–9's three components say that just because people pass through life unscathed by suffering they should not assume that therefore they please God. Tragedy is no sure sign of sinfulness, just as absence of tragedy is no sure sign of righteousness. All alike—those whose lives are tragic and those whose lives are tranquil—are sinners and all alike must repent (change directions in life) before God's judgment does come upon them.

Luke 13:10–21, the healing of the stooped woman, freeing her from the bondage of Satan, is a sign of the presence of God's kingdom (cf. 11:20). Though, like the rising cloud (12:54) or the south wind (12:55), it is seemingly small and insignificant, this single defeat of Satan, like the cloud and wind, signals a certain result—ultimate universal victory over evil (13:18–21).

The challenge to the multitudes is clearly put. Do not misinterpret your freedom from misfortune as a sign of your righteousness: it is God's last opportunity for you to repent. Do not miss the presence of God's rule in Jesus' healings: they are signs pointing to a certain result. Be at least as astute in these matters as you are in your reading of the weather and in your avoiding the judgment of the courts. Repent!

THE RESPONSE
OF ELDER BROTHERS

15:1–32

Luke 15 contains an introduction (vss. 1–3) followed by three parables (vss. 4–7; 8–10; 11–32), two of which are peculiar to the gospel (vss. 8–10; 11–32); the third has a parallel in Matt 18:12–14. The first two parables (vss. 4–7; 8–10) possess a common surface structure: (1) what man/what woman; (2) one sheep lost/one drachma lost; (3) sheep found/coin found; (4) calls friends and neighbors, saying, "Rejoice with me for I have found the lost sheep"/calls friends and neighbors, saying, "Rejoice with me for I have found the lost coin"; (5) Just so, I tell you/Just so, I tell you. The two stories are joined by a simple "or," just as the two parables of 14:28–32 and the two incidents of 13:1–5 were. The three parables are linked together by the key words "joy" (vss. 6–7; 9–10; 23–24, 32), "because the lost is found" (vss. 6; 9; 24; 32), and "repentance" (vss. 7; 10; 18). The entire chapter is joined by an inclusion: the elder son's complaint about the father's receiving the prodigal and giving him a feast (vss. 27–30) echoes the murmuring of the Pharisees and the scribes over Jesus' receiving sinners and eating with them (vss. 1–2).

The chapter is put together with techniques characteristic of the evangelist. (1) The pattern is similar to what we find elsewhere in Luke: an action of Jesus (vs. 1) evokes an assault on him (vs. 2), to which he responds (vss. 3–32)—cf. 13:10–17; 11:37–44, 14–23; 5:29–32, 17–26) (2) Luke 5:36–39 introduces a series of three parabolic sayings with the singular, "He told them a parable also," just as 15:3 does. (3) Luke 13:1–9 has two short, similarly constructed sayings of Jesus followed by a longer parable, just as chapter 15 does. Luke 15, taken as a whole, is a Lukan composition, meant to be read as a unit.

The introduction to the chapter (vss. 1–3) contains two components: the occasion (vss. 1–2) and a transition (vs. 3). The occasion is the Pharisaic criticism of Jesus' association with outcasts ("sinner" has a connotation that goes beyond our usual moralistic interpretation and involves a disreputable social status). The stance of the Pharisees (5:29ff.; 7:39; 15:1–2) reflects the OT warning about association with evil-doers (Prov 1:15; 2:11–15; 4:14ff.; Psalm 1; Isa 52:11; cf. 2 Cor 6:14–18) which was crystallized in the rabbinic dictum "Let not a man associate with the wicked, not even to bring him to the Law" (Midrash Rabbah on Exodus 18:1 [65a]). In contrast, Jesus eats and drinks with outcasts because "I have not come to call the righteous, but sinners to repentance" (5:32). He enters their houses because "the Son of Man came to seek and save the lost" (19:10). The verb *prosdechomai* (receives) in 15:2 may indicate that here Jesus is hosting sinners, an even more serious offense to a Pharisee than merely eating with them. Given the Pharisaic criticism of his behavior, the transition (vs. 3) tells us that Jesus spoke a parable (consisting of three stories).

The first of these three stories, the parable of the lost sheep (cf. Ezek 34; Ps 119:176), is paralleled in Matt 18:12–14. Luke's point is clarified by a comparison with the Matthean parallel. Matthew 18 is the fourth of five large teaching sections in the first gospel; it is concerned with the relationships of disciples to one another in the church and is addressed specifically to disciples. Verses 12–13 appear as part of a unit, 18:1–14, which deals with "the little ones" in the church (that is, the rank and file disciples who are in constant danger of deception from proud and clever people). The point of the unit is twofold: (1) do not cause a rank and file Christian to sin (vss. 6, 7–9), and (2) if one goes astray, go after him/her (vss. 5, 10–14). Note that in Matt 18:12–13 the sheep is not lost; it *goes astray*. In 18:14, the conclusion, the meaning is that the heavenly Father does not want any *little ones* to perish. In the first gospel, therefore, the parable of the sheep gives directions to disciples for dealing with straying Christians. In Luke, however, the one sheep is *lost* (15:4, 6). Furthermore, the interpretation (vs. 7) appended to the parable (vss. 4–6) makes clear the meaning of "lost." Verse 7 reads, "Just so, I tell you, there will be more joy in heaven over one *sinner* who repents than over ninety-nine righteous persons who need no repentance." The lost in Luke are sinners, the outcasts with whom Jesus eats.

In the Lukan story of the lost sheep, the rejoicing of the shepherd is matched by the rejoicing of friends and neighbors over his having found the lost animal. If his associates join the shepherd in his rejoicing when a lost sheep has been found, how much more should the

Pharisees join heaven in its joy over the repentance of a sinner. Can you join me, says Jesus to his critics, in my rejoicing over the reclamation of any of the outcasts with whom I eat and drink?

The second story, the parable of the lost coin, is little more than an alternative way of saying the same thing. The repetition is for emphasis. Joy over finding the lost coin (not a coin used as an ornament but one that was part of the woman's savings) is the center of concern. The picture of an oriental woman in her house with no windows and a dirt floor lighting a tiny lamp and sweeping until she finds her lost coin climaxes with a conclusion (vs. 10) similar to that of the preceding story: "Just so, I tell you, there is joy before the angels of God over one sinner who repents" (15:10). Taken together the parables of the lost sheep and the lost coin justify Jesus' association with outcasts by appeal to the joy in heaven over the repentance of even one sinner. Those two stories say, You know how you feel if you are a herdsman and you find a lost sheep or if you are a housewife and you recover a lost coin; well, that is how God feels when a sinner repents. You know how your friends and neighbors join you in rejoicing over your find; well, that same kind of communal rejoicing is heaven's response to a sinner's being reclaimed. A question is implicit: Can you share that joy? Will you join with God and heaven's hosts in their rejoicing?

The third story, the parable of the two sons, is perhaps the best known of the gospel parables. This story falls into two parts, the first focusing on the prodigal (vss. 11–24), the second on the elder brother (vss. 25–32). In both parts of the parable the focus is first on the son and then on the father.

In the first part of the story, the portrayal of the prodigal evokes negative feelings. (1) The boy treated his father as if he were dead. According to the laws of property, it was possible for children to receive a division of the father's capital during his lifetime (cf. Sir 33:19–21), but a son had the right of disposal of the property only after the father's death. (2) The prodigal had dissipated his means of caring for his father in case a necessity arose (vss. 18, 21): He had violated the commandment to honor one's father and mother (Exod 20:12; Deut 5:16). (3) He had associated with a Gentile (vss. 15–16) instead of going to the Jewish community for help. He had, moreover, made his living in what for a Jew was a sinful way (feeding pigs). The polite way a Mid-Easterner gets rid of unwanted hangers-on is by assigning them a task he knows they will refuse. Not even this work, which practically precluded the practice of his religion, got rid of the youth. Here then is a portrait of a despicable youth about whom one's feelings are similar to those of a Pharisee for a tax collector. He was uncouth, unclean, and contemptible.

The portrayal of the father in the first part of the story evokes amazement. (1) The father would be expected to refuse the younger son's request (vs. 12), but instead he grants it. (2) The expected response from the father upon the younger son's return home is mirrored in the prodigal's request: "Treat me as one of your hired servants" (vs. 19). A typical Jewish father might have considered this expedient until the son's reformation had been confirmed. It would, moreover, allow the youth to make reparations required by repentance (cf. Luke 19:8). Instead, the father came out of the house and in a dramatic demonstration showed an unexpected love publicly, even to the point of humiliating himself. The father's actions were without restraint. He ran. Even if he were in a great hurry, for an aged oriental to run would be beneath his dignity. (Sir 19:30 says, "A man's manner of walking tells you what he is.") Yet he ran. The embrace would stop the prodigal from going to his knees. A kiss on the cheek was a sign of reconciliation and forgiveness, the best robe a sign of honor, the ring a sign of authority (cf. Esth 3:10; 8:2; Gen 41:42), the shoes a sign of a free man—slaves went barefoot—and the feast a sign of joy: "Let us eat and make merry; for this my son was dead, and is alive again; he was lost, and is found" (vss. 23–24). Here is the same note of joy over the recovery of the lost that we met in the interpretations of the two earlier parables (15:7, 10). Joy over a recovered sheep or coin is understandable. They are valuable and we benefit from their being found. But the "excessive joy" of the father at the prodigal's return makes no sense. At the very least, one stands puzzled at the father's joy.

Just as in the case of the prodigal, the elder brother in the second part of the story (vss. 25–32) evokes negative feelings. (1) In addressing his father (vs. 29) with no title, he insults him publicly. (2) He accuses his father of rank favoritism (vss. 29–30). (3) He declares he is not part of the family (cf. "my friends" in vs. 29b; "this son of yours" in vs. 30). (4) If, moreover, all that is left belongs to the elder brother,. and if he complains about not being able to dispose of it yet as he wants to do, then he also wants the father dead and gone. In other words, although the elder son has carried out orders (vs. 29b), he has been lawless within the law—not physically but spiritually. If the prodigal was an overt sinner, the elder brother has been a covert one. He is certainly not a lovable figure.

Again in the second part of the parable the father's response is provocative. Reacting to the elder brother's anger, the father goes out (vs. 28) and says, "Son, you are always with me, and all that is mine is yours. It was fitting (*edei*—cf. 2:49; 4:43; 9:22; 13:16, 33; 17:25; 19:5; 22:37; 24:7, 26, 44) to make merry and be glad, for this your brother was dead, and is alive; he was lost, and is found" (vss. 31–32). Given the context the statement should be taken to mean that it was a divine necessity to rejoice over the recovery of the lost (cf. 15:7, 10). Joy is the appropriate (as defined by God's behavior) response to a sinner's repentance.

In taking this stance the third story stands in continuity with the first two. (1) The joy in heaven over a sinner's repentance is greater than a shepherd's happiness over the recovery of a lost sheep (vs. 7). (2) There is joy in heaven over a sinner's repentance just as there is when a woman finds her lost coin (vs. 10). (3) Heaven rejoices over a sinner's reclamation just as the father did over the return of the prodigal, even though it is difficult to accept. In one respect, however, the third story stands in discontinuity with the first two: it remains open. The elder brother's response to the father's joy is not given. Will the elder son accept the father's invitation to rejoice with him over the recovery of the prodigal as the shepherd's friends and the women's neighbors did with them? This is left open for each "elder brother" who hears the parable to decide.

As in all double-edged parables, the emphasis lies in the second half, the climax, which comes to us as a query: Will you share in the communal joy over the prodigal's return? If not, why not? Chapter 15, then, is a threefold statement of God's joy over a sinner's repentance followed by a query: Can you participate in that joy? If not, why not? Can you not rejoice at the efforts to effect a sinner's repentance? If you were able to feel the joy of the shepherd and the woman, why are you unable to feel the joy of the father? Do you get more excited about money and animals than about people (12:15–16; 14:5)? Who are you, in your relation to God and humans, in light of your absence of joy? Why are you not able to participate in the divine necessity to rejoice?

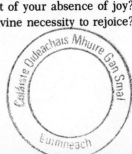

Jesus' response to the assault on his behavior (vs. 2) is to raise a question about his accusers. As has been noted, the conclusion is missing in vs. 32. The hearers must decide their response.

When the parables are used to question the hearers in this way, the christological question is just below the surface. One is forced to ask, "Who is this who professes to know the mind of God?" The Pharisees of vss. 1–2 would not only be forced to ask themselves, "Are we elder brothers?" but also, "What right does Jesus have to make the judgments he does?"

THE USE AND
MISUSE OF WEALTH

16:1–31

The unity of the chapter is apparent first of all from the concern with possessions that runs through it. The chapter falls into two parts, 16:1–13 and 16:14–31, each dominated by a parable beginning "There was a rich man" (vs. 1; vs. 19). The first part is addressed to disciples (vs. 1), the second to Pharisees (vs. 14—cf. 17:1 where the audience switches back to disciples).

The first part of chapter 16, vss. 1–13, is composed of a parable with some interpretations (cf. a similar phenomenon in 18:6ff.). Verse 1a is a Lukan introduction; vss. 1b–8a give the parable; vs. 8b is one interpretative comment about the story; vs. 9 is a second interpretation; vss. 10–12 are an elaboration of the second interpretation; vs. 13 is a conclusion to the second interpretation and its elaboration (vss. 9–12). These separate pieces are held together by a complex web of interlocking devices. Verse 8a reads, "The master commended the steward of *unrighteousness* because he *acted shrewdly*" (*tēs adikias hoti phronimōs epoiēsen*). Each of the italicized words serves as a link with what follows: (1) vs. 8b says, "for the sons of this world are *shrewder* (*phronimōteroi*) in their own generation than the sons of light"; (2) vs. 9 tells the disciples, "*make* (*poiēsate*) friends for yourselves by means of the mammon *of unrighteousness* (*tēs adikias*); furthermore, vs. 9's reference to being received (*dexōntai*) into eternal habitations echoes the being received (*dexōntai*) into the houses of earthly associates in 16:4); (3) vs. 10's "he who is dishonest (*adikos*) in a very little is dishonest (*adikos*) also in much" echoes the *adikias* (unrighteousness) of vss. 8a, 9. In addition to these links with vs. 8a, there are other links between later verses. Verse 11's unrighteous mammon (*adikō mamōna*) ties it to vs. 9. The occurrence of "faithful" links vss. 10 and 12. Verses 11 and 12 are linked by a similar structure: "If you have not been faithful . . . who . . . ?" Verse 13 again uses mammon. By means of such links the evangelist has constructed a unit from diverse materials in vss. 1–13. He issues a call for Jesus' disciples to be wise in their use of wealth and gives reasons why such wisdom is desirable.

The Lukan call for a wise use of wealth by disciples is located in the parable of the steward (vss. 1b–8a) and its first interpretation (vs. 8b). The parable has provoked much controversy, often unnecessarily. The story is about a man who, when confronted with a crisis, acted shrewdly (cf. 12:57–59). Caught in the act of wasting his master's goods, the steward received notice of the termination of his job. Not strong enough to do manual work and too proud to beg, with prospects of future employment virtually nil, the steward acted to guarantee his future. How? There are two possible ways of reading the remainder of the story that are worthy of attention. (1) Some say that as an agent, he was entitled to a commission. Seeing he was to be dismissed, he decided to forego his commission in order to get the people who would benefit to reciprocate (cf. 6:32) and receive him into their houses when he was unemployed (vs. 4). In this act there was no dishonesty, only prudence to prepare for the future. (2) Others claim the key to the situation is that no one yet knows the steward has been fired. He summons the debtors who therefore assume the entire bill-changing is legitimate. They assume the master authorized the reductions in what they owed and that the steward talked him into it. The steward then delivered the changed accounts to his master. The master looked at them and reflected on his alternatives. Either he could go to the debtors and explain—in which case he would be cursed—or he could be silent, accept the debtors' praise, and allow the clever steward to ride high on the wave of popular enthusiasm. He chose the latter course of action and said to the steward, "You are a wise fellow." Either way the steward acted to guarantee his future by means of his use of the wealth under his control. When the master (the rich man, not Jesus) commended the steward's shrewdness, it was no praise of his original waste. It was rather an acknowledgment that the steward's subsequent actions had wisely guaranteed his future. The first interpretation of the parable (vs. 8b) notes that non-Christians are shrewder in their use of money than are disciples. That is, they, like the dishonest steward, use it to guarantee their future. This serves as a call for disciples of Jesus to act as wisely in their use of the wealth under their control.

What would constitute a wise use of wealth by disciples? Verse 9 explains what is implied in vs. 8b. If a dishonest manager could provide for his future by a shrewd use of possessions, how much more should the sons of light, by giving alms (unrighteous mammon means worldly wealth, not possessions acquired dishonestly), provide for their future in heaven ("they" is a circumlocution for God; cf. *Mishna*, Yoma 8:9— "He who says, 'I will sin and repent, and sin again and repent,' to him give they no opportunity to repent."). Wise use of money will gain one's welcome in heaven ("eternal habitations"—cf. 1 Enoch 39:4; 2 Esdr 2:11). Verses 10–12 elaborate on this. If disciples have not been faithful in their use of earthly wealth which is on loan from God (*Pirke Abot* III:7), how can they be trusted with the true riches of eternal life? This is one of the few places in the NT where the idea of stewardship is applied to material possessions.

Why is disciples' use of wealth tied to their future in heaven? Verse 13 tells us plainly: One's use of wealth points to whom one serves. Jesus says, "You cannot serve God and mammon." Given this, Christians need to answer the call to manifest a shrewdness in the use of wealth under their control. Affluence in the hands of disciples is to be used sacramentally as a means of expressing love, both to God and to other people who have needs. The church in Acts embodies a proper response to Jesus' call. There was first a spontaneous (Acts 2:44–45; 4:32, 34ff.) and then an organized (Acts 6:1ff.) sharing of wealth within the community to meet needs. Sharing was carried on between congregations some distance from one another (Acts 11:27ff.). This Lukan spirit reflects that of the early church fathers generally. Justin Martyr (*Apology* I, 67) says,

> And they who are well to do, and willing, give what each thinks fit; and what is collected is deposited with the president, who succours the orphans and widows, and those who, through sickness or any other cause, are in want, and those who are in bonds, and the strangers sojourning among us, and in a word, takes care of all who are in need.

Tertullian (*Apology* 39:10) says, "We do not hesitate to share our earthly goods with one another. All things are common among us but our wives." A shrewd use of wealth by disciples would be to use it for meeting the needs of others. Such use signals an end to the worship of money and the existence of one's service of God. It also opens the door to a warm reception by God in heaven.

The second part, 16:14–31, is addressed to the Pharisees (vss. 14–

15), those who held that possession of wealth points to the one whom God loves. The section, which is an attack on the Pharisaic assumptions about wealth, is organized into a two-pronged group of sayings (vss. 14–18), followed by a double-edged parable (vss. 19–31). Verses 19–26 of the parable are an exposition of vss. 14–15, while vss. 27–31 serve as an illustration of vss. 16–18 (E. E. Ellis, *The Gospel of Luke*, p. 201, following a hint by John Calvin). This pattern gives unity to the section.

The first of the double-pronged group of sayings, vss. 14–15, makes two points. (1) Verses 14–15a emphasize that it is not the outer appearance of righteousness and its rewards that counts but what God sees in the heart. The Pharisees scoff at Jesus' statement, "You cannot serve God and mammon" (vs. 13). Given their assumptions, this was predictable. For them tragedy is a sign of God's displeasure; success (e.g., financial prosperity) is evidence of one's righteousness and of God's pleasure. It is no wonder they scoffed at Jesus' "either God or money" stance (cf. 18:24–26 where the disciples, after being told of the difficulty of a rich man's being saved, ask, "Then who can be saved?"). Money for them was a sign, a sure sign, of God's favor and of their place in the kingdom. Their position had roots in their scriptures (e.g., Deut 28:12–13 where wealth and plenty are a sign of God's blessings). Jesus' response to their scoffing was to contrast their outer-public appearance with their inner-private reality (cf. 11:39–41; 18:9–14). (2) In their inner selves they were exalted (that is, self-sufficient, independent of God). This is a stance God hates (vs. 15b). Jesus was speaking out of another strand of OT thought which saw the poor as symbolic of total dependence upon God and the rich as symbolic of independent self-sufficiency. These rich ones oppressed their poor brethren and thereby violated the covenant (Amos 8:4–6), instead of giving alms (Deut 15:11). Jesus' point, therefore, is that prosperity is an ambiguous sign—only a knowledge of the heart can tell for sure whether or not one is righteous.

The first part of the parable of the rich man and Lazarus (vss. 19–25; 26 is a transition) amplifies the two themes of vss. 14–15. (1) The first is that wealth is not necessarily a sign of righteousness. In the parable the rich man who was clothed in purple and fine linen and who feasted sumptuously every day is an example of the misuse of wealth. He neglected the law relating to the poor. Deut 15:4 says there should be no poor person in Israel's midst. So generosity toward the poor was counted as righteousness (Prov 11:23–24; 21:26; 29:7). It was regarded as a good thing to help the poor and weak through kindness (Prov 14:31; 17:5), loans (Prov 19:17), and liberality (Prov 11:25; 21:26). In Sifre Deuteronomy 116–18, we find a rabbinic commentary on Deut 15:7–11. From vs. 9 of Deuteronomy 15 the lesson is drawn: "Be careful not to refuse charity, for every one who refuses charity is put [by the text] in the same category with idolaters, and he breaks off from him the yoke of Heaven, as it is said, *wicked*, that is, without *yoke*." In the mainline Jewish tradition it was believed one should not withhold needed relief for the poor. In this parable, however, Lazarus received only the leftovers from the table that fell on the ground—what the dogs ate—and was not the object of any significant charity. The rich man, then, was definitely not righteous (cf. 1 John 3:17).

If wealth is no guarantee of one's righteousness, then poverty is no proof of another's evil. This is the only parable of Jesus that names a character. The name, Lazarus (he whom God helps), is symbolic of the beggar's piety. Moreover, ritual uncleanness is no evidence against piety (the unclean dogs who licked his sores rendered him unclean, from a Pharisaic perspective—cf. Luke 10:29–37; Acts 10). A parable that portrayed its hero as an unclean beggar must have been as startling to Pharisaic assumptions (clean plus rich equals righteous) as one that depicted a Samaritan as hero. The first part of the parable, then, illustrates the initial theme of vss. 14–15—prosperity is an ambiguous sign.

(2) The first part of the parable also elaborates the second point of vss. 14–15: God who looks on the heart regards anyone who is proud-exalted as an abomination. The rich man accordingly ended in torment, crying for Abraham to send Lazarus to dip the end of his finger in water to cool his tongue since he was in anguish in the flame. The proud rich man who demonstrated no charity to the poor in this life finds his status reversed in the next. The Lukan God is the opponent of the exalted (self-sufficient who are insensitive to the needs of the poor). Luke 16:19–25 says plainly that the failure to use one's wealth on behalf of the poor in this life leads to torment in the afterlife. The first half of the parable of the rich man and Lazarus, then, illustrates both themes of vss. 14–15.

The second of the group of sayings, vss. 16–18, likewise makes two points. (1) Verse 16 speaks of the inclusiveness of the kingdom. A very different version of the saying is found in Matt 11:12–13. The Lukan version says that since John the Baptist the kingdom of God has been proclaimed as good news (cf. 4:18; Acts 1:21–22). Two possible consequences of this are worth our attention. (a) Is it that everyone (*pas*— cf. 3:6; 4:25–27; 7:1–10; 8:26ff.) is pressing hard (*biazetai* taken as middle voice means "to overpower by force, to press hard, to act with violence") into it? (b) Or is it that "everyone is expressly invited to come in" (*biazomai* taken as passive voice with the meaning found in the LXX—e.g., Gen 33:11—means "to be begged earnestly, to be urged")? Either way, in the Lukan context the emphasis is on the universality of the kingdom's outreach and the option for everyone to enter it (cf. Acts 13:48; 28:28). (2) Verse 17 (cf. Matt 5:18) affirms the continuing validity of the law (cf. Acts 20:27–28). In this context doubtless the evangelist is thinking of the law that teaches about the care of the poor. One should remember that in the OT laws relating to the care of the poor dealt not only with an individual's giving alms or assistance but also with structural provision for the poor within society at large (e.g., Leviticus 25 equalizes land ownership every fifty years; Deuteronomy 15 gives Hebrew slaves their freedom in the sabbatical year; Ruth 2 indicates the law of gleaning was designed to prevent debilitating poverty among the people of God and the sojourners in the land).

The second part of the parable (vss. 27–31) amplifies the two themes of vss. 16–18. (1) The first theme is that there is a universality in the kingdom's composition. Everyone enters it. This is certainly illustrated by the story of the unclean beggar Lazarus. Who, in this life, would have thought he, of all people, would end in Abraham's bosom and be asked to go to warn the rich man's brothers of their fate? If Lazarus succeeded, the kingdom is certainly inclusive. (2) The second theme is that the law is still in force, in particular that law dealing with the treatment of the poor. In the parable, when the rich man asks father Abraham to send Lazarus to warn his five rich brothers of their destiny unless they change, Abraham answers, "They have Moses and the prophets; let them hear them" (vs. 29). If the law and the prophets do not call the rich to repentance, then even if someone goes to them from the dead it will make no difference. They will not repent. Once again the parable serves to illustrate themes set forth earlier in the chapter (vss. 16–18). Since in double-edged parables the second part receives the emphasis, the evangelist wants to accent the point about the continuing validity of the law and its teaching on the use of wealth on behalf of the poor.

In Luke 16 the evangelist issues a call and gives a warning. On the one side, he calls for disciples to be as wise as the steward in their use of wealth to guarantee their future. On the other side, he warns that one not assume wealth to be so much a guarantee of one's being approved by God that one neglects the less fortunate, failing to follow the guidance of Moses and the prophets, and thus finds oneself cast out.

THE POSSIBILITY
OF AN IMPOSSIBLE DEMAND

17:1-10

L uke 17:1-10 is a small collection of four independent sayings of Jesus directed to disciples: (1) 17:1-2 (Matt 18:6-7; cf. Mark 9:42); (2) 17:3-4 (Matt 18:15, 21-22); (3) 17:5-6 (Matt 17:20); and (4) 17:7-10 (only in Luke). The collection focuses on two questions: (a) What are disciples called to do? and (b) Are they able to do it? The first two sayings (vss. 1-2, 3-4) answer the initial question, the second two logia (vss. 5-6, 7-10) respond to the latter query.

What does Jesus expect of his disciples in their life together? The answer is given in the first two sayings, which are tied together by their common focus on sin. The first, vss. 1-2, deals with one's offences against others; the second, vss. 3-4, is focused on another's offences, either generally (vs. 3) or against one specifically (vs. 4). (1) Verses 1-2 are a woe pronounced on disciples who cause one of the little ones to stumble (cf. 1 Cor 8:9ff.; 10:32; Rom 14:13-21; 1 John 2:10; Rev 2:14). The issue is Christian influence. That we find material about the perils of influence here, in Matthew 18, in two letters of Paul, in 1 John, and in the Apocalypse indicates the issue was a serious one in early Christianity. Here Jesus holds his disciples responsible for their influence on weaker Christians. (2) Verses 3-4 are a call first to reproof and then to forgiveness of others who sin. Christians' reproof of one another derives from Christ's activity (Acts 10:15; cf. Rev 3:19), as does their forgiveness (Luke 23:34; 22:54-62 with 24:34). In Luke the twofold activity is to be part of the spontaneous life-style of the individual disciple, whereas in Matthew 18 it is a Christian duty ordained in a code of church discipline. Paul, in Acts 15:36-41, may embody reproof but it is unlikely the evangelist regarded him as incarnating forgiveness. The disciples of Jesus are called to a responsible use of their influence and to a limitless forgiveness of those who sin against them who then repent.

Are we able to do what is asked of us? The call to cause no little one to stumble and to forgive repentant sinners without limit is so demanding the apostles ask Jesus for more faith (cf. 11:1). Jesus' response is typically oriental in using a vivid and extreme image, which the RSV translates, "If you had faith as a grain of mustard seed, you could say to this sycamine tree [a black mulberry with an extensive root system], 'Be rooted up, and be planted in the sea,' and it would obey you" (vs. 6). The implication derived from this translation is that the apostles do not have faith, but if they had even a little bit it would work wonders. In the Greek text, however, the best reading is, "If you have faith [and the assumption is that you do], you could say to this sycamine tree, 'Be plucked up by the root' . . ." That is, since you have faith, even the minutest amount, the impossible is possible (Nigel Turner, *Grammatical Insights into the New Testament* [Edinburgh: T. & T. Clark, 1966], pp. 51–52). In the RSV translation the point is that if the apostles had the least bit of faith the impossible would be possible. In the second, and correct, reading the point is that the apostles have at least some faith, which is enough to do the impossible.

Further insight into the meaning of 17:6 comes from an examination of the parallels to this saying in Matt 17:20; 21:21 // Mark 11:22–23. These parallels occur in different contexts and have slightly different contents. (a) Matt 17:20 is part of the climax to the healing story that follows the transfiguration in all three synoptic gospels. Whereas Mark 9:29 says the disciples' failure was due to the fact that "this kind cannot be driven out by anything but prayer," and although Luke 9:37–43 does not even deal with the issue of the disciples' failure except by allusion (9:41), Matt 17:20 says the disciples failed "because of your little faith. For truly, I say to you, if you have faith as a grain of mustard seed, you will say to this mountain, 'Move hence to yonder place,' and it will move; and nothing will be impossible to you." (b) Matt 21:21 and Mark 11:22–23 have a similar saying in the context of the cursing of the fig tree. Matthew's connection is explicit. The disciples ask Jesus how the miracle happened. His response is, "Truly, I say to you, if you have faith and never doubt, you will not only do what has been done to the fig tree, but even if you say to this mountain, 'Be taken up and cast into the sea,' it will be done" (cf. Jas 1:6–8).

Luke's use is different from the two uses of the saying in Matthew and the one in Mark in two ways. First, Luke refers to a sycamine tree, not to a mountain. Second, the Lukan context uses the saying to support the possibility of the disciples' moral behavior (17:1–4), whereas Matthew and Mark use it to explain the success of Jesus' miraculous activity and to promise such success to his disciples. In the case of all three synoptics and both forms of the saying, however, faith is associated with the manifestation of awesome power in the lives of Jesus' disciples, whether it be moral or miraculous.

In order to make sense of the saying, in whatever form, it is necessary to understand what is and what is not meant by faith. (a) It is important to note that "faith is not a magic by which we control God. . . . We cannot use it to back God into a corner and force him to produce a sensational show which will enable us to make the headlines" (Malcolm Tolbert, "Luke," *Broadman Bible Commentary* [Nashville: Broadman Press, 1969], 9:134). In magic one acts to gain control of the spiritual powers so they will do one's bidding. The NT, especially Paul, makes it clear that faith is always a person's response to God's initiative. In Luke 17:11–19, for example, the Samaritan who was healed saw God in the cure effected by Jesus and responded with thanksgiving and praise. Faith is always a human response. (b) It is also important to see faith as a response to God in the context of a relationship; it is personal response to personal initiative. Again, Paul and Luke 17:11–19 speak to this point.

If faith is a disciple's personal response to the personal initiative of God in relationship, then vs. 6 is intelligible in its context. God relates to the sinner with forgiveness (15:11–32). The disciple, a forgiven sinner to whom God has shown and is showing mercy, in faith responds with mercy and forgiveness to those who sin against the disciple (6:35–38; 11:4). In response to the apostles' request for more faith so they would be able to forgive unceasingly, Jesus says, You are living out of a response to God's initiative with you, however limited your response may be. Since God is constantly forgiving you, if you are responding in faith, forgiving without end, though it may seem impossible, is possible to you.

In the version of the logion found in Matthew and Mark, Jesus says that when God has taken the initiative to tell the disciple what God wants to do, an unwavering response of the disciple in that direction results in miracles. If, however, God does not take the initiative in a given situation, it is magic for the disciple to take the initiative and to try to force God's hand by his undoubting belief that God will do what the disciple tells God to do. Faith is not the coercion of God into action by our believing that he will do our bidding. Rather it is the cooperation with God in the action, which, by his initiative, he has indicated that he wills to perform. For Luke such divine initiative was part of Christians' ongoing religious experience (cf. Acts 4:19–20, 31; 5:19–20, 29; 7:55–60; 8:26, 29; 10:9ff., 44–48; 11:15–17; 13:1–3; 16:6–10.).

The train of thought in 17:1–6 to this point has been: (1) if a disciple is never to cause another to stumble and is always to be forgiving, surely the disciple needs an increase in faith; (2) since the disciple is living out of the response to how God has and does treat him or her, this impossible demand is possible, even with the most minute amount of faith (the assumption is that God's gracious initiative is so generous that even a response to a part of it would result in wonderful behavior in human relationships). Luke believed those who live in faith were able to do what has been asked of them.

If disciples are able to do what is required, they are not able to do more than is required. This point is made in the parable of 17:7–10. Here we meet a man with only one slave, who was forced to do double duty. He worked both as a farm hand (plowing and keeping sheep) and as a domestic servant (preparing supper, serving). After a long day of work, the slave did not expect to be thanked by the master. He had simply done what he had been commanded to do. So, says Jesus, when the disciples "have done all that is commanded" (never being a stumbling block; forgiving unceasingly) they should recognize they have done no more than was commanded. No room is left here for any notion of moral superiority or merit. If, given the enormity of God's gracious initiative, there is even the slightest response of faith on the part of the disciples, the commandments are achievable. Nevertheless, no achievement is ever able to go beyond what is expected.

ESCHATOLOGY, FAITH, AND PROSPERITY

17:11—19:44 (A. 17:11—18:30)

Luke 17:11—19:44 is a long thought unit consisting of a mix of uniquely Lukan traditions together with materials having parallels elsewhere in the synoptic tradition. The pattern of this section is ABCD:A'B'C'D'. (1) 17:11 refers to the movement to Jerusalem; so does 18:31–34. (2) Each reference to the journey to the holy city is followed by a healing story (17:12–19; 18:35–43). The two healings are structurally similar: (a) "Jesus, have mercy" (17:13; 18:38); (b) "your faith has made you well" (17:19; 18:42); (c) give/gave praise to God (17:18, 15; 18:43). The first healing story is two pronged, the second half dealing with salvation; the second healing is followed by another story (19:1–10), related to it by the theme of salvation. (3) After the healings come two sections that deal with eschatology (17:20—18:8; 19:11–27). Both aim to protect against an over-realized eschatology; both focus on the parousia and on the necessary faithful posture of those who wait for the Lord's coming. (4) After these two sections are units that focus on the problem of human response to God. Luke 18:8b raises the problem with which 18:9–30 deals: "When the Son of Man comes, will he find faith on earth?" Luke 18:9–30 contains several traditions that illustrate what it means to be rightly related to God in the here and now. Similarly, 19:27 raises the problem with which 19:28–44 deals: "as for these enemies of mine who did not want me to reign over them. . . ." Two pericopes at 19:28–44 illustrate the rejection of Jesus by Israel. It would seem then that the evangelist has taken a variety of materials and has organized them into a coherent pattern in order to serve his own purposes.

The next section of this book will deal with 18:31—19:44. In this section we will focus on 17:11—18:30, in three stages: (1) 17:11–19; (2) 17:20—18:8; and (3) 18:9–30. Luke 17:11–19 deals with the relation between healing and salvation (Cf. H. D. Betz, "The Cleansing of

* the Ten Lepers [Luke 17:11-19]," *Journal of Biblical Literature* 90:314-28 [1971]).

Luke 17:11-19 is a miracle story introduced (vs. 11) by the evangelist's location of the incident between Samaria and Galilee. This is doubtless to make plausible the reference to the Samaritan in vs. 16. Its local color is accurate: lepers grouped together (2 Kgs 7:3), avoided physical contacts with other people (Lev 13:45f.; Num 5:2), but stayed close to where people lived so they could receive charity. The unusual feature of the story is that it is a two-part miracle story: vss. 11-14 tell of the cleansing of ten lepers, while vss. 15-19 follow up the cleansing of one of them, recounting the Samaritan's conversion. There is a prototype of such a two-part story about the healing and the conversion of a leper in 2 Kings 5. Naaman the Syrian is healed as he goes and washes seven times in the Jordan River in obedience to Elisha's command. When he sees he is healed, he returns to Elisha and confesses his faith in the God of Israel. The OT story tells how a miracle of healing is the occasion for the conversion of a foreigner. Luke 17:11-19, likewise, narrates a miracle of Jesus which serves as a catalyst for the conversion of the Samaritan. Verse 19 should be translated, "Rise and go your way; your faith has saved you (*sesōken se*). "Saved" here does not refer to physical cleansing only. The other nine were healed. His salvation was linked to the Samaritan's both seeing the giver in Jesus' gift of healing and responding appropriately. Since in such a story the climax comes in the second part, Luke's emphasis is on the faith of the Samaritan. The evangelist is concerned with the attitude of the person who was cured. The mere experience of being healed did not save. It was acknowledging what God had done through Jesus ("he fell on his face at Jesus' feet, giving him thanks"—vs. 16) that enabled him to experience a salvation beyond the physical cure. Healing issues in salvation, Luke is saying, only when God's gracious initiative is recognized and when one's response to that initiative is faith so that a relationship results.

The evangelist is also saying that often the most unlikely persons recognize the divine approach and respond appropriately. The leper who returned after his healing with praise to God and submission to Jesus was a Samaritan; nine Jews made no such response. The faith of foreigners is a Lukan concern (e.g., 7:9; 10:25-37; Acts 10-11), as is the contrast between their faith (cf. Acts 26:16-18 where the Gentiles' eyes are opened) and the unbelief of Jews who are unable to see

God's work in Jesus (cf. Acts 28:26–27 where the Jews do not see). This story, then, foreshadows the rejection of the gospel by the Jews and its enthusiastic reception by foreigners which we see in the narrative of Acts and which was already established at the time Luke-Acts was written.

Luke 17:20—18:8 is a composite passage that deals with three problems of eschatology: (1) the attempt to calculate when the kingdom of God will come; (2) an over-realized eschatology; and (3) the doubt regarding an ultimate, cosmic settling of accounts by God.

The pronouncement story of vss. 20–21 functions as a rejection by Jesus of the attempt to say when the kingdom of God will come. The Pharisees raise the question. The initial part of Jesus' answer indicates that the question assumed the kingdom's coming would be preceded by certain signs. The answer expected would take the form, "The kingdom of God will come when you see such and such taking place." Jesus rejects this assumption, saying instead, "the kingdom of God is in the midst of you" ("within you" though linguistically possible seems inappropriate since Jesus is talking to Pharisees). Luke would understand this to refer to the presence of the Holy Spirit in Jesus' ministry (cf. 11:20; 4:18–19, 1; 3:22). Luke makes two points. (a) Although one may speak about the nearness of the kingdom (e.g., 10:9), it is illegitimate to try to calculate the time of the End (e.g., Acts 1:6–7). This is a rejection of apocalyptic speculation (the attempt to use historical events and natural disasters to determine a blueprint of what is going to happen and when). In his *City of God* (18:53), Augustine spoke to the point:

> In vain, then, do we attempt to compute definitely the years that may remain to this world, when we may hear from the mouth of the Truth (Jesus) that it is not for us to know. . . . But on this subject He puts aside the figures of the calculaters.

The Markan Jesus speaks the same way: "But of that day or that hour no one knows, not even the angels in heaven, nor the Son, but only the Father" (13:32). (b) The only signs of the kingdom proper to look for are those characteristic of the Spirit-empowered ministry of the earthly Jesus (e.g., 4:18–19).

The composite discourse (17:22–37) which follows the pronouncement story of vss. 20–21 functions as protection against an over-realized eschatology. The discourse is linked to the pronouncement story both formally and logically. Formally, the "Lo, here," and "there" in 17:21 are echoed in "Lo, there," and "Lo, here," in 17:23. Logically, the link relates to the emphasis on the presence of the kingdom. Verses 20–21 speak of the kingdom being present in Jesus' ministry. In vss. 22–23 the disciples, desiring to experience the parousia ("one of the days of the Son of Man" is a Christianization of the Jewish "days of the Messiah" or OT "those days" or "latter days"—that is, the messianic or New Age), are told it is already present (they will say to you, "Lo, there!" or "Lo, here!"). The disciples are not to believe such claims. It would appear from this logical connection that vss. 22–37 are to interpret vss. 20–21 in a way that prevents their being read in terms of an over-realized eschatology. Apparently some in Luke's church were using vss. 20–21 to support the claim that it was possible to experience the eschaton in a secret way in the present. Verses 22–37 guard against such an interpretation by focusing on the nature, the time, and the place of the parousia.

When the disciples hear some say that the parousia is already present in a secret way, not obvious to all, they should not follow them (vss. 22–23). The parousia as an event will not be spatially restricted but will be universal and instantaneous (vs. 24). It will occur after Jesus' passion (vs. 25). It will occur at a time when people are preoccupied with the common ventures of life: eating, drinking, marrying, buying, selling, planting, building (vss. 26–27; 28–30). The proper attitude to have at the parousia is an absolute indifference to all worldly interests. There can be no looking back (vss. 31–33). When it comes the parousia will be a great divider (vss. 34–35). Jesus' response to the disciples' query about where the parousia will take place comes in vs. 37: "It is as senseless to ask for a map of what will happen as it is to ask for a timetable: just as the location of a corpse in the wilderness is obvious from the crowd of circling vultures, so the Son of Man will appear for judgment in an unmistakable manner, and there will be no need to ask where he is" (I. H. Marshall, *The Gospel of Luke*, p. 656).

The evangelist has used an eschatological collection that focuses on the parousia of the Son of Man to prevent an interpretation of vss. 20–21 in terms of an over-realized eschatology. The presence of the kingdom (the Holy Spirit in this instance) in the ministry of Jesus cannot be used to legitimate Christian claims that the parousia has already occurred. The parousia is a future event, cosmic in scope.

The problem of an over-realized eschatology was widespread in early

Christianity. Outside the NT we read of it in numerous sources. (a) Irenaeus, in speaking of those who belong to Simon and Carpocrates, says they hold "that the resurrection from the dead is simply an acquaintance with the truth which they proclaim" (*Against Heresies,* 2:31:2). (b) Irenaeus also says Menander claims that "his disciples obtain the resurrection by being baptized into him" (*Against Heresies,* 1:23:5). (c) Hippolytus reports the Naassenes think that "being born again spiritual" is the resurrection (*Refutation of all Heresies,* 5:3). (d) Hippolytus also claims that the Italian wing of the Valentinians—Heracleon and Ptolemaeus—held a similar position. They regarded the baptism of Jesus as the moment of his resurrection and, correspondingly, the baptism of Christians as the time of their resurrection (*Refutation,* 6:30). (e) In the Gospel of Thomas from Nag Hammadi, in logion 51, the disciples ask Jesus, "When will the new world come?" Jesus answers "What you expect has come, but you know it not." (f) In another Coptic document, *De Resurrectione,* we read, "already you have the resurrection." (g) The Gospel of Philip 121:1-5 says, "Those who say 'They will die first and rise again' are in error. If they do not first receive the resurrection while they live, when they die they will receive nothing." Within the NT a similar problem is echoed in various places. (a) 2 Tim 2:17b-18 is the most explicit statement of the problem: "Among them are Hymenaeus and Philetus, who have swerved from the truth by holding that the resurrection is past already." (b) 1 Cor 4:8 (cf. 15:12ff.) echoes the same view. (c) The same stance is warned against in Phil 3:12-15 (cf. vss. 11, 12, 20) and 2 Thessalonians 2 (cf. vs. 2). The problem with which Luke struggles was widespread in the early church.

The evangelist's response to such an over-realized eschatology is to say first that certain stages or events precede the End, and second that the parousia has a nature different from the experience claimed in the present. A similar response can be found in Tertullian's *On the Resurrection of the Flesh,* 19, and in 1 Cor 15:22ff., Phil 3:12ff., and 2 Thes 2:1ff.

Luke here attempts to prevent a misunderstanding of the experience of the Holy Spirit as the experience of the eschaton. Wherever the experience of the Spirit was identified as the experience of the parousia in early Christianity serious problems resulted: for example, (1) a perfectionism that claimed it was possible for Christians to live sinless lives (1 John 1:8, 10); (2) a spirituality that believed Christians had transcended their sexuality (1 Cor 7; 11:2–16); (3) a triumphalism that regarded Christian experience as beyond persecution, deprivation, sickness, and weakness (1 Cor 4:8–13; 2 Cor 12:1–10). In the generation before Luke, Paul had stood against such an over-realized eschatology. For the apostle the Christian faith involved the believer in sharing Christ's sufferings as well as his resurrection life (Rom 8:17; 2 Cor 1:5; 4:10; Phil 3:10f.; Col 1:24). The experience of the Spirit for him was an experience of power in weakness (2 Cor 4:7; 12:9ff.; 13:3f.), not of power that transcended and left behind the limitations of this present existence. Luke shares Paul's understanding. Although Luke is especially concerned to emphasize the experience of the power of the Holy Spirit in the lives of Jesus and his followers, it is power experienced within the bounds of this age (cf. 4:18 with 9:21, 44; cf. Acts 2 with 14:22). For Luke, as for Paul, there is a "now" and a "not yet" to Christian existence in the world.

Luke 18:1–8 functions as an exhortation not to lose heart. This pericope is an expansion of the eschatological discourse begun at 17:20: (a) 18:1 indicates that the disciples are still being addressed, and (b) the reference to the Son of Man's coming (18:8) echoes 17:22, 24, 26, 30. Here we confront the problem of doubt about whether the parousia will ever take place and the behavior that such doubt induces (cf. 12:45–46; 2 Pet 3:4ff.; 1 Clem 23:3—24:1; 2 Clem 11:1–7). Is the Son of Man really coming? After all this time can we really believe God will vindicate his people? We have been praying "Thy Kingdom come" for years and nothing has happened. The parable in 18:1–8 was told, says Luke (vs. 1), to encourage the disciples to pray and not lose heart (cf. 21:36). As it stands in its context, the story functions as an encouragement to Christians not to give up hope for the parousia but rather to go on praying "Thy Kingdom come." If a corrupt judge, unconcerned about human need and divine law, would grant an insistent widow justice merely to get rid of her, how much more will God, the righteous judge, speedily vindicate his elect when they cry to him. Pray for the parousia because God is faithful and will vindicate his people.

The pericope also raises a question about those who are plagued with doubt. Will disciples remain faithful until the End (cf. Heb 6:11–12; 10:36–39; 2 Pet 3:11–14; Rev 21:7)? The introduction to the parable (vs. 1) tells how faith is maintained. One does not lose heart because one prays. The maintenance of faith depends on persistence in prayer. This is so because "in prayer we enter into the realm of reality

and see things as they really are, from God's point of view"
(H. A. Williams, *The Simplicity of Prayer* [Philadelphia: Fortress, 1977],
p. 69). "The less we pray, the less we experience life in the Christian
way. We move into another mental world" (J. Neville Ward, *The Use
of Praying* [New York: Oxford University, 1977], p. 141). Hence the
Lukan directive: always pray (cf. Phil 4:6–7).

Luke 18:9–30 is a composite unit that deals with the issue raised by
vs. 8b: "Nevertheless, when the Son of Man comes, will he find faith
on earth?" It illustrates appropriate and inappropriate responses to
God/Jesus in the period before the parousia and falls into two loosely
parallel parts, each part involving both the unmasking of unbelief in
an unlikely situation and the identification of faith in an improbable
person(s).

(1) Luke 18:9–17, the first part, consists of a parable (vss. 9–14)
and a story that illustrates a point of the parable (vss. 15–17). The
parable sets before us two men praying in the temple, a Pharisee (vss.
11–12) and a tax collector (vs. 13). The Pharisee belonged to the most
liberal, pious, and dedicated of Judaism's sects in the first century.
This individual, moreover, went beyond even what was required of a
Pharisee. He fasted twice a week and tithed all that he bought. His
prayer follows Jewish liturgy (cf. Ps 17:3–5). He recognized God as
the source of his lot in life (a point missed by the editorial introduction
of 18:9). He thanks God and does not ask for anything. What fault can
possibly be found with this man or his prayer? He represents the best
in the religion of his time.

The tax collector, on the other hand, was among the most despised
of all of Palestine's inhabitants because of his dishonesty, his disloyalty
to the Jewish people, and his uncleanness (of which his stance shows
he was aware). This individual's prayer also follows Jewish liturgy (cf.
Psalm 51). It is an outburst of despair, a petition for mercy. His situation is indeed hopeless. If he repented, he had to make restitution plus
one-fifth. If he ended his defilement, he lost his livelihood and earned
Roman hostility. This man represents the worst of his times. What
could possibly be right about him? Yet Jesus said, "I tell you, this man
went down to his house justified ("forgiven"—cf. 2 Esdr 12:7 where
"justified" is synonymous with "to be heard in prayer") rather than the
other" (vs. 14a).

The story fits into the general theme of status reversal in the third
gospel. The New Age will overturn the values and structures of the

present evil age. We meet this theme in the birth narratives (1:51–53) and in the Sermon on the Plain (6:20–26). In the travel narrative (9:51—19:44) Jesus' teaching anticipates this eschatological reversal even now in overturning the estimate of what is virtue and what is vice. Consider 10:29–37 (good Samaritan/bad priest and levite); 10:38–42 (good inactive Mary/bad active Martha); 11:37–41 (good unclean/bad clean); 12:13–34 (good poor/bad rich); 14:7–11 (good humble/bad exalted); 15:11–32 (good prodigal/bad elder brother); 16:19–31 (good Lazarus/bad rich man); 18:18–30 (good poor/bad rich). Into this thematic context 18:9–14 fits (good tax collector/ bad Pharisee) as another example of Jesus' reversal of values. How can it be? What is wrong with so obviously good a man as the Pharisee? What can be right about so obviously perverse a person as the publican?

The parable functions first of all as the unmasking of unbelief in an unlikely situation. The introduction (vs. 9) exposes the problem. The parable is told to those who (a) trusted in themselves that they were righteous (self-assured piety) and (b) despised others (spiritual condescension). Such a stance is described by the conclusion (vs. 14) as exalting oneself. This was the plight of the Pharisee. He was self-assured about his righteousness (vs. 12), condescending about his superiority to others (vs. 11). He trusted in what he had done and not done and was proud of who he was. It is such a person whom God humbles.

The Pharisee's posture is unmasked as idolatry. He was usurping the prerogatives of God, which is how the devil acts. To judge is God's prerogative (cf. 1 Cor 4:5), not ours. Proper thanks to God for one's lot in life never involves condescension toward others. Salvation by grace means one can never feel religiously superior to another. Faith never expresses itself as despising others. Spiritual arrogance is presumption, assuming that one stands in God's place, able to judge. It is this exaltation of oneself that God overturns.

The parable functions secondly as the identification of faith in an improbable person. It was the despicable tax collector whose prayer was answered. Why? (a) He trusted not in who he was but in who God was (merciful). (b) He hoped not in what he had but in what he might receive (forgiveness). This stance the conclusion describes as humility (vs. 14).

The same point is made in the very next pericope, 18:15–17. Whereas Mark 9:40 uses this same material as part of a series of traditions giving teachings about marriage, children, and possessions, Luke uses it as part of a unit describing what is involved in becoming a disciple and being found faithful when the Son of Man comes. Receiving the kingdom of God in a childlike manner in this context refers to humility (cf. Jas 4:6–10; 1 Pet 5:6–10 where humility means submission to God).

If you think God is one who delights in the spiritually superior, then God is not who you think he is. If you think God shuns the despicable sinner who has no one else to turn to, then God is not who you think he is. Why is this so? With the "I tell you" of vs. 14a, Jesus claims to know God's judgments and dares to say what God is like and how he acts. He claims to know the mind of God.

(2) Luke 18:18–30, the second part of vss. 9–30, consists of a recognition story (vss. 18–23) and a dialogue between Jesus and his disciples (vss. 24–30). The two components give an example of one who was exalted before God and of some who were humbled before him. The recognition story (a narrative in which a person recognizes something about himself he did not know before) unmasks the ruler's unbelief. A ruler inquires of Jesus about what style of life would place him among the people of God who will inherit the New Age. Following the spirit of Deut 30:15–20, Jesus refers to the commandments. When the ruler professes to have kept them since childhood, Jesus says, "One thing you still lack. Sell all that you have and distribute to the poor, and you will have treasure in heaven; and come, follow me" (vs. 22). From this the ruler learned something about himself he did not formerly know. He learned he was an idolater. Though he attempted to worship God and mammon at the same time, when the test was put to him he saw that his wealth was really his god. "Jesus always requires from one just that earthly security upon which one would lean" (E. E. Ellis, *The Gospel of Luke*, p. 217). He did not really keep the first and greatest commandment so his lack of faith was exposed. Jesus' response was that it would be impossible for a rich man to enter the kingdom were it not for God's grace (vss. 24–27).

The dialogue between Jesus and his auditors (vss. 24–30) identifies as faith a life detached from idolatrous relationships and attached to Jesus. Peter says the disciples have fulfilled the calling the ruler refused: "Lo, we have left our homes and followed you" (vs. 28; cf. 5:11, 28). It is this detachment from everything and every relationship for the sake of the kingdom that constitutes the humility (submission to

God) the Son of Man at his parousia recognizes as faith (cf. 9:57–62; 14:25–33). The one who has left family for the sake of the kingdom will receive more back in this life (vs. 30), perhaps a reference to the new family in the church. The principle is that one gives everything to God and then receives back from him what he wants to give. Luke, unlike Mark 10:30 and Matt 19:29, does not promise wealth but only community ("house" in vs. 29 refers to family; "wife, brothers, parents, children" to the various parts of the family). The evangelist does not connect prosperity with piety in any kind of necessary cause and effect relationship (cf. Acts 11:27–30; 24:17). For him the pious are often poor (Luke 2:24; 14:21; 16:19ff.). This raises the issue of the larger biblical perspective about wealth and poverty.

There is a variety of attitudes towards wealth and poverty in the OT. (a) In some circles affluence was connected with righteousness and poverty with wickedness: for example, in the Deuteronomic theology (Deut 28:12ff.; 8:7–10; 26:1–9) and in some Wisdom circles (Prov 6:6–11; 10:4; 28:19). (b) In other circles affluence was associated with evil, while the poor could be regarded as the righteous whom God vindicates: for example, in the prophetic writings (Amos 8:4ff.; Mic 2:1–5; Jer 5:28) and in some Wisdom circles (Prov 28:6; Sir 10:21–23). (c) In still other circles the ideal was neither poverty nor wealth—because each was subject to perversion—but for just enough to meet one's needs (Prov 30:7–9). There is, then, no one viewpoint.

There is a neutral attitude towards wealth and possessions in the NT: neither prosperity nor poverty is a value. This stance is intelligible given its theological context. Though affluence was God's intention in creation (that is, apart from sin, cf. the garden of Eden) and is his intention in the New Age beyond the resurrection (cf. Matt 8:11–12, or any description of the messianic banquet), in the present time affluence and poverty are both affected by the fallenness of the creation. God's objective is now first and foremost to free his creation from its sin (idolatry and injustice). Hence there is no guarantee of affluence to a believer in this life. (3 John 2 does not refer to financial prosperity any more than John 10:10 does. Mark 10:29–30 probably refers to what is available to the Christian from the resources of the Christian community. Paul speaks in Phil 4:10–13 of poverty and plenty as matters of indifference.) Rather God uses poverty and plenty for his ends and our good (that is, ultimate salvation—Rom 8:28). If it takes a miracle of abundance to communicate with us, he will do it; if it takes a bare subsistence to heal us of some imperfection, he will see to it; if he sees we can handle plenty, then it is his will we share with the less fortunate. In the NT, then, there are two main concerns regarding possessions: first, that the individual's heart be right, that there be no idolatrous attachments to things; second, that the structures of life in the community of faith reflect the values of the faith. At no point does the NT claim prosperity is guaranteed to believers in the here and now—that would be to fall into an over-realized eschatology.

ON BEING PART
OF THE PEOPLE OF GOD

17:11—19:44 (B. 18:31—19:44)

L uke 18:31—19:44 is the second part of a balanced longer section that begins at 17:11. Each part begins with a reference to Jesus' movement towards Jerusalem, followed by a healing story, then an eschatological section, and finally a passage focusing on the problem of the human responses to God.

After the notice of Jesus' movement towards Jerusalem (18:31-34), are two stories (18:35-43; 19:1-10) connected with Jericho (18:35; 19:1), dealing with the salvation Jesus brings (18:42—*sesōken se*, it has saved you; 19:9–*sōtēria*, salvation), which focus on the importance of the human response in the appropriation of Jesus' gifts (18:43; 19:8). The two stories function as paradigms of what conversion entails. The first, 18:35-43, has parallels in the synoptic tradition in Matt 20:29-34 (two blind men) and Mark 10:46-52 (blind Bartemaeus). Common to all three versions is the request of the blind one(s): "Son of David, have mercy on me/us," and "Let me/us receive my/our sight." This is what is desired from Jesus. Jesus answers this request by healing the blindness. The healing evidently opened the door to a perception of yet another problem because, as a result of the healing, he/they followed Jesus. Here Jesus' answer to one question on one level led to awareness of another issue on another level to which Jesus also could supply a solution. Jesus took him/them where he was/they were, and brought him/them to where he/they needed to be. The crucial difference between Luke's version of the story and that of Matthew and Mark comes at 18:43 // Matt 20:34 // Mark 10:52. Matthew reads, "and immediately they received their sight and followed him." Mark reads, "And immediately he received his sight and followed him on the way." Luke reads, "And immediately he received his sight and followed him, *glorifying God.*" This Lukan distinction is similar to the reaction of the cleansed leper in 17:15, 18 (cf. 7:16). The human response to the

175

healing and to conversion is vertical, that is, praise to God (cf. 7:36–50). The meeting of a physical need led to a spiritual conversion and produced an outpouring of praise. Here is one paradigm of conversion then and now.

The second paradigm of what conversion entails is found in 19:1–10. This is a conflict story (Jesus' act, vss. 1–6, meets with criticism, vs. 7, to which Jesus responds, vss. 9–10) which has many similarities to the narrative of the call of Levi in Luke 5 (in both Jesus is going somewhere; there is a tax collector; Jesus issues an invitation; a positive response is given; Jesus then enters the tax collector's house; an objection is brought; Jesus responds, justifying his behavior; an "I came" saying is appended). Verse 8, on first reading, presents a problem. It interrrupts the sequence between vs. 7 where the people murmur because "he has gone in to be the guest of a man who is a sinner," and vs. 9b where Jesus responds (to the people about Zacchaeus): "Today salvation has come to this house, since he also is a son of Abraham." Verse 8, further, seems characteristically Lukan: "Lord" and "repentance" (cf. 5:32). It appears the evangelist added vs. 8 to a story from the tradition. The story originally told of table fellowship between Jesus and Zacchaeus in which Zacchaeus' joyful reception of Jesus signaled his being a son of Abraham (cf. 7:36–50). By the addition of vs. 8, the evangelist spelled out the appropriate response to the grace Jesus brought to this rich tax collector through their table fellowship. It was a horizontal one. Zacchaeus said, "Behold Lord, the half of my goods I give to the poor; and if I have defrauded any one at anything, I restore it fourfold." In the OT, when a defrauder confessed and made a voluntary restitution, the amount stolen plus a fifth was sufficient (Lev 6:5; Num 5:7). When a man was compelled to make reparation for a deliberate act of robbery, if the animal was alive he must pay double, but if dead or sold he must pay fourfold or fivefold (Exod 22:1, 3b–4; 2 Sam 12:6). Zacchaeus was willing to treat his wrong acts as belonging to the latter category. This action demonstrated a new attitude toward wealth. What was impossible with man had become possible with God (18:27). In vs. 9 Jesus pronounces the reality of salvation in Zacchaeus' life as demonstrated by the tax collector's response in vs. 8 (cf. 7:36–50). He really was what his name said he was, a righteous or pure one.

If one remembers that the traditions about the historical Jesus have been shaped by the church's experience with the risen Lord, it will enable one to read this edited conflict story in a new way as a paradigm of what conversion entails. (a) The pericope shows how Jesus draws a person (vss. 1–4): "The Lord often . . . inspires in men a blind feeling which brings them to Him although He is still hidden and unknown. . . . He does not disappoint them but in time reveals Himself to them" (*Calvin's Commentaries: A Harmony of the Gospels*, trans. T. H. L. Parker [Grand Rapids: Eerdmans, 1972], 2:281). There was something about Jesus that drew Zacchaeus to climb the sycamore for a glimpse of one who was as yet unknown.

(b) The story also says Jesus comes in to a person (vss. 5–7). The risen Christ in Rev 3:20 verbalizes the reality: "Behold, I stand at the door and knock; if anyone hears my voice and opens the door, I will come in to him and eat with him, and he with me." The language of indwelling is widespread in Paul (e.g., Gal 2:20; Col 1:27) and the fourth gospel (e.g., 14:23; 15:5). When Jesus came into the sinner Zacchaeus' house, he brought forgiveness.

(c) The passage, in addition, says Jesus confirms the person (vss. 8–9), giving assurance of the reality of what has transpired in the secret of the human soul. This assurance rests on two things: a transformed life (vs. 8) and the witness of Jesus (vs. 9). The author of 1 John says he wrote "that you may know that you have eternal life" (5:13). He appeals to the same two bases. On the one hand, there is the evidence of a transformed life: "we know we have passed out of death into life, because we love the brethren" (3:14; cf. 4:12b). On the other hand, there is the inner witness: "By this we know that we abide in him and he in us, because he has given us his own Spirit" (4:13; cf. 3:24b; cf. Rom 8:15–17; 2 Cor 1:22). The third evangelist, in this story of the earthly Jesus, is echoing the same postresurrection reality. Here is a second paradigm of what conversion entails.

Luke 19:11–27 consists of at least three components: (1) vss. 11–12a (through "He said therefore") which are Lukan transitional and introductory material; (2) a parable about a man going away and leaving his affairs in the hands of three servants (// Matt. 25:14–30); and (3) a political parable in vss. 12, 14, 15a, 27, and possibly with fragments in 17b and 19b (F. D. Weinart, "The Parable of the Throne Claimant [Luke 19:12, 14–15a, 27] Reconsidered," *Catholic Biblical Quarterly*, 39:505–14 [1977]). These components are joined together into an allegory of salvation history, making three points.

(1) Here, as in 17:22ff., the evangelist wants to protect against an

over-realized eschatology. The introduction indicates that "because he was near to Jerusalem, they supposed that the kingdom of God was to appear immediately." The allegory which follows says the End is not yet. First Jesus goes away to receive kingly power (cf. Acts 1:11; 2:36); later he will return (cf. Acts 3:20–21). Why would Luke stress a point obvious to his readers after Easter? If one views 19:11 as a reflection of problems in Luke's church, then it may be that some disciples were regarding the events in Jerusalem (Jesus' resurrection and ascension) as the parousia. In response the evangelist is saying, "not yet." There is a difference between the resurrection/ascension and the parousia (and, by inference, between one's dying and rising with Christ on the one hand, and one's resurrection on the other).

(2) The major focus of the allegory is on the accountability of the three servants upon the nobleman's return (vss. 15b–26). Here Luke is addressing the question, what is the responsibility of Jesus' servants in the interim between the ascension and the parousia (cf. 12:35–48)? They are expected to be faithful to their commission. Faithful servants are those who are productive, who make the most of what they have been given. They will receive a reward. Not everyone has the same resources with which to work: that difference is taken into account. The unproductive servant, however, will be punished. Luke, though, has nothing like Matt 25:30: "And cast the worthless servant into the outer darkness; there men will weep and gnash their teeth." Like Paul in 1 Cor 3:10–15, the third evangelist seems to think the unfaithful servant's work will be burned up, but "he himself will be saved." The judgment at the parousia for disciples will focus not on whether they make it into the kingdom but whether or not they receive a commendation and reward.

(3) Though Luke does not discuss the ultimate punishment of the third servant, he does speak about the destiny of those who refused to have the nobleman reign over them (vss. 14, 27). It is probable that in vs. 14 the story is making use of contemporary events. In 4 B.C. Archelaus went to Rome to obtain the kingdom which his father, Herod the Great, had left him. The Jews revolted and sent an embassy of fifty to oppose him at Rome (Josephus, *Antiquities*, 17:8:1 § 188; 17:9:3 § 222; 17:11:4 § 317; *War*, 2:6:1, 3 § 80, 93). Luke's allegory uses these current events to speak about the Jewish (and unbelieving Gentile?) rejection of Jesus' kingship (cf. 23:2, 36–37). The result at the parousia for those who rejected Jesus' sovereignty will be judgment (vs. 27:

cf. 12:8–9; Acts 17:30–31): "As for these enemies of mine, who did not want me to reign over them, bring them here and slay them before me" (vs. 27). Verse 27 sets the stage for the rejection of Jesus by Jerusalem which is the major focus of 19:29–44.

Luke 19:29–44 contains a record of three events: (1) Jesus' ride on a colt which evokes an ovation (vss. 29–38 // Matt 21:1–9 // Mark 11:1–10); (2) the Pharisees' protest (vss. 39–40 // Matt 21:15–16); and (3) the lament over Jerusalem (vss. 41–44). The first and second of these units are joined by the term "disciples" (vss. 37, 39); the first and third by "peace" (vss. 40, 44).

(1) In 19:29–38 Jesus approaches Jerusalem as the peaceable king. The tradition of Jesus' ride on a colt is set at the Mount of Olives (19:29). This location may echo Zech 14:4 and thus have eschatological overtones. In Luke, given 19:11–27 and 17:22ff., this must not be thought of in terms of the eschaton. Furthermore, the ride on a colt (only an animal that had never been used as a beast of burden was suitable for sacred purposes—Num 19:2; 1 Sam 6:7) most likely echoes Zech 9:9 (Matt 21:5 and John 12:15 make it explicit). Jesus comes not in war but in peace (cf. 2:1–20). A number of distinctive Lukan traits tells us the author's special concerns. (a) In Luke there are no branches (Matt 21:8 // Mark 11:8 // John 12:13). Since the branches had nationalistic overtones (2 Mac 10:7), the omission serves to emphasize the absence of any revolutionary element in Jesus' movement. (b) So, even if the disciples call Jesus "King" (vs. 38—probably to pick up 19:12, 15), it would not justify the charges of 23:2. (c) In Luke the disciples set Jesus on the colt (vs. 35—Matt 21:7 // Mark 11:7 // John 12:14 say Jesus sat on the animal). The evangelist is saying the disciples were acclaiming Jesus king: Jesus does not claim kingship for himself. (d) In Luke it is the disciples (not the crowds as in Matt 21:9 // John 12:12) who give Jesus the ovation. They understand something of his identity (8:9–10) because of the mighty works they had seen (cf. 18:43; 7:16), though they still do not understand the necessity of suffering (18:34; 24:25–27). The ride on the colt in the third gospel sets Jesus forth as the peaceable king who is recognized as such by his disciples (cf. 20:21–26; 23:2–4). In Jesus God had come calling on Jerusalem (19:44).

We may think of time either in terms of duration or of content: for example, (a) duration—chronological time that can be measured on a clock or a calendar; (b) content—the character of the time, that which fills the moment, so the time of planting or meal time. The latter kind of time confronts us with an opportunity and demands of us a response. In 19:44 Jesus speaks of "the time of your visitation." He means that in his ministry God had come calling, had visited his people (cf. 7:16). The content of the time of Jesus' career was a divine visitation (17:21; 11:20; 10:9). The visit of God in the ministry of Jesus was recognized by his disciples who set him on the colt (vs. 35).

(2) The protest of the Pharisees in 19:39–40 (only in Luke) speaks of the rejection of the peaceable king by the Jewish leadership (cf. Acts 13:27). (3) The lament over the city in 19:41–44 (cf. Isa 29:3; Ps 137:9) ties the destruction of Jerusalem to the Jewish rejection of Jesus (cf. 13:34–35; 21:20, 21, 24; 23:27–31). The tragedy is that Jerusalem did not know the time of her visitation by God (vs. 44; cf. 1:78; 7:16). God had come calling but his visit had gone unrecognized. It is as though the Lukan community after A.D. 70 was saying that when the Jewish people rejected the peaceable king, they opted for Zealot violence which resulted in the destruction of the city of peace (cf. 23:18–19, 25). This point raises the larger question of how the evangelist regards Israel.

The Lukan estimation of Israel may be summarized in five steps. (1) Before Israel's refusal of the gospel, Luke regards her as a reality existing on two levels: first, as a historical people defined by race and nationality, the Jewish nation (e.g., 7:5; 23:2; Acts 10:22; 24:10, 17; 26:4; 28:19); and second, as the people of God (e.g., 1:68; 2:32; 7:16; Acts 7:34; 13:17).

(2) The evangelist makes much of the Jewish rejection of Jesus and the Christian message (e.g., 2:34; 4:28–29; 13:34; 19:14, 39, 44; 20:13–16; 23:102, 18–19, 23; 24:20; Acts 4:1–2, 17–18; 5:17–18, 40; 7:58; 13:45; 14:19; 17:5–9, 13; 18:5–6, 12–17; 19:8–9; 20:3; 21:27–30). At the same time Luke makes it clear that the earliest believers were Jewish (Acts 1:13–14, 21) and that there were many Jewish converts to Christianity (Acts 2:41, 47; 4:4; 5:14; 6:7; 13:43; 17:4, 12; 21:20) both in Jerusalem and elsewhere. Hence Luke shows the Christian movement divided Israel into two groups: the repentant and the unrepentant (2:34–35). Israel has not rejected the gospel but has become divided over the issue.

(3) In the Lukan perspective the repentant portion of the Jewish nation is Israel, the people of God. It is to and for these believing Jews the promises have been fulfilled. This restored Israel is the presuppo-

sition of all the missionary work to the Gentiles (Acts 15:15–18). God first rebuilds and restores Israel and then, as a result, the Gentiles seek the Lord. The unrepentant portion of the nation, however, has forfeited its membership in the people of God (Acts 3:23). A formal statement of rejection of the unrepentant portion of the Jewish nation is delivered three times, once in each main area of missionary activity. Acts 13:46 has Paul and Barnabas say to the unbelieving Jews in Antioch of Pisidia, "It was necessary that the word of God should be spoken first to you. Since you thrust it from you, and judge yourselves unworthy of eternal life, behold, we turn to the Gentiles." In Acts 18:6, in Corinth, when the unbelieving Jews opposed him, Paul says, "Your blood be upon your heads. I am innocent. From now on I will go to the Gentiles." Finally, in Acts 28:25–28 Paul says to the unbelieving Jews, "Let it be known to you then that this salvation of God has been sent to the Gentiles; they will listen."

(4) It is incorrect to say that for Luke it is only when the Jews have rejected the gospel that the way is open to Gentiles. It is equally incorrect to say that only when Israel has accepted the gospel that the way to the Gentiles is opened. Both, however, are parts of the total view of Luke. That is, both Acts 15:15–18 on the one hand, and Acts 13:46, 18:6, and 28:25–28 on the other, are parts of the total perspective of the evangelist. In the first place, the Jewish Christian community in Jerusalem, as the restored Israel, is the means through which salvation comes to the Gentiles (Acts 15:15–18), who are incorporated into believing Israel. They are, however, incorporated without circumcision and the law, without first becoming proselytes (Acts 15). In the second place, the explanation as to why the Lukan church feels no obligation to evangelize the national-racial entity of Israel is that these unrepentant ones have excluded themselves from Israel, the people of God (Acts 13:46; 18:6; 28:25–28). Hence, in Luke's view, by the end of Acts the people of God is no longer a race or a nation but those who believe (Luke 20:9–18). The unbelieving Jews remain a historical people who experience the fall of Jerusalem and the destruction of the temple (13:35a; 19:41–44; 21:20–24; 23:28–31), but they do not belong to Israel, the people of God. The destruction of the temple and the holy city, moreover, are understood as the consequence of the rejection of Jesus by the racial-national Israel. (Cf. Eusebius, *Ecclesiastical History*, 3:5:3–6, for an explicit statement of this Christian point of view. For an analogous interpretation of a historical disaster as result-

ing from the martyrdom of an innocent man, see Josephus' statement about the destruction of Herod's army as a just punishment for his treatment of John the Baptist in *Antiquities*, 18:5:2 § 116–19.)

(5) The question whether Luke, like Paul in Romans 9–11, envisioned a final conversion of the entire Jewish people prior to the parousia, prompted by the inclusion of the Gentiles in the people of God, is debatable. Most scholars think the Lukan Paul of Acts 28:25–28, unlike the historical Paul of Romans 11, seems resigned to a Gentile church. A few scholars think Luke, like Paul in Rom 11:20, looked forward to a time when the Jews as a people would be reinstated (e.g., A. W. Wainwright, "Luke and the Restoration of the Kingdom to Israel," *Expository Times* 89:76–79 [1977]). Acts 1:6; Luke 21:24, 28; 22:28–30 are about the only supports for this stance. There is enough question about these texts, however, to make it improbable that the Gentile Christian community from which Luke-Acts came expected the final conversion of the nation as a whole before the parousia. The evangelist would not have ruled out the conversion of any individual Jew, but as far as the direction of the church's mission was concerned, it was to Gentiles. In this Luke is akin to Justin Martyr who believed that in the second century a remnant of Jews were still being saved by conversion to Christianity (*Dialogue with Trypho*, 32;55;64). These Jewish Christians, who lived within the church, Justin allowed to practice the law (*Dialogue*, 47:2).

The Lukan position with reference to Israel may be summed up in three propositions: first, Christianity is completed Judaism; second, the nation-race no longer is synonymous with the people of God—there is no future hope for the nation as such; third, one becomes a part of God's people by individual decision for Jesus.

Luke 19:45–24:53

MARTYRDOM
AND VINDICATION

INTRODUCTION

The fourth major section of the gospel is 19:45—24:53, the narrative of the last events in Jerusalem. In order to gain some perspective about how the evangelist views this section, we look first at its pattern, then at how this period is seen in the speeches of Acts, and finally at the correspondences between this last period of Jesus' earthly career in the gospel and the corresponding period in Paul's career in Acts.

(1) Luke 19:45—24:53 falls into two large sections: 19:45—21:38, Jesus' teaching in the temple, and 22:1—24:53, the Passion itself. The first large division is held together not only by its location in the temple but also by an inclusion, 19:47 and 21:37. Luke locates more of this material in the temple than do the other synoptic writers. For example, Luke 21's apocalyptic speech occurs in the temple, whereas Mark 13 locates it outside. The temple functions in Luke's section as a site for Jesus' teaching. By suppressing the temple cleansing—for the most part—and by inserting vs. 47 in chapter 19, Luke has caused the plot of the rulers to be a response to Jesus' teaching in the temple, and not to its cleansing. This fits: later Luke omits the charge that Jesus said he would destroy the temple.

The second large division is the Passion proper. (a) In the gospel the Passion of Jesus is portrayed as the supreme assault of Satan (22:3, 31, 53). (b) Throughout there is a pro-Roman and an anti-Sanhedrin thrust. Whereas Jesus' answers before the Sanhedrin were to exclusively religious issues, the Jewish leaders distort his replies and in their report to Pilate use a political charge. Pilate, however, is not able to discover enough evidence either in the Jewish charges or in Jesus' answers to proceed with a criminal trial. The shaming of Jesus is transferred from Pilate to the half-Jew Herod and his Jewish guard. Pilate is prepared to let Jesus go with a warning (*paideusas*, 23:22, being the lightest form of Roman beating; contrast Mark 15:51b's *phragellosas*, the most severe whipping). In 23:47 the centurion pronounces the final verdict for Rome: he is innocent. This pro-Roman sentiment was not likely to persuade some Roman that the Christians were innocent but was likely designed to persuade Christians that Roman justice was advantageous to them (P. W. Walaskay, "The Trial and Death of Jesus in the Gospel of Luke," *Journal of Biblical Literature* 94:81–93 [1975]). (c) In the Passion narrative there is an effort to minimize the failure of the Eleven. Luke has shaped the material so it is a "promise of ultimate victory after passing failure, especially for Peter," rather than of complete collapse as in Mark (R. H. Lightfoot, *History and Interpretation in the Gospels* [New York: Harper & Brothers, 1934], 174–75). (d) Luke locates all of the resurrection appearances in Jerusalem, in contrast to the other gospels.

(2) Since the speeches of Acts are most likely Lukan compositions, it is helpful to examine them to see what emphases they contain about Jesus' days in Jerusalem. Their focus is on Jesus' death and resurrection. Nothing is said about his teaching in the temple. About his death we hear: (a) Jesus could not be charged with anything deserving death (12:28); (b) the Jews delivered him up (2:23; 3:13; 13:28); (c) the Jews asked Pilate to kill him (3:13; 13:28); (d) Herod was involved against Jesus (4:27); (e) instead of Jesus the Jews asked for a murderer (3:14); (f) Jesus was laid in a tomb (13:29); (g) these events were in accord with prophecy (13:27; 3:18).

About his resurrection, the speeches say, (a) God raised Jesus (2:24; 5:30; 10:39–40; 13:30); (b) God made him manifest (10:39–40), or he appeared (13:31) to Galileans (13:31), witnesses who ate and drank with him after the resurrection (10:39–40); (c) the resurrection is in fulfillment of prophecy (2:25–28). One recognizes immediately that the references to Herod and to witnesses eating and drinking with Jesus after the resurrection are peculiar to Luke-Acts.

(3) The remarkable correspondences both in content and sequence between the events and persons found in Luke and those in Acts constitute the primary architectonic pattern in Luke-Acts (C. H. Talbert, *Literary Patterns*, pp. 15ff.). This pattern of correspondences is especially clear in the final sections of both Luke and Acts. The following examples are representative:

19:37 Jesus receives a good reception and the people praise God for the works they have seen.	21:17–20a Paul receives a good reception and God is glorified for the things done among the Gentiles.

19:45–48	Jesus goes into the temple. He has a friendly attitude toward it.	21:26	Paul goes into the temple. He has a friendly attitude toward it.
20:27–39	The Sadducees do not believe in the resurrection. The scribes support Jesus.	23:6–9	The Sadducees do not believe in the resurrection. The scribes support Paul.
22:19a	At a meal, Jesus takes bread, gives thanks, and breaks it.	27:35	Paul has a meal in which he takes bread, gives thanks, and breaks it.
22:54	A mob seizes Jesus.	21:30	A mob seizes Paul.
22:63–64	Jesus is slapped by the priest's assistants.	23:2	Paul is slapped at the high priest's command.
22:26; 23:1; 23:8; 23:13	The four trials of Jesus (Sanhedrin; Pilate; Herod; Pilate).	Chps. 23; 24; 25; 26	The four trials of Paul (Sanhedrin; Felix; Festus; Herod Agrippa).

Some of the details in the trials of Jesus in the gospel and of Paul in Acts correspond:

23:4, 14, 22	Three times Pilate declares Jesus innocent.	23:9; 25:25; 26:31	Three men, Lysias, Festus, and Agrippa, declare Paul innocent.
23:6–12	Pilate sends Jesus to Herod for questioning.	25:13–26:32	Herod hears Paul with the permission of Festus.
23:16, 22	Pilate says he will release Jesus.	26:32	Herod says, "This man could have been released."
23:18	The Jews cry, "Away with this man."	21:36	The Jews cry, "Away with him."
23:47	A centurion has a favorable opinion of Jesus.	27:3	A centurion has a favorable impression of Paul.

These correspondences function in the interests of the Lukan belief that Jesus is the pioneer or leader (*archēgos*) of the Christian Way. His career is, then, prototypical for his followers. Throughout the Passion one should be alert to the recurring emphasis on Jesus as the model for Christian existence.

TESTED IN THE TEMPLE

Luke 19:45—21:38 (A. 19:45—21:4); 2:1-7; 11:37-54; 14:1-24

L uke 19:45—21:38 constitutes a large thought unit in the gospel, 19:47 ("he was teaching daily in the temple") and 21:37 ("every day he was teaching in the temple") functioning as an inclusion to hold the material together. In 19:45–46 Jesus enters not the city but the temple. The temple functions in this section as the site for Jesus' teaching (cf. 2:41–51), which teaching serves as a confrontation between God's accredited agent and the Jewish people. The outcome is the rejection of God's messenger (cf. 4:16–30; Acts 3—4; 5:12–42; 13:13–52; 18:1–11) which issues in God's judgment on those who have rejected Jesus. The teaching in the environs of the temple falls into two parts: (1) 19:45—21:4, and (2) 21:5–38. In this chapter, the focus will be on the former part.

Luke 19:45—21:4 has, for the most part, parallels in the other synoptics. All of this material, however, has been shaped to fit Luke's "teaching in the temple" motif.

In 19:45—20:18 the material has become a warning to the leaders of religious establishments. Four points are made in the warning. (1) God will not allow the religious leadership of his people to fail to nourish the flock. The entry into the temple (19:45–46) functions to indict the religious leadership for allowing the temple's purpose to be perverted (cf. Isa 56:7; Jer 7:11). Jesus' act and word testify that the religious establishment has not been faithful to its charge to nourish God's people.

(2) When the sheep are not fed, others may be expected to come to remedy the deficiency. Jesus' teaching in the temple daily (19:47a) appears to be in response to the failure of the Jewish leaders.

(3) There follows a predictable twofold response by the religious establishment (20:1–19). The leaders question the reformer's authority: "Tell us by what authority you do these things, or who it is who gave you this authority" (vs. 2). When such a challenge is put to him, Jesus responds with a question of his own: "Was the baptism of John from

188

heaven or from men" (vs. 4)? That is to say, "Can you recognize God's presence anywhere else than in the official structures?" The people are able to recognize it (vs. 6b). There is also the temptation characteristic of every bureaucracy, including the religious ones, to forget to whom the vineyard belongs. Jesus tells the people (note the contrast between the favor of the people, 19:48, and the opposition of the leaders, 20:19) a parable directed against the religious leadership. The story is actually another allegory of salvation history as Luke sees it (cf. 14:16–24; 19:11–27). Time after time the tenants (the religious bureaucracy) fail to recognize God's authority in his prophets (e.g., John the Baptist—20:4–7) and have repeatedly expressed hostility to God's messengers (13:34; Acts 7:52). Now they have rejected even the beloved Son (3:22; Acts 7:53): "This is the heir; let us kill him, that the inheritance may be ours" (vs. 14). The allegory implies that the bureaucracy recognized him but rejected him because they were unwilling to relinquish control over the vineyard to its rightful owner. They had ceased to be stewards of another's property and had begun to seek to function as owners in their own right.

(4) Such a rejection of the Son results in an overthrow of the established leadership. The allegory says that for rejecting God's Son, the tenants will be severely punished: "He will come and destroy those tenants, and give the vineyard to others" (20:16; cf. 19:27). This is not a reference to the destruction of Jerusalem and to the shift of the good news to the Gentiles. It is an attack on the religious bureaucracy (vs. 19) and says that because of their rejection of Jesus, their positions as caretakers of God's people are cancelled and in their place others are appointed (in the Lukan context, the apostles—22:28–30; Acts 1:15–26). One's response to the beloved Son is absolutely decisive: "Every one who falls on that stone will be broken to pieces; but when it falls on any one it will crush him" (vs. 18). This verse, which is peculiar to Luke, is a statement similar to that of the rabbi cited in Midrash Rabbah on Esth 3:6: "Should the stone fall on the crock, woe to the crock. Should the crock fall on the stone, woe to the crock. In either case, woe to the crock" (cf. Luke 2:34; 12:8–9; Acts 4:12). One's place in the religious establishment hinges on one's acquiescence in the claims of the beloved Son as owner of the vineyard. This is the criterion by which every religious establishment is judged by God.

The first attempt to discredit Jesus having failed, a second effort was made at 20:20–26, so they could "deliver him up to the authority and jurisdiction of the governor" (vs. 20; cf. 18:32). At issue here is the attitude toward the state advocated by Jesus. Our appreciation of vss. 20–26 is enhanced if we first look at some background material from the rest of the gospel. Luke 2:1–7 is crucial, with the data relevant to our purposes related to the census in vs. 2. There are two possible translations of this sentence. (1) The usual way is to render it, "This was the first enrollment, when Quirinius was governor of Syria" (RSV). If one translates in this fashion, there is a problem of chronology. Quirinius did not become governor until A.D. 6. At that time he conducted a census together with Coponius, the procurator of Judea. This innovation was widely resented and led to a Zealot uprising under Judas the Galilean (Josephus, *Antiquities*, 18:1:1, 6 § 4–10, 23–25). The difficulty is that 1:5 locates the annunciation of John the Baptist's birth in the days of Herod, king of the Jews, presumably Herod the Great who died in 4 B.C. Since Luke 1:26 locates the annunciation of Jesus' birth in the sixth month of Elizabeth's pregnancy, presumably Jesus too would be born under Herod the Great, as Matthew 1—2 also claims. This makes a discrepancy in dating of a minimum of ten years (4 B.C.– A.D. 6). If so, then the evangelist has made an error, whether unconsciously or purposefully (Horst Moehring, "The Census as an Apologetic Device," in *Studies in the New Testament and Early Christian Literature*, ed. D. E. Aune [Leiden: Brill, 1972], pp. 144–60). (2) An alternate translation of vs. 2 is offered by Nigel Turner (*Grammatical Insights into the New Testament* [Edinburgh: T. &. T. Clark, 1966], pp. 23–24), who observes that the Greek of the period often used "first" when "former" or "prior" would have been more grammatical. If so, then it would be possible to translate, "This enrollment was before Quirinius was governor of Syria," or "This enrollment was prior to (the enrollment) when Quirinius was governor of Syria" (cf. John 5:36; 1 Cor 1:25 for similar compressions). If this reading is adopted, there is no chronological error on Luke's part. Then the question would be, Why would the evangelist have wanted to refer to Quirinius and possibly his census?

Which ever of the two translations one accepts, the reason for Luke's reference to Quirinius is obvious. His census was the occasion for a rebellion led by Judas of Galilee, from which came the Zealot movement. That Acts 5:37 mentions Judas the Galilean's revolt in connection with the census indicates the associations that were in the evangelist's mind when he mentioned a census and Quirinius together in

Luke 2:2. The actions of Judas apparently were part of a general pattern of rebelliousness among Galileans. Returned to the Jewish state by the Hasmoneans, the Galileans after 63 B.C. aimed to reestablish the Hasmonean state. There were instances of rebelliousness under Ezekias (47 B.C.), in the uprising of Antigonus (40–37 B.C.), at the death of Herod (4 B.C.), in Judas' opposition to the census (A.D. 6), under the Roman procurators, and in the Jewish revolt of A.D. 66–74 (F. Loftus, "The Anti-Roman Revolts of the Jews and the Galileans," *Jewish Quarterly Review* 68:78–98 [1977]). For Luke to depict the Galilean family of Jesus doing its civic duty would be significant. Joseph, like Jesus and his later followers, was obedient to Roman rule. Jesus' family did not participate in the Galilean spirit of rebellion that oftentimes brought recrimination from Roman officials (cf. 13:1–2).

The one who was born a peaceable king (2:1–20) entered Jerusalem on the same note. Jesus came riding on a colt (a sign of peace), with no nationalistic trappings (the absence of the branches), amid the acclamation of his disciples: "Peace in the heavens and glory in the highest." Furthermore, Jesus' entrance into the temple (19:45–46) is told by the evangelist in a way that eliminates almost all details of violence. It is against this background that one must read 20:20–26. In A.D. 6 Judas of Galilee (Josephus, *Antiquities,* 18:1:6 § 23–25; 20:5:2 § 102) had denounced the payment of taxes to Caesar as treason against God. Now the spies ask Jesus, "Is it lawful (that is, scriptural) for us to give tribute to Caesar or not?" No matter how he answers, they think, he will offend someone. Asking for a coin, Jesus inquired about whose image was on it. When his opponents said, "Caesar's," he said, "Then render to Caesar the things that are Caesar's, and to God the things that are God's." In this context, the logion points in two directions.

(1) The saying affirms the sovereignty of God. From Luke's point of view the authority of the political realm belongs to God who then delivers it to whom he wishes (cf. 4:6—"for it has been delivered to me," that is, by God). A ruler who does not give glory to God but rather usurps God's prerogatives is subject to God's judgment (cf. Acts 12:20–23). A disciple, when confronted with the choice, must obey God rather than humans (Acts 4:19–20; 5:29). From the evangelist's perspective there are not two realms, Caesar's and God's, but rather only one, God's. The only areas in which Caesar can expect allegiance from Jesus' disciples are those in which his patterns are in conformity with God's desired patterns. That the Roman officials in Acts provided protection

for the preachers of the gospel doubtless accounts for the positive portrayal they receive from the evangelist (cf. Acts 13:7, 12; 16:35–39;
18:12–17; 19:35–41; 21:31–39; 22:25–26; 23:19–24, 31–32; 27:42–
43).

(2) The logion speaks a word of assurance about Christian political
intentions. It is very difficult not to see vss. 24–25 as affirming the
payment of taxes. Give Caesar his money. Those who use Caesar's
money will have to pay Caesar's taxes (cf. Rom 13:6–7). The evangelist would see this saying as falsifying the Jewish charge that Jesus
was "forbidding us to give tribute to Caesar" (23:2). Jesus was not
hostile to the state as such. Within the context of total submission to
God, Jesus advocated submission to the state. Given Roman protection
of the church from mob violence, both Gentile and Jewish in origin
(e.g., Acts 18—19), in the early years of the Christian movement, it is
no surprise that many Christians heard this emphasis primarily (Rom
13:1–7; 1 Tim 2:1–2; Tit 3:1–2; 1 Pet 2:13; 1 Clement 61; Pol Phil
12:3; Justin, *Apology I*, 17:3; Tertullian, *Apology*, 30). The attitude of
loyalty and moderation toward Rome largely characterized the church
through the second century. Yet faced with emperor worship and the
persecution which followed Christian reluctance to participate in it,
the author of Revelation developed his resistance to the state from the
former point: "Render to God the things that are God's."

This passage raises a larger question: what kind of political and social stance does Luke attribute to Jesus? A recent book, *Jesus, Politics,
and Society* (Maryknoll, N.Y.: Orbis Books, 1978), by Richard Cassidy,
portrays the Lukan Jesus as a Gandhi-like figure advocating nonviolent resistance. Cassidy works with three possibilities: (a) nonresist-
ance (where people refrain not only from physical violence but also
from directly confronting those responsible for existing ills; they identify with those suffering from such evils; they offer no defense if they
themselves are subjected to violence by those who have power; their
hope is that their example will eventuate in changes in the attitudes
and actions of others); (b) nonviolent resistance (where people avoid
violence to persons but confront in a nonviolent way those responsible
for existing social ills; their hope is that the challenge will serve to
create a dialogue which may eventually result in a favorable change of
behavior); and (c) violent resistance.

These or similar stances had their representatives among the Jewish
population at the time of Christian origins. (a) The Zealots were the

advocates of armed revolution against Rome. (b) Josephus gives two examples of nonviolent resistance in Jesus' time. The first is found in *Antiquities* 18:3:1 § 261–309 and *War* 2:9:3 § 184–203, an account of a five day sit-in to protest Pilate's introduction of images into Jerusalem. When threatened with death if they did not end their protest, the Jews cast themselves on the ground and bared their throats, declaring they gladly welcomed death rather than violate their law. The protest caused Pilate to remove the offensive images from the city. The second is found in *Antiquities* 18:8 § 244–72 and *War* 2:10 § 184–98, and tells of the action of the Jews who left fields untilled in the sowing season for more than a month. The protest prevented Caligula's statue being erected in the temple. (c) Although during the Hasmonean rule at least some of the Pharisees functioned as a political party, from the rise of Herod the Great until the end of the first Jewish revolt against Rome, the Pharisees seem to have moved from direct political involvement to an attitude of indifference regarding rulers and the forms under which they ruled. It seems likely that the Pharisees did not oppose Roman rule in Judea. Their concern was with the proper ordering of the life of God's people according to the law.

The Lukan Jesus' portrayal is more complex than Cassidy's description allows. Three components must be recognized in Luke's picture of Jesus' social and political posture. (a) Although Jesus shows no deference towards political rulers (e.g., 13:31–33), this does not mean he is involved, Gandhi-like, in a nonviolent resistance to them. Like the Pharisees Jesus manifests an indifference to the political rulers. For someone who believed that all power and authority resided with God and all history unfolded according to his purpose, such rulers were of little consequence. Since the rulers shared no common assumptions that would facilitate dialogue with Jesus, he opted for silence in their presence. (b) Toward the Jewish structures, however, Jesus showed no indifference. Here he was involved in nonviolent resistance. Confrontation between Jesus and the Jewish leaders was frequent (e.g., 5:12—6:11; 11:37–54; 13:10–17; 14:1–24; 16:14–15; 19:47—20:47). Only at 19:45 is there any hint of possible violence, but the evangelist has so shaped the cleansing story that it becomes merely Jesus' entry into the site of his subsequent teaching (19:47—21:38). Moreover, 22:49–51 has Jesus explicitly reject violence against Jewish authority. Nonviolent confrontation aimed at dialogue and change of behavior seems the best description of Jesus' stance toward the Jewish structures (the people of God). This was doubtless because Jesus and the Jews shared common assumptions about God and about religious values. With such people dialogue could be profitable. (c) Jesus' primary vehicle for social change was the structure of life in the community of his disciples. Among his disciples Jesus sought a revolutionary change in social attitudes. They were to live in the present in light of God's reversal of all human values in the eschaton. Such a stance, of course, was regarded by some as "turning the world upside down" (Acts 17:6). By embodying structures of social relationships to reflect the new life in the Spirit under the lordship of Jesus, the Christian community functions in the larger society as an agent of social change.

The third attempt to discredit Jesus as a teacher came from the Sadducees, who denied the resurrection (cf. Acts 23:8; Josephus, *Antiquities*, 18:14 § 16–17; *War*, 2:8:14 § 164–65). Posing resurrection riddles was a favorite way for Sadducees to torment Pharisees. For example, they might ask whether or not those who will allegedly be resurrected will require ritual cleansing since they were in contact with a corpse (b. Niddah 70b). Or they inevitably inquired where in the Pentateuch Moses taught resurrection from the dead, since they accepted only those five books as scripture. Luke 20:27ff. reflects just such a Sadducean ploy. The problem they pose is based on Deut 25:5–10, the law of levirate marriage. If a brother died childless, a surviving brother was to take the widow and beget children for his dead brother. The firstborn of such a union was to bear the name of the deceased (cf. Gen 38:8; Ruth 3—4). Though the law of levirate marriage was not enforced in the time of Jesus, the question was raised to show that since resurrection would imply polyandry, which was unacceptable, it was excluded by the law of Moses.

Jesus' answer is twofold. (1) In vss. 37–38 he says the inference drawn by the Sadducees from their posed problem is inaccurate because it does not reckon with the continuing nature of the relationship between God and his people. The form of Jesus' answer resembles rabbinic argument. In the Talmud (e.g., b. Sanhedrin 90b–91a), we read again and again the question, "How is resurrection derived from the Torah?" The rabbis appealed to numerous passages for support (e.g., Num 18:28; 15:31; Exod 6:4; 15:1; Deut 31:16). In one first century example sectarians asked R. Gamaliel, "Whence do we know that the Holy One will raise the dead?" Gamaliel appealed to Deut 31:16, Isa 26:19, and Cant 7:9, all to no avail. They were not satisfied until he quoted Deut 11:21, "Which the Lord swore unto your fathers to give to them," and pointed out that the text said not "to you" but "to them." Since the promise could only be fulfilled by the patriarch's resurrection, resurrection is derived from the Torah (Pentateuch). Luke 20:37–38 follows this type of rabbinic argument, appealing to Exod 3:6, which called the Lord the God of Abraham, Isaac, and Jacob. Since Yahweh is not God of the dead but of the living, the patriarchs must either be in some sense alive or they will be raised. The meaning is basically that when God has a relationship with someone, that relationship is not terminated by death: God will not allow an enemy of his, death, to destroy that which means so much to him (cf. Rom 8:35–39).

(2) In vss. 34–36 (considerably longer than Matt 22:30 // Mark 12:25) Jesus says the problem posed is inappropriate because it does not take into account the difference between life on earth and life beyond the resurrection. Human life in this world is mortal, and our sexuality guarantees the survival of the human race. Beyond the resurrection, however, people do not die, so the type of sexual unions appropriate in this life do not apply (cf. 2 Baruch 51:10; 1 Enoch 104:4, 6; 1 QSb 4:24–28; 1 QH 3:21ff.; 6:13). (Given this line of reasoning, if the Corinthians believed they had already been raised from the dead—1 Cor 4:8—then their attitudes toward marriage are understandable—1 Corinthians 7.) The one who knows the mind of God therefore knows what life in the other world will be like (cf. Luke 6:20–26; 13:28–29; 16:19–31).

The scribal commendation of Jesus (vs. 39) that follows the discomfiture of the Sadducees becomes the occasion for a twofold critique: (a) of scribal theology (vss. 41–44), and (b) of the scribal way of life (20:45–47; 21:1–4). The critique of their theology is addressed to the scribes (vs. 41, cf. vs. 39); the critique of their way of life is addressed to the disciples (20:45). (a) Luke 20:41–44 poses a puzzle for the scribes very much in the same manner the Sadducees had presented Jesus with a riddle. The pericope assumes first that "the Lord" is God, that "my Lord" equals the Messiah, and that David is the author of the psalm (vs. 42); and second, that, according to oriental mores, a son did not surpass his father. Given assumption two, how could the Messiah be David's son (vs. 44)? David would not address a son of his as Lord. No answer to the riddle is given, but Luke's readers would have their own answer. The one who is David's son (1:69; 2:4; 3:23–38) became

David's Lord by virtue of his resurrection-ascension-exaltation (Acts 2:34–36; 13:22–23, 33–37).

(b) The critique of the scribal way of life echoes, in part, earlier attacks on the Pharisees, scribes, and lawyers (11:37–54; 14:1–24). In order to gain perspective it will be helpful to examine these earlier passages briefly. Luke 11:37–54 is a meal setting (vs. 37) in which there are two parallel units:

Provocation by Jesus (vs. 38)	Provocation by Jesus (vs. 45)
Response by the Pharisee (vs. 38)	Response by the lawyer (vs. 45)
Three woes on the Pharisees (vss. 39–44)	Three woes on the lawyers (vss. 46–52)

It closes with a statement about the scribes' and Pharisees' conspiracy against Jesus (11:53–54).

The passage functions as an expose of the disparity between outer appearance and inner reality in the life-style of Pharisees and lawyers. Two excerpts give the thrust of the meaning: "Now you Pharisees cleanse the outside of the cup and of the dish, but inside you are full of extortion and wickedness. You fools! Did not he who made the outside make the inside also?" (vss. 39–40); "Woe to you! for you are like graves which are not seen, and men walk over them without knowing it" (vs. 44).

Luke 14:1–24 is set at dinner in a Pharisee's house. The dinner scene is a literary device (cf. Plato, *Symposium;* Esther; Ep Artist § 182–294; Plutarch, *Nine Books of Table Talk*) to provide a unified setting for four separate traditions (14:1–6, 7–11, 12–14, 15–24). These four traditions fall into a clear chiastic pattern:

A Unconcern about others (humans) while giving an appearance
   of being religious (14:1–6)
 B Self-seeking as a guest (14:7–11)
  B' Self-seeking as a host (14:12–14)
A' Unconcern about others (God) while giving the appearance of
   being religious (14:15–24)

This passage also functions as an expose of the disparity between outer appearance and inner reality. The first tradition (vss. 1–6) assumes the Pharisee and his guests were opposed to healing the man with dropsy on the sabbath. Jesus' behavior and words expose their callous unconcern for the man even while they profess to protect the rituals of religion. Something in vs. 5 has fallen into an artificially constructed well (*phrear;* Exod 21:33 shows such accidents were by no means uncommon). The best textual tradition reads, "son or ox." Jesus asks, "Which of you, having a son or even an ox that has fallen into a well, will not immediately pull him out on a sabbath day?" Would this have been the case? Jewish attitudes toward assistance on the sabbath varied. At Qumran it was taught that a person could be pulled from a pit so long as no implements were used, but an animal could not be lifted out on the sabbath (CD 11:13–17). In the Talmud (b. Shabbath 128b) two rulings are given: the mild ruling allows helping an animal out of a pit; the harsh one allows only the provision of fodder to it. It would seem, then, that even the most severe opinion would allow human beings to be pulled out even on the sabbath, though there was a difference of opinion about animals. Luke 14:5 assumes the Pharisees allow both people and animals to be pulled out on the sabbath. Jesus' argument runs from the lesser to the greater: if pulling an animal or a son out of a pit on the sabbath is permitted by Jewish logic, then how much more should a man in the pit of illness be extricated from his plight. The effect of the argument is to expose the callousness of the Pharisees, who have an appearance of being religious (keeping the sabbath) but are unconcerned about people in need.

The second and third traditions (vss. 7–11; 12–14) expose the self-seeking of the people at the meal. Verses 7–11 begin with the note that the guests were seeking the places of honor at the dinner (vs. 7). The prescription of Jesus ("go and sit in the lowest place") is based on the way God acts: "Every one who exalts himself will be humbled, and he who humbles himself will be exalted" (vs. 11; cf. 1:48, 52; 3:5; 18:14; 6:20–26). Verses 12–14 assume the host has invited only those who could benefit him in the future: his self-seeking as a host is exposed. Jesus' prescription ("invite the poor, the maimed, the lame, the blind") is based on the way God will act: "You will be repaid at the resurrection of the just" (vs. 14).

The fourth tradition (vss. 15–24) opens with a pious utterance by one of those present: "Blessed is he who shall eat bread in the kingdom of God" (vs. 15). The allegory of Jesus given in response exposes the hollowness of the words. It follows the outline of salvation history presented in the narrative of Luke-Acts. The many in Israel had been invited to the messianic banquet through God's messengers (the prophets). When the time for the banquet came, God sent his servant (Jesus—Acts 4:27; 3:26; and his disciples) to say, "Come," but when the announcement was made, those invited refused because they were preoccupied with the common ventures of life (cf. Luke 17:26–30). Faced with refusal by the Jewish leaders, the Lord turned first to the outcasts among the Jews (cf. 15:1–2), then to the Gentiles. The pious profession of vs. 15 masks the unconcern which such a one had for God and his kingdom. The allegory exposes the disparity between profession and practice. It is as though Jesus looks through spectacles that allow him to penetrate the outer appearance and lay bare the inner reality of one's life. It is against this background one may turn to 20:45ff.

In 20:45–47 Jesus critiques the scribal way of life. In their outer appearance they are ostentatiously religious. Yet the reality of their situation is stated in vs. 47a: "who devour widows' houses" (that is, by taking them as pledges for debts which cannot be paid). This is the disparity between outer profession and inner reality of which the disciples are to beware (vs. 45–46a). What the disciples are to emulate is found in 21:1–4. Since it was not possible under Jewish law to offer less than two mites, the widow was making the smallest offering possible. Yet she is praised by Jesus above the rich (like the scribes). For Jesus "what matters is not the amount that one gives but the amount that one keeps for oneself" (I. H. Marshall, *The Gospel of Luke*, p. 750). Beware the scribes! Emulate the widow! The latter is whole; the former are hollow.

With this, the first part of Jesus' teaching in the temple ends. Challenged by many, he was overcome by none.

ON PERSECUTION
AND PERSEVERANCE

19:45—21:38 (B. 21:5–38);
12:1–12; 14:26–35

M uch of the material in 21:5–38 has parallels in the other synoptics, but the evangelist has shaped the total unit to reflect
his own conceptions. For example, whereas Matt 24:1–3 and Mark
13:1–4 locate the discussion outside the temple on the Mount of Olives
and specify the disciples (Matthew) or four named disciples (Mark) as
the auditors of the discourse, Luke keeps Jesus inside the temple and
makes the teaching public (20:45; 21:37–38). If, as the contents indicate (21:12–19), at least part of the teaching is intended for disciples,
they are instructed in the hearing of all the people. Luke 21:5–26,
thereby, functions as the second part of the public teaching of Jesus
in the temple in Jerusalem (19:45—21:38).

The occasion for the teaching in Luke 21 is an admiring remark
made by someone about the adornments of the temple (vs. 5). In response (cf. 14:15) Jesus utters a prophetic oracle: "As for these things
which you see, the days will come when there shall not be left here
one stone upon another that will not be thrown down" (vs. 6). This
echoes the prophecy of the destruction of the temple by Micah (3:12)
and Jeremiah (7; 22:5) in earlier times. The oracle prompts two questions: "when will this be, and what will be the sign that this is about
to take place?" (vs. 7). The questions are answered in an apocalyptic
discourse (vss. 8–36) which sets the fate of the temple in a much
larger context, concerned with other issues. The dialogue falls into the
following pattern:

A The time of the eschaton, warning not to be misled (vss. 8–9)
 B Political upheavals (vs. 10)
  C Cosmic disturbances (vs. 11)
   D The time of testimony (which comes before all this)
    (vss. 12–19)

199

> B′ Political upheavals (of which the fall of Jerusalem is a part)
>   (vss. 20–24)
>   C′ Cosmic disturbances (vss. 25–26)
> A′ The time of the eschaton, warning to be ready (vss. 27–36).

If we arrange the items into an ordered series, it would run as follows: (1) a time of testimony (vs. 12a indicates this period comes *before* all the rest); (2) the emergence of false messiahs; (3) political upheavals (including the fall of Jerusalem); (4) cosmic disturbances; and (5) the coming of the Son of Man. From this apocalyptic timetable we can extract the Lukan answers to the two questions raised in vs. 7. When will the temple be destroyed? It will occur as part of the political disturbances prior to the End. What will be the sign when this is about to take place? The sign will be when you see Jerusalem surrounded by armies (vs. 20). Though it was the oracle about the temple's destruction that prompted the questions which evoked the discourse, the evangelist's concerns are broader in this chapter than the fall of Jerusalem and the temple's demise (though the fall and the demise are a part of the recurrent theme in Luke: 13:31–35; 19:28–44; 23:26–31).

Two primary concerns, in addition to the destruction of Jerusalem, are evident in Luke 21: (1) persecution, which is the time of testimony (vss. 12–19), and (2) perseverance or readiness for the Son of Man's coming (vss. 34–36).

Proper appreciation of Luke's treatment of persecution requires looking first of all at an earlier passage that also dealt with this problem: 12:1–12, which serves as background for the examination of 21:12–19. In 12:1–12 the combination of sayings is so ordered that its message is directed to the church's life after the resurrection of Jesus. (1) The section begins with a warning against hypocrisy, that is, not being on the inside what one appears to be on the outside (vs. 1). Such a life is futile because at some point (in a time of persecution?) it will be exposed (vss. 2–3). (2) The disciple should not acquiesce because of a fear of those whose ultimate power is their ability to kill only the body (vs. 4). Rather they should fear God who has power over one's destiny after death (vs. 5). Gehenna, originally a valley near Jerusalem where children were sacrificed to Molech (Jer 7:31–32), was, after Josiah's reform, turned into a garbage dump (2 Kgs 23:10), and ultimately became a symbol of punishment reserved for God's enemies (Rev 14:7–13; cf. Mark 9:43–48; 1 Pet 4:17–19). This one who has power over your ultimate destiny cares for you. Do not fear your persecutors (vss. 6–7). (3) One's ultimate destiny depends upon the relation to Jesus: "Everyone who acknowledges me before men, the Son of Man also will acknowledge before the angels of God; but he who denies me before men will be denied before the angels of God" (vss. 8–9). The only way to avoid a contradiction between this principle and the qualification in vs. 10 is by understanding the crucial difference in the Lukan mind between the period of Jesus, in which only he enjoys the abiding presence of the Holy Spirit, and the period of the church when the promised Spirit is bestowed on the disciples. The general principle of vss. 8–9 may be qualified by saying that hostility to or denial of the earthly Jesus is forgiveable—so Peter who denied Jesus (22:54ff.) was forgiven by the risen Lord (24:34) and the Jewish people who acted in ignorance are offered a second chance after Jesus' resurrection (Acts 3:14–15, 17, 19, 26; 5:30–31). After the resurrection of Jesus reviling the Holy Spirit is not forgiveable (vs. 10). For the unbelievers rejecting the Christian message is resisting the Holy Spirit (Acts 7:51; cf. 28:25–28). The disciples, who are the evangelist's primary concern here, would be rejecting the Spirit's inspiration when, required to testify before persecutors, they would, in direct opposition to the Spirit's influence deny Christ (vss. 11–12; cf. 21:14–15; Acts 4:8, 19–20; 5:30). By denying Christ the disciples deny the Holy Spirit within and blaspheme the only one who can mediate God's forgiveness. This Lukan exhortation to stand firm in the face of persecution functions as the background for 21:12–19.

The chronology of the events described in 21:8–19 does not coincide with the order of their appearance in the text where a warning not to be misled by false messiahs and other signs into thinking the End has arrived (vss. 8–9), and references to political upheavals (vs. 10) and cosmic disturbances (vs. 11) precede the section on persecution (vss. 12–19). Chronologically, however, the persecutions precede the other items (cf. vs. 12a—*pro de toutōn pantōn*, "but before all these things"): that is, in the interim before the eschaton the disciples will experience persecution (cf. 6:22–23; 8:13; 12:11; Acts 4—5; 12; 16; 18; 21).

The persecution will be of two types (cf. Luke 12:11): Christians will be brought before Jewish synagogue courts (vs. 12a), and they will be brought to trial before kings and governors (vs. 12b). This, of course, is exactly the case in the narrative of Acts (e.g., 4—5; 9:1 for Jewish arrests; 24; 25—26 for trial before governor and king). That the account in Acts conforms to historical reality, at least in the case of Paul, may be seen from 2 Cor 11:23ff. Such a moment of persecution from church and state is "a time for you to bear testimony" (vs. 13).

In this time of testimony the disciples need have no anxiety about what to say, "for I will give you a mouth and wisdom, which none of your adversaries will be able to withstand or contradict" (vs. 15). A similar promise was given in Luke 12:11–12, with the Holy Spirit teaching the disciples what ought to be said. Luke 21:15's "I will give you" may be designed to echo Exod 4:15. Again the promise is fulfilled in Acts (4:8–13; 6:10, "But they could not withstand the wisdom and the Spirit with which he spoke.").

The persecution will find even one's closest family and friends as betrayers (vs. 16a), which gives impact to the logion in 14:26 (cf. Acts 21:27; 22:1; 23:12—kinsmen). Persecution for some will result in death (cf. Acts 7:58–60; 12:1–2). Martyrdom is a real possibility for Jesus' disciples. Given this, how can the distinctively Lukan saying in vs. 18 ("But not a hair of your head will perish") be understood? Are we take vs. 16 as referring to only a few martyrs and vs. 18 as referring to the safety of the church as a whole? Or does vs. 16 refer to the threat to the bodies of the disciples and vs. 18 to the safety of their essential being? Because of 12:4ff. the latter seems the better option. Though they kill the body, that is all they can do: God preserves the life. Knowing this, the disciples' endurance (faithfulness to the end) gains them their lives (since 14:14 and 21:35 point to Luke's belief in resurrection only of the righteous, this would mean "resurrection lives"). In the early church endurance was a key quality encouraged in Christians who faced persecution (cf. Heb 10:32–39; Rev 2:2; 21:7–8; Jas 1:2–4; Rom 5:3–4).

The second of the evangelist's primary concerns in Luke 21 is the perseverance of the disciples, their readiness for the Son of Man's coming (vss. 34–36). Proper appreciation of what Jesus is saying in this chapter depends upon seeing it against the background of what has been said earlier in the gospel. In 14:25–35 Jesus addresses the multitudes who have been given an invitation to the table of God (14:23) in such a way as to discourage hasty enthusiasm. Perseverance depends upon counting the cost before one embarks upon the Way. Luke 14:26–35 says one should do this because the demands of discipleship are rigorous, and it is tragic not to be able to follow through on what has been begun. (1) Verses 26–27 give two parallel sayings about the demands of discipleship. Both sayings end with the refrain, "it is not possible to be my disciple." (a) The "hating" of one's family and one's own life in vs. 26 is a Semitic way of expressing absolute and total detachment. When disciples are confronted with a conflict of loyalty, they will give priority to the commitment to Jesus (9:59–62; 18:28–30; cf. Deut 33:9). (b) Verse 27 is basically the same logion as 9:23. The bearing of one's cross is an expansion of the idea of hating one's own life in vs. 26. When one is confronted with a conflict between his or her commitment to Jesus and his or her own unredeemed desires, the unredeemed self is treated as dead and one's commitment to Jesus reigns supreme: "Discipleship is not periodic volunteer work on one's own terms and at one's convenience" (Robert J. Karris, *Gospel of St. Luke* [Chicago: Franciscan Herald Press, 1974], p. 59). Absolute detachment from all else and total commitment to Jesus are what is demanded of disciples. Given this rigorous demand it would be advisable to count the cost before accepting the invitation to the messianic banquet.

(2) Three sayings speak to the tragedy of not being able to follow through on what one has begun. (a) In vss. 28–30 this tragedy is expressed in terms of embarrassment. Be like the farmer who sits down first and counts the cost of building a tower to guard his vineyard against marauders at harvest season. He does this to avoid the embarrassment of not being able to finish what he has started. (b) In vss. 31–32 it is stated in terms of subjection to a foreign king. Be like the king who sits down first and reckons his chances of winning before venturing forth into battle against a foe who cannot be beaten. He does this to avoid subjection to an alien rule. (c) In vss. 34–35a the tragedy is discussed in terms of discarded salt. Salt in Palestine was obtained by evaporation from the Dead Sea. Since the water of the Dead Sea contained many substances evaporation produced a mixture of crystals of salt and gypsum or carnallite. The mixture would taste salty even though it was not pure salt. If, however, in the process the salt crystals were dissolved, what was left might appear to be salt but would have no salty taste. This residue would serve no useful purpose and so would be thrown away. Though Matt 5:13 addresses a form of this saying to disciples, Luke uses it to speak to a group of would-be disciples (the multitudes—vs. 25). He says, "Count the cost before you accept the invitation because to fail to persevere is to be as useless as tasteless salt and to be subject to the same judgment."

The evangelist has arranged the materials of 14:25–35 to set forth the demands of discipleship, call for sober calculation of what is involved before setting out on the Christian Way, and tell of the tragedy involved in failure to finish what one has begun. Perseverance is essential for disciples. If 14:25–35 addressed this word about perseverance to would-be disciples, 21:34–36 speaks to those who are already disciples. The accent on perseverance is the same, however.

Luke's concern for the readiness of Christians (vss. 34–36) is set in the context of an apocalyptic scheme: (1) political upheavals, of which the fall of Jerusalem is one part (vss. 20–24); (2) cosmic disturbances (vss. 25–26); (3) the coming of the Son of Man in a cloud (9:34; Acts 1:9): "Now when these things begin to take place, look up and raise your heads, because your redemption is drawing near" (vs. 28). For the Lukan church, that looked back on the destruction of Jerusalem and lived in a world with cosmic signs aplenty, all that would be left in this apocalyptic timetable would be the coming of the Son of Man. Luke's readers should know that just as the fresh foliage in spring signals the coming of summer, so the disasters and cosmic disturbances signal the nearness of the End (vss. 29–31). Since the evangelist believed that all had taken place in the apocalyptic scheme except the Son of Man's coming, the End was near. In light of this, the simplest way to read vs. 32 is that Luke believed the End would come before "this generation" (that is, his own) passed away (of course, IQpHab 2:7; 7:2, indicates the "last generation" could mean "several lifetimes"). In this belief Luke was one with most of the early church (e.g., 1 Thes 4:15; 1 Cor 15:51–52; Mark 9:1; Heb 10:25, 37; 1 Pet 4:7; Jas 5:8–9; Rev 22:7, 12, 20). Luke 21:33 is the basis for believing vs. 32: "Heaven and earth will pass away, but my words will not pass away."

In the context of this statement of the impending coming of the Son of Man (the cosmic judge), the evangelist exhorts his readers to watch (be prepared) at all times (cf. 12:35–40; 18:8). Being prepared means two things in this passage. On the one hand it means to pray (vs. 36b; cf. 11:4b; 22:40, 46). In Luke's mind prayer was the opposite of losing heart (18:1). It signaled intense persistence. On the other hand being prepared means allowing nothing to distract one from his or her primary concern (vs. 34). Two dangers are cited as of special importance: (a) sensuality (here "dissipation and drunkenness"—cf. 8:14; 12:45–46; Rom 13:11–14), and (b) preoccupation with the cares of this life (cf. 8:14; 14:15–24; 17:26–27, 28–30). Persevere! Be prepared! It is certain everyone will have to render an account to the cosmic judge (vs. 35; cf. 19:11–27; Acts 17:31; Rev 20:11–13; 1 Pet 4:5; Rom 2:5–11; 14:12; Matt 12:36; Jude 14–15).

MEALTIME FAREWELLS

22:1—23:56 (A. 22:1–38)

M uch of the material in 22:1–38 has at least loose parallels in the other synoptics but the overall impact of the material is distinctly Lukan. The setting shifts from the temple where Jesus taught daily (19:45—21:38) to the city. The battle between Jesus and the Jewish leadership moves from the intellectual sphere (chap. 20) to a plot to capture Jesus in the absence of the multitude (22:1–6). Satan joins the fray (22:3) and the Passover season (22:1) becomes the hour of the power of darkness (22:53). Satan manipulates Judas by means of the latter's attachment to money (22:5; Acts 1:18a; John 12:4–6).

Luke 22:7–38 is arranged as a supper scene in two parts: the preparation (vss. 7–13), and the meal itself which functions as the occasion for a farewell speech (vss. 14–38). (1) In the preparation scene Jesus takes the initiative, sending Peter and John to prepare the meal. A prophecy by Jesus tells them how to find the place where the group will eat. When they enter the city they will confront a man carrying a jar of water (an unusual thing because women normally carried water jars). This man will lead them to a spot where a room would be available: "And they went, and found it as he had told them; and they prepared the passover" (cf. 19:32). The fulfillment of Jesus' words so exactly in this instance would instill confidence in Luke's hearers that the predictions of Jesus which dominate vss. 14–38 would be fulfilled. (Deut 18:22 gives as a way to recognize a false prophet that his predictions do not come true.)

(2) The interpretation of the meal itself depends first of all upon how the textual question of vss. 19b–20 is settled. The Western Text omits the words, " 'which is given for you. Do this in remembrance of me.' And likewise the cup after supper, saying, 'This cup which is poured out for you is the new covenant in my blood.' " These words are included by most other manuscript evidence. The external evidence for the longer text is overwhelming. The weakness in its claim to originality is in accounting for the origin of the shorter text. Until about

1950 there was widespread scholarly agreement in favor of accepting the shorter form. Since then P⁷⁵ (the Bodmer papyrus of Luke dating from about A.D. 200) has strengthened the argument in favor of the longer text, which will be accepted here.

The meal itself consists of two sets of sayings about eating and drinking (vss. 15–18, 19–20). (a) In the first set there are two parallel sayings.

> 1) I have earnestly desired to eat this passover with you before I suffer; *for I tell you I shall not eat it until* it is fulfilled in the *kingdom of God.* (vss. 15–16)

> 2) Take this [cup] and divide it among yourselves; *for I tell you that from now on I shall not drink* of the fruit of the vine *until* the *kingdom of God* comes. (vss. 17–18)

These verses are specifically linked to the Passover (vs. 15): Jesus says he will eat no more Passovers until the kingdom of God comes. The sayings are, therefore, oriented to the future. If we had only vs. 16, one would inevitably understand the reference to be to the messianic banquet (cf. 13:29; 14:15). Verse 18, however, is sufficiently general that it could be fulfilled in the references to postresurrection appearances where Jesus ate and drank with disciples (24:41–42; Acts 1:4; 10:41; cf. Luke 9:27). Both postresurrection appearances and the post-parousia banquet are probably involved. Repeatedly in the gospel Jesus has warned his disciples of his approaching fate (9:33, 44; 12:50; 13:32–33; 17:25; 18:32–33). Now he tells them the time has come. He will depart this life, an exodus (9:31) to be accomplished at the season that celebrated the Exodus from Egypt (Exodus 12).

In this context vss. 15–18 function in the interests of the farewell speech to come in vss. 19–38. In the farewell speeches characteristic of Jewish and Christian materials certain factors are constant: a hero figure knows he is going to die (cf. 2 Pet 1:15 where the apostle describes his death as an exodus); he gathers his primary community together and gives a farewell speech with two standard components—there is first a prediction of what will happen after he is gone and then there is an exhortation about how to behave after his departure. The evangelist has turned the meal into a farewell speech setting. In 22:15–18 Jesus says he is about to die; vss. 19–38 give the predictions and exhortations of the speech proper; vss. 7–13 lend credibility to the predictions by showing a prophecy of Jesus in another regard fulfilled to the letter. The desire to use a farewell speech, therefore, determines the shape of his material in 22:7–38. The distinctively Lukan words at the Last Supper (vss. 15–18) are included and placed first to allow Jesus to say he is about to die just before he gives his last words to the apostles. They are not eucharistic as such. In their Lukan context they are Jesus' prediction of impending death.

(b) In vss. 19–20, the second set of parallel sayings, we find two more items.

> 1) And he took bread, and when he had given thanks he broke it and gave it to them, saying, "This is my body which is given for you. Do this in remembrance of me." (vs. 19)

> 2) And likewise the cup after supper, saying, "This cup which is poured out for you is the new covenant in my blood." (vs. 20)

These verses are not explicitly linked to the Passover. Here Jesus asks his disciples to repeat the meal in his personal memory (vs. 19) and says his death is the seal of the new covenant (vs. 20). The orientation is to the past. The similarities to the Pauline tradition of the Lord's Supper in 1 Cor 11:23–25 are striking.

What is the view of Jesus' death reflected in these words? Three expressions need analysis if we are to arrive at an adequate answer: "new covenant," "in my blood," and "given for you." In the first place, Jesus speaks of a new covenant related to his death. The reference is to Jer 31:31–34 where Yahweh declares he will make a new covenant with Israel: "I will put my law within them, and I will write it upon their hearts" (vs. 33). A similar kind of promise is found in Ezek 36:26–27, though the expression "new covenant" is missing: "A new heart I will give you, and a new spirit I will put within you. . . . And I will put my spirit within you, and cause you to walk in my statutes and be careful to observe my ordinances." In 2 Cor 3:3, 6 is a Pauline appropriation of the thought of Jeremiah 31:

> You show that you are a letter from Christ . . . written not with ink but with the Spirit of the living God, not on tablets of stone but on tablets of human hearts. (vs. 3)

> God . . . has qualified us to be ministers of a new covenant, not in a written code but in the Spirit; for the written code kills, but the Spirit gives life. (vs. 6)

Jeremiah saw the new covenant as involving an urge from the inside to be faithful to the relationship with God in contrast to the old command from the outside. Paul specified that the urge from the inside came from the Spirit. Luke 22:20 uses this new covenant mentality.

The necessity for a new covenant lay in the sinfulness of God's creatures (v., Jer 17:9—, "The heart is deceitful above all things, and desperately corrupt"). In the new covenant God himself assumes responsibility for enabling one "to will and to do his good pleasure" (Phil 2:13). The new covenant prophesied by Jeremiah and Ezekiel and spoken about by Paul and the Lukan Jesus is new in the sense that God now assumes responsibility for enabling humans to relate faithfully to him.

In the second place, Jesus says the new covenant is sealed by his blood, which echoes the covenant ceremony of Exod 24:3–8 where Moses, after throwing the blood on the people, said, "Behold the blood of the covenant which the Lord has made with you" (vs. 8). Jesus says his coming death will seal the new covenant in the heart so that there would be an urge from within to obey God. In Lukan theology, as in Pauline, the instrument of this inner power is the Holy Spirit. In the emptying of the cup Jesus saw the promise of a new relation to God, one controlled by the Holy Spirit within the disciple which would be sealed by his death. If the death of Jesus is in any way to be regarded as sacrificial in Luke-Acts, it is as a sacrifice that seals a covenant (cf. Gen 15:8–21; 17): it is not an atonement for sin.

In the third place, the expression "which is given for you" in the saying over the bread should not be understood in terms of an atoning sacrifice. Although "given" (*didomenon*) can be used with reference to sacrifice (e.g., Exod 30:14; Lev 22:14), it can also be used for martyrdom (Isa 53:10). The same is true of "for you" (*huper*), which can be used of a martyr's actions (2 Mac 7:9; 8:21; 4 Mac 1:8, 10) as well as of a sacrificial offering (Lev 5:7; 6:23). Since the dominant thrust of Luke's understanding of Jesus' death is that of martyrdom, it seems preferable to understand the language here in those terms as well. Here we are told that Jesus' martyrdom would have beneficial effects for the disciples—exactly what was said in the remarks about a new covenant.

Taken as a whole the words of Jesus over the bread and wine in 22:19–20 speak of Jesus' death as a martyrdom which seals the new covenant characterized by life in the Spirit. Jesus asks that this death be memorialized in a repeated meal observed by his disciples. The foundational event in the community's life must not be forgotten.

Viewed in their immediate context vss. 19–20 function as part of the farewell speech form into which the evangelist has cast his material: in vss. 15–18 Jesus predicts his imminent death; in vss. 19–20 he predicts that it will seal the new covenant and exhorts his apostles to repeat it as a memorial to him. The other components in vss. 21–38 function similarly.

Luke 22:21–23 functions as a prediction. Someone at the table with Jesus will betray him. Luke, unlike Matt 26:21–25 // Mark 14: 18–21, locates this prediction of betrayal (Ps 41:9) after the meal, thereby saying it is possible to eat with Jesus and still betray him. Similar points are made in 1 Corinthians 10 and John 13, indicating this was a serious problem in early Christianity (cf. A. Vööbus, *The Prelude to the Lukan Passion Narrative* [Stockholm: Este, 1968], p. 24). Presence at the Lord's table is no guarantee against apostasy. The meal possesses no magical powers. Here is a warning for Luke's community about a danger for which to be alert.

Luke 22:24–27 functions as exhortation. Luke, unlike Matt 20:25–28 // Mark 10:42–45, has the disciples' dispute over greatness not on the way to Jerusalem but after supper with Jesus, thereby saying it is possible for disciples to eat with Jesus and still be involved in strife among themselves because of their desire for places of status (cf. 1 Cor 3:1–4; 12—14; John 13; Matt 23:1–11; again, this points up a real problem in the early church). The correction for this strife is located in the reversal of values so characteristic of Luke: "let the greatest among you become as the youngest, and the leader as the one who serves." The basis for this reversal is the example of Jesus: "I am among you as one who serves." This passage presupposes a community with leaders who are overly impressed with their authority (cf. 12:41–48). Here is another warning for Luke's church. The supper guarantees neither a lasting vertical relationship nor a harmonious horizontal one.

Following the two warnings Jesus gives two promises to comfort his disciples. The first, 22:28–30, is prediction. The apostles who have continued with Jesus in his trials will participate both in the messianic banquet (cf. 13:28–29; 14:15) and in the last judgment (cf. Matt 19:28; 1 Cor 6:2, 3): Jesus promises ultimate vindication for those who walk his way.

Luke 22:31–34, the second promise, functions as both prediction and exhortation. Jesus predicts the satanic attack on the disciples (the "you" is plural in vs. 31; cf. Job 1—2; Zech 3:1–3) and assures Peter of his intercession on his behalf (the "you" is singular in vs. 32; cf. John 17:15; Rom 8:34; Heb 7:25). He predicts the threefold denial that is coming so soon. Peter's slip is not regarded by Luke as apostasy. Operating from his confidence that Peter will repent, Jesus exhorts him to strengthen his brethren when he is able. Satan tries to secure the apostasy of Jesus' disciples, but Jesus' prayer protects them. This can only be seen as a foreshadowing of the risen Lord's heavenly intercession for his saints. It is a comforting promise.

Luke 22:35–38, an exhortation based on a prediction, closes the farewell speech. The prediction is that now the conditions of the Lord's passion ("he was reckoned with transgressors," that is, treated as a criminal—23:39ff.) apply to his followers. The peaceful conditions of the first missions (9:1ff.; 10:1ff.) no longer apply. Since this is so, there is an exhortation: be ready for hardship and self-sacrifice, a part of Jesus' Way (cf. Luke 9). Its purpose is the refinement of one's faith. 1 Pet 1:6–7 puts it well: "Now for a little while you may have to suffer various trials, so that the genuineness of your faith, more precious than gold which though perishable is tested by fire, may redound to praise and glory and honor at the revelation of Jesus Christ." Failing to grasp the point, the disciples take Jesus' words literally and produce two swords. Frustrated, Jesus breaks off the conversation: "Enough of this."

The farewell speech of 22:14–38 relates that Jesus' disciples need warnings about the dangers of apostasy, strife, denial, and persecution as part of the lives of those who eat at Jesus' table. Disciples receive not only exhortation to right behavior but also assurances. Jesus' death has sealed a new relation with God through the Spirit; he is praying for his own; and he promises his disciples ultimate vindication with him.

A MODEL FOR MARTYRS

22:1—23:56 (B. 22:39—23:25)

Luke 22:39—23:25 has parallels for much of its material in the other synoptics; again, however, the shape of the material is distinctively Lukan. The distinctive thrust of this section is best understood against the background of the Lukan view of Jesus' death as a martyrdom which is a model for his disciples. First, two things need to be said about Jesus' death. On the one hand, in contrast to other NT witnesses (like Paul e.g., 1 Cor 15:3; 2 Cor 5:21; Rom 3:25, and Matthew e.g., 26:28), Luke avoids any connection between Jesus' death and the forgiveness of sins. (a) In the speeches of Acts both Peter (2:38; 3:19; 5:31; 10:43) and Paul (13:38; 17:30; 26:18) preach the forgiveness of sins as the risen Christ directed (Luke 24:47). Yet neither combines the forgiveness of sins with the death of Jesus on the cross. (b) In contrast to Mark 10:45 ("For the Son of man also came . . . to give his life as a ransom for many"), Luke 22:27b ("I am among you as one who serves") avoids any mention of an atoning death. (c) In 22:37 (Isa 53:12) and Acts 8:32–33 (Isa 53:7–8), although Isaiah 53 is quoted, there is no mention of the sacrificial death of the servant. (d) In Luke-Acts, neither baptism (Acts 2:38, 41; 8:12, 13, 16; 8:37–39; 9:18; 10:47–48; 16:15; 19:5; 22:16) nor the Lord's Supper (Luke 22:16–20; 24:30ff.; 24:41ff.; Acts 2:42–46; 20:7, 11; 27:35) is connected with Jesus' atoning death (contrast Rom 6:3ff. and 1 Cor. 11:23ff.). In Luke-Acts forgiveness of sins flows from the earthly Jesus, especially at mealtime (Luke 19:7f.; 15:1ff.; 5:29–32), and after the resurrection from the exalted Lord (Acts 3:28; 4:11; 5:31—"God exalted him at his right hand as Leader and Savior, to give repentance to Israel and forgiveness of sins.").

On the other hand, Luke portrays the death of Jesus as a martyrdom, the unjust murder of an innocent man by the established powers due to the pressure of the Jewish leaders. (a) Jesus is innocent of the charges against him (23:4, 14, 15, 22, 41, 47). (b) He is delivered by the Jewish chief priests and scribes (Luke 22:66; 23:1–2, 10, 13, 18,

21, 23, 24; cf. Acts 5:27, 30; 13:27) and executed by Gentiles (Luke 23:34; Acts 4:27). (c) His death is parallel to the sufferings of the prophets of old at the hands of the Jews (Luke 13:33; Acts 7:52— "which of the prophets did not your fathers persecute? And they killed those who announced beforehand the coming of the Righteous One, whom you have now betrayed and murdered"). So Jesus stands at the end of a long line of martyrs. (d) Like the martyrs in 2 Mac 7:2, 11; 4 Mac 6:1; 10:23, Jesus is silent before his accusers (Luke 23:9). As in the Martyrdom of Isaiah, Jesus' martyrdom is due to the devil (Luke 22:3, 53). As in the case of the martyrs slain by Herod (Josephus, *Antiquities*, 17:6:2–4 § 167), there is an eclipse at Jesus' death (Luke 23:45). (e) His demeanor in his martyrdom leads to the conversion of one of the thieves crucified with him (Luke 23:40–43). (f) Jesus' martyr death is a fulfillment of OT prophecies (Luke 23:25–27, 46; Acts 13:27–29), a part of God's plan (Acts 2:23).

Secondly, the martyrdom of Jesus is viewed as a model for his disciples. This becomes clear when we note that the story of Stephen's death in Acts parallels that of Jesus in the gospel. (a) Both are tried before the Council (Luke 22:66f.; Acts 6:12f.). (b) Both die a martyr's death. (c) Acts 7:59, "Lord Jesus, receive my spirit," echoes Luke 23:46, "Father, into thy hands I commit my spirit." (d) Acts 7:60, "Lord, do not hold this sin against them," echoes Luke 23:34, "Father, forgive them; for they do not know what they are doing." (e) Both stories contain a Son of Man saying: Luke 22:69; Acts 7:56. This is remarkable since Acts 7:56 is the only occurrence of the title Son of Man outside the gospels and on any lips except those of Jesus. (f) Both men's deaths issue in evangelistic results (Luke 23:39–43; Acts 8:1ff.; 11:19ff.). Moreover, the story of Stephen's martyrdom fulfills Jesus' words: Luke 21:12–19, especially vs. 16 ("some of you they will put to death"; cf. also 12:1–12). The deaths of both Jesus and Stephen are portrayed as martyrdoms in Luke-Acts, the former being the model for the latter.

It is against the backdrop of the Lukan view of Jesus' death as a martyrdom which serves as a model for his followers that one reads 22:39—23:25. This passage pictures Jesus, on the way to martyrdom, as an example for his community. There are a number of facets to the example offered. (1) Luke 22:39–46, the first of two episodes set on the Mount of Olives, portrays Jesus as an example in his use of prayer as protection against the temptation to lapse. The evangelist has shaped the prayer scene for his own ends. First, he specifies that the disciples "followed him" (vs. 39). There is not the effort in Luke to put distance between Jesus and the disciples that we find in Matthew and Mark. They are with him in his trials (23:28; Acts 14:22). For the evangelist the apostles' perseverance is as important as their being present throughout Jesus' career for their testimony's reliability after Easter. Second, Luke frames the account of Jesus' prayer with an exhortation to those who follow him "to pray that you may not enter into temptation" (vss. 40, 46; cf. 11:4—"enter into" means "succumb to"). The present imperative has durative force: "go on praying." Prayer is the weapon of a disciple as well as his master in the face of satanic attack in an hour of darkness (21:36; 18:7–8). This framing device gives the story a parenetic function: Jesus is teaching his disciples to pray in the face of trouble and attack (cf. Acts 4:23–31). This command is given in the context of the problem of the disciples' lapsing (Luke 22:22, 32, 34, 54–62). Third, the evangelist uses Jesus as a model of the praying Christian. Verses 43–44, absent in the other synoptics, are textually questionable. In spite of the strong evidence for their omission, however, there is equally strong internal evidence for their inclusion. It is, for example, a Lukan tendency to have prayer followed by some type of heavenly manifestation (e.g., Luke 3:21–22; 9:28–31; Acts 10:1–7). Also, the best parallels for a strengthening angel are in Dan 10:18–19 and Genesis Rabbah 44, words to or about the potential martyrs of the Maccabean period, and the best parallels for the themes of sweat and blood are in the story of Eleazer's martyrdom in 4 Mac 6:6, 11; 7:8. The use of these two items fits with the overall tendency in Luke to depict Jesus as a martyr. It seems preferable to include the verses. Jesus prays and an angel from heaven appears to strengthen him so he can pray more intensely. Here Jesus is no more forsaken by his Father than he is by his disciples. Heaven sends a strengthening angel to equip him for his martyrdom. Jesus carries out his own admonition to pray in times of crisis (cf. Acts 14:23–31; 12:1ff; 16:25ff.). By teaching and by example Jesus instructs disciples about how potential martyrs face the power of darkness (J. Warren Holleran, *The Synoptic Gethsemane* [Rome: Universita Gregoriana Editrice, 1973], chaps. 3, 6, 7). Finally, the content of the prayer is submission: "not my will, but thine, be done." Temptation to lapse is overcome by the intense prayer of surrender (cf. Eph 6:18; Col 4:2). Jesus' prayer is the disciples' model.

(2) The second episode, 22:47–53, also presents Jesus as teacher and model for his community. In this version of the arrest, two related variations from the other synoptics point to the evangelist's intent. (a) In vs. 49, when Jesus' disciples see what is about to happen, they ask, "Lord, shall we strike with the sword?" (b) Then in vs. 51, after one of the disciples had cut off the right ear of the high priest's slave, Jesus responds, "No more of this." Then he touches the ear and heals it. By means of these two episodes Jesus is presented as one who does not sanction physical violence as a means of escaping from martyrdom: violence as self-defense is renounced.

(3) In 22:54—23:25, the trials of Jesus, are several more examples in which Jesus serves as a model for his community in a time of crisis. In contrast to Matthew and Mark, who have three trials (Sanhedrin at night; Sanhedrin in the morning; Pilate), Luke has four (22:66—Sanhedrin, 23:1—Pilate; 23:8—Herod; 23:13–Pilate), probably to parallel the four trials of Paul in Acts (Acts 23—Sanhedrin; 24—Felix; 25—Festus; 26—Herod Agrippa). (a) Though Luke has Jesus taken to the high priest's house at night after his arrest (vs. 54), there is no nighttime trial. As the reader waits for daybreak, the denial of Peter is described (vss. 54b–62). Satan is sifting Peter (22:31), but a distinctive Lukan look by Jesus (vs. 61a) brings tears of repentance (vs. 62; though omitted by some, this verse is supported by such strong external evidence it should be included). Here the martyr, Jesus, is concerned to return straying disciples to the fold (22:32). Even in times of personal crisis, Jesus is concerned for others. In this he is a model for his community. He also is one whose faithfulness evokes our own (cf. 1 Tim 6:13–14).

(b) Though Jesus was submissive to the Father's will (22:42), he did not seek martyrdom. The trials make this clear. When day came Jesus was brought before the Council (22:66) briefly in what appears to be a preliminary investigation. The case against him was based solely on what Jesus himself said. There were no false witnesses as in Matt 26:60 // Mark 14:56–57. The issue was his identity: Are you the Christ? Are you the Son of God? There was no mention of the destruction of the temple as in Matt 26:61 // Mark 14:58. Jesus' answers were evasive: the first (vss. 68–69) said that though the Jewish leadership would not believe, God would vindicate his servant (cf. Acts 2:33–36; 5:31; 7:56); the second simply said, "That is what you say" (vs. 70). In his evasiveness Jesus acted in accord with general cultural norms. Martyrdom was not to be sought. Pagan teachers like Seneca (*Epistle* 24:25) said, "Above all, . . . avoid the weakness which has taken possession of many—the lust for death." Jewish teachers denounced overeagerness for martyrdom as self-annihilation (Genesis Rabbah 82) and argued that under duress evasion was acceptable. Early Christians reflected the same stance: the *Martyrdom of Polycarp,* 4, stated, "we do not approve those who give themselves up, for the gospel does not teach us to do so"; the *Acts of St. Cyprian* put it, "our discipline forbids anyone to surrender voluntarily." Jesus had no lust for death, was not bent on self-annihilation, but submitted to his Father's will. If that led to martyrdom, so be it. In this he functions as a pattern for his disciples.

(c) The Jewish Council in Luke does not condemn Jesus to death as in Matt 26:66 // Mark 14:64; they bring him to Pilate for the second trial (23:1). In 23:1–5 the Jewish leaders register their charges against Jesus. They have nothing to do with the previous examination, but are specifically political: 1) perverting the nation; 2) forbidding payment of taxes to Caesar; and 3) claiming to be a king (vs. 2). Of course, Luke intends the reader to see the charges as false (cf. 19:41–44 where Jesus is for peace; 20:21–25 where taxes are not prohibited; 22:67–70 where his answers are ambiguous about his identity). In being the object of false witness Jesus' experience is prototypical for his followers. It was the question of kingship that would most concern a Roman official (cf. Acts 17:7–8). So Pilate asks, "Are you the king of the Jews?" Jesus' answer (vs. 3) is the same as that given to the Sanhedrin (22:70): he is evasive. Pilate's evaluation is different from the Council's: "I find no crime in this man." The Jewish leadership is insistent: "He stirs up the people, teaching . . . from Galilee even to this place." Mention of Galilee is part of their propaganda against Jesus because Galilee was a hot-bed of revolutionary activity. By implication they bear false witness against Jesus. It is something with which Jesus' disciples will have to live.

(d) When Pilate learned that Jesus was a Galilean, he sent him to Herod, who happened to be in Jerusalem then (vss. 6–7) and who was eager to see Jesus (cf. 9:9). The third trial of Jesus, before Herod (vss. 6–12), is peculiar to Luke. It serves three possible functions. 1) It provides a second official witness to Jesus' innocence and so satisfies the demands of Deut 19:15. This seems indisputable in light of 23:14–15. Jesus is not guilty of sedition. The two officials agree on that. 2) It may serve to fulfill Ps 2:1ff. quoted in Acts 4:25–26 and in vs. 27 of that chapter is applied specifically to Herod and Pontius Pilate who collaborated to kill Jesus. It seems better to say, however, that the gospel regards Herod and Pilate favorably because of their judgment on Jesus' innocence, while Acts 4 regards them hostilely as involved in Jesus' death. 3) Like Ephesians, where Christ's death is the reconciliation of human hostility, particularly of the division between Jew and Gentile, 23:12 may indicate that the Jewish ruler (Herod) was reconciled to the Gentile (Pilate) on the very day of the shedding of Jesus' blood (John Drury, *Tradition and Design in Luke's Gospel* [Atlanta: John Knox, 1976], pp. 16–17). Though this third option is possible, it is not explicit in the Lukan scheme. The primary function of 23:6–12 seems to lie in the first explanation, Luke's preoccupation with the innocence of Jesus. Here again, he is a model for disciples: "For it is better to suffer for doing right, if that should be God's will, than for doing wrong. For Christ also died . . . the righteous for the unrighteous" (1 Pet 3:17–18).

(e) The emphasis on the innocence of Jesus is continued in the fourth and final trial (23:13–25), where Pilate appears more as an advocate who pleads Jesus' case than as a judge presiding over an official hearing: "I did not find this man guilty . . . neither did Herod. . . . I will therefore chastise him and release him" (vss. 14–16). The chastisement was a light beating accompanied by a severe warning (cf. Acts 16:22–24; 22:24). Pilate was saying in effect that he would give Jesus a suspended sentence. The opponents of Jesus, which now include the people along with the chief priests and rulers (23:13—but not the Pharisees), all cry out for Jesus' death and Barabbas' release (vs. 18). This is part of the irony of the gospel story: those who sought Jesus' death because of his alleged sedition called for the release of one guilty of an insurrection started in the city and of murder (vs. 19). Pilate tries once more to release Jesus: "I have found in him no crime deserving death" (vs. 22). "But they were urgent, demanding with loud cries that he should be crucified. And their voices prevailed" (vs. 23)—Pilate released Barabbas the insurrectionist and delivered Jesus to their will. The impression made by the trials as a whole is that an innocent man has been condemned, and Jesus goes to his death a martyr.

In this story of Jesus' progress toward death, his disciples are intended to see certain things relating to their lives as well. Although innocent, Christians may be given over to the will of their opponents with their vindication coming only after suffering (Acts 16:19–39) or death (Acts 7). At such a time it is important that the Christians have prayed and continue to do so in order to escape the temptation to lapse (22:39–46). Martyrdom is not to be sought, but neither is violence to be used to escape. The disciples may expect false witness to be borne against them. Note the irony: that with which one is charged is often that of which one's accusers are guilty. In such times of crisis Jesus is one's model.

INNOCENT AND OBEDIENT

22:1—23:56 (C. 23:26–56a)

While the material in 23:26–56a has parallels in the other synoptics, for the most part, its overall purpose is quite different. The clue to the distinctive Lukan development of the material is found in the very first pericope of the unit, vs. 26, the reference to Simon of Cyrene. The evangelist has shaped this statement so Simon carries the cross "behind Jesus." Thereby the pericope not only speaks about the nature of discipleship (cf. 9:23; 14:27—taking the cross and following Jesus), but also about who Jesus is (*archēgos,* pioneer, leader, one who goes before and opens the way for others to follow—cf. 19:28; Acts 3:15; 5:31; also Heb 2:10; 12:2). Jesus has gone before the disciples (19:28); they are to follow after him in the way he has opened. Simon is a symbol for disciples who share Jesus' trials (22:28). The NT sometimes refers to Jesus as an example (e.g., John 13:15; 1 Pet 2:21), as does this book; whenever this is done the term is intended in the sense of this leader-follower pattern. This picture of Jesus sets the stage for what follows.

In vss. 32–56 Jesus' way is described in terms of both horizontal and vertical relationships. In his horizontal relations with others Jesus' innocence is accented. In his vertical relationship with the Father, Jesus' obedience is highlighted. Though these threads often run together in the narrative, one does not truly perceive Jesus' way unless both are seen. The one who as a lad "increased . . . in favor with God and man" (2:52) now ends his career with the emphasis on just those two relationships. The implication throughout is that the one so described is intended to function as a model for the disciples who follow him. The pattern can be anticipated as one reads the following paragraphs.

Luke 23:32–43 records Jesus' crucifixion among the transgressors (22:37), together with a variety of responses to the event. Several components of the narrative stand out. (1) Although vs. 34a, "And Jesus said, 'Father, forgive them, for they know not what they do,'" is omitted by many manuscripts, it is almost certainly a legitimate part of the text. The language and thought are Lukan (Father—10:21; 11:2; 22:42; 23:46; forgive because of ignorance—Acts 3:17; 13:27; intercede for executioners—Acts 7:60). Also sayings of Jesus are found in each main section of the crucifixion narrative (23:28–31, 43, 46). If one were missing here the pattern would be disturbed. It could have been omitted because either it was believed to have conflicted with vss. 28–31 or it was thought that the events of A.D. 66–70 showed it was not answered. The prayer seems to echo Isa 53:12: "he . . . made intercession for the transgressors." In so doing Jesus was modeling what he had taught (6:27–28; 17:14): he not only taught God's will but was also obedient to it.

(2) The responses of the rulers (vs. 35), the soldiers (vss. 36–37), and one of the criminals crucified with him (vs. 39) combine to form a threefold temptation of the crucified Jesus much like the earlier threefold temptation in the wilderness (4:1–13): "If you are the Christ, the king, save yourself." Though Jesus' power was still with him (22:51), as in the wilderness, he refused to use it for himself even to save his life. This episode needs to be set in the context of the overall development of Jesus' career. The temptation in the wilderness (4:1–13) followed his empowering by the Holy Spirit after his baptism and in response to his prayer (3:21–22; cf. 4:16–21). Then the question was whether or not Jesus would use the divine power for his own benefit, for his self-aggrandisement, or for the advancement of his cause. By a Spirit-directed use of scripture Jesus overcame the temptation. Thereafter his power was used for the benefit of others. The temptation on the cross (23:35–39) comes near the climax of Jesus' career which began at 9:18. Since then Jesus has been walking the way of rejection, suffering, and now death. It is a way that perfects his obedience to God by stripping him of every possible idolatrous attachment. Now at the end, hanging on the cross, his life ebbing away, the same question is raised again: Will you use the divine power with which you are endowed for self-preservation? The final attachment in this world to which one is tempted to cling in an idolatrous way is life itself, mere continuance of physical existence: "If you are the Christ, the king, save yourself." The crucified criminal adds, "and us" (vs. 39). The crucified Jesus will not cling even to physical existence and thereby make it an idolatrous attachment. He is obedient unto death (Phil 2:8). He is willing to die rather than sin (i.e., be an idolator). In this his obedience is perfected (Heb 5:8–9; 1 Pet 4:1–2).

(3) The second criminal crucified with Jesus responded differently, he accepted his punishment as justified, an expression of penitence if taken in a Jewish context (vss. 41–42), pronounced Jesus innocent (vs. 41b), and said, "Jesus, remember me when you come in your kingly power" (vs. 42). The plea is to be acknowledged by Jesus at the parousia (9:26; 12:8–9; 18:8b; 19:15; 21:27, 36b), but Jesus responded, "Truly, I say to you, today you will be with me in Paradise" (vs. 43), promising immediate bliss. Paradise originally meant a garden or park such as a king would possess. In intertestamental Judaism it was used of the realm reserved for the righteous dead (Levi 18:10). In 2 Cor 12:4; Rev 2:7 it refers to the realm of bliss in heaven. Luke would regard it as being synonymous with being "in Abraham's bosom" (16:22). He has an interest in individual eschatology, that is, in what happens to a person at death (e.g., 12:4–5, 16–21; 16:19–31; 23:43; Acts 7:55–60), a concern with roots in ancient Judaism. The Apocalypse of Abraham 21 says the righteous dead proceed straight to Paradise where they enjoy heavenly fruits and blessedness, while the wicked dead go immediately to the underworld. 1 Enoch (60:8, 23; 61:12; 70:4) indicates the righteous already dwell in the garden of life. Paul apparently accepted this notion (e.g., 2 Cor 5:8; Phil 1:23), as does Luke-Acts. The exchange indicates that the martyrdom of Jesus performed an evangelistic function which is best understood against the background of ancient thinking about martyrdom.

Any appreciation for the Lukan understanding of Jesus' martyrdom must come from a knowledge of pagan, Jewish, and early Christian attitudes towards martyrdom. With pagans, on the one hand, martyrdom was regarded positively in many circles in antiquity. (a) It was a commonplace that true philosophers lived their doctrine as well as expounded it. The philosopher's word alone, unaccompanied by the act, was regarded as invalid (e.g., Seneca, *Epistle,* 52:8–9; Dio Chrysostom, *Discourse,* 70:6). Some very harsh things were said about philosophers' sincerity—or lack of it—in antiquity. Josephus (*Against Apion,* 1:8) exaggerated when he said no Greek philosopher would ever die for his philosophy. The same sentiments are found, however, in Lucian (*The Fisherman,* 31): "in their life and actions . . . they contradicted their outward appearance and reversed [philosophy's] practice." Epictetus (*Discourses,* 1:29:56) says, "what, then, is the thing lacking now? The man . . . to bear witness to the arguments by his acts." Seneca (*Epistle,* 23:15) joins the chorus: "there is a very disgraceful charge often brought against our school—that we deal with the words, and not the deeds, of philosophy." In view of this cyncism about philosophers' sincerity, sometimes only the willingness to die or actual death could validate a philosopher's profession.

The *Life of Secundus the Silent Philosopher* furnishes an example of a philosopher's sealing his profession with his willingness to die. Secundus, because of an incident that had caused his mother's suicide, put a ban on himself, resolving not to say anything for the rest of his life—having chosen the Pythagorean way of life. The Emperor Hadrian arrived in Athens and sent for Secundus to test him. When Secundus refused to speak, Hadrian sent him off with the executioner with instructions that if he did speak his head should be cut off; if he did not speak, he should be returned to the Emperor. When he was returned to Hadrian after having been willing to die for his vow of silence, Secundus was allowed to write answers to the twenty questions asked by the Emperor—which answers were then put in the sacred library. His willingness to die had validated his philosophy.

(b) The sealing of one's profession in death as a martyr sometimes issued in furthering the cause of the philosopher. Plato's *Apology* tells the story of Socrates' death. In chapter 39 Socrates says, "I would fain prophesy to you; for I am about to die, and that is the time when men are gifted with prophetic power. And I prophesy to you who are my murderers, that immediately after my death punishment far heavier than you have inflicted upon me will surely await you." What is meant in the context is that there will be more accusers than there are now: his position vindicated by death, Socrates' disciples will attack the Athenians as never before.

On the other hand, Greco-Roman teachers warned that martyrdom does not provide certain results; it may win some but not necessarily others (Lucian, *Peregrinus*, 13; Marcus Aurelius, 11:3:2). Above all, as noted above, martyrdom that was sought was regarded as lust for death and was not persuasive (Seneca, *Epistle*, 24:25).

The view of martyrdom in ancient Judaism had similarities to the Greco-Roman stance though there were also differences. On the one side, there was a positive attitude toward martyrdom. (a) Two streams of thought ran parallel. One stream spoke of the prophets dying as martyrs at the hands of God's people (e.g., *Lives of the Prophets; Martyrdom of Isaiah;* cf. also Matt 23:31–39; Heb 11:36ff.; 1 Thes 2:15; Mark 12:1–12). The emphasis is on the sinfulness of God's people (cf.

Luke 13:33–34; Acts 7:52). The other stream spoke of the faithful among God's people dying as martyrs at the hands of the Gentiles. Here, as in Greco-Roman paganism, it was believed the true prophet sealed the truth of his testimony with death. In 4 Maccabees 7 the aged scribe Eleazer refused to eat swine's flesh as demanded by the Syrians or even to pretend to eat it (cf. 2 Mac 6:18ff.). Instead he endured willingly the scourge, the rack, and the flame (2 Mac 7:4). 4 Mac 7:15 cries out, "O life faithful to the Law and perfected by the seal of death."

(b) Sometimes the martyr's actions made converts to Judaism. One tradition (b. Abodah Zarah, 18a) tells of Rabbi Hanina ben Teradion who, in the time of Hadrian, was arrested for teaching Torah to groups. As a punishment he was burned to death. After watching, the executioner then threw himself into the fire, whereupon a *bath qol* exclaimed, "Rabbi Haninah and the executioner have been assigned to the world to come."

On the other hand, as we have seen, Jewish teachers give the same types of cautions about martyrdom found in Greco-Roman paganism: martyrdom is no guarantee of another's conversion (e.g., 2 Mac 6:29). Above all, overeagerness for martyrdom is denounced as self-annihilation (e.g., Genesis Rabbah 82).

Ancient Christianity was deeply indebted to both pagan and Jewish views about martyrdom. On the one hand, there was a positive attitude towards martyrdom. Like pagans and Jews, most Chrisitans believed the truth of their profession must be sealed in blood if it came to that (e.g., Revelation; Justin, *Apology II*, 12). Only some Gnostics refused to undergo martyrdom (e.g., Irenaeus, *Against Heresies,* 1:24:3–6— Basilides; Tertullian, *Against All Heresies,* 1—Basilides). Christians, even more than pagans and Jews, believed martyrdom had "evangelistic" benefits: it helped to spread the gospel. Justin, *Dialogue,* 110, says, "the more we are persecuted, the more do others in ever-increasing numbers embrace the faith." Tertullian, *Apology,* 50, agrees: "we conquer in dying. . . . The oftener we are mown down by you, the more in number we grow; the blood of Christians is seed." The Epistle to Diognetus 6:9 says, "Christians when they are punished increase the more in number every day." In 7:7–8, it proclaims, "Can you not see them thrown to wild beasts, to make them deny their Lord, and yet not overcome? Do you not see that the more of them are punished, the more numerous the others become?" Lactantius (d. c. A.D. 325), *Di-*

vine Institutes, 5:19, says, "It is right reason, then, to defend religion by patience or death in which faith is preserved and is pleasing to God himself, and it adds authority to religion."

On the other hand, Christians also shared the pagan and Jewish reservations about martyrdom: martyrdom, while very persuasive, was certainly not a proof. (Cf. *The Acts of the Christian Martyrs,* ed. H. Musurillo [Oxford: Clarendon Press, 1972], passim.) Overeagerness for martyrdom was denounced (e.g., *Martyrdom of Polycarp,* 4). Not only did such a lust for death violate the Christian belief that life belonged to God, it also detracted from the persuasiveness of the act.

The narrative of Jesus' death in the third gospel comes alive against this background: Jesus did not die because of a lust for death (cf. 22:42); he sought to avoid it, if God would permit it. In dying he legitimated his profession as he sealed it with his blood. He was absolutely sincere in his stance. This legitimation is evidenced in the conversion of the criminal on the cross: Jesus' martyrdom had such evangelistic benefits (cf. Acts 8:1, 4; 11:19ff. for the evangelistic benefits of Stephen's martyrdom). Such a death is persuasive because it testifies to a selfless commitment.

That the one who was converted was a crucified criminal means that this story fits into the motif of Jesus' mediating forgiveness to the outcasts of society (5:29ff.; 7:36ff.; 15:1–2; 18:9–14; 19:1–10). That the conversion and its confirmation by Jesus come before Jesus dies means that this story fits into the theme that it is the Jesus who lives— whether in his earthly life or after his resurrection, e.g., Acts 5:31— who grants forgiveness. Though the evangelist has no doctrine of forgiveness being made available through the death of Jesus, as do Paul and others, he does see forgiveness mediated by the Jesus who lived and who lives. The death of Jesus in Luke-Acts is his rejection by the leaders of Israel. The Passion narrative in the gospel is basically a rejection story, very much like the stories about Stephen and Paul in Acts. Jesus dies as a martyr and his blood does seal a new covenant (22:20), but it is not an atoning sacrifice.

(4) Luke 23:44–56 tells of Jesus' death and burial. Several facts stand out in the account of Jesus' death (vss. 44–49). (a) From noon until three o'clock there was darkness (cf. Amos 8:9). In the Greco-Roman mentality events with cosmic significance were attested by cosmic signs (e.g., Lucan, *Civil War,* 7:199–200, says that at the battle of Pharsalia the "sorrowing deity in heaven gave notice of the battle by the dimness and obscurity of the sun"). This was a time of the power of darkness

(22:53). (b) When Jesus dies, it is with the uniquely Lukan words, "Father, into thy hands I commit my spirit" (vs. 46), an echo of Ps 31:5. Absent are the words, "My God, my God, why hast thou forsaken me?" (Matt 27:46 // Mark 15:34). Jesus dies quietly, full of trust, a model for Christian martyrs to follow (Acts 7:59). This calm assurance in God at the moment of his death was enough to convince the centurion of Jesus' innocence. Unlike Matt 27:54 // Mark 15:39, who have the centurion say, "Truly this man was the Son of God," Luke's guard says, "Certainly this man was innocent" (vs. 47—*dikaios*). Whereas in the other synoptics the centurion was a christologist, in Luke he is an apologist. (c) Verse 49 proclaims that the Galileans witness Jesus' death. These people who will be present throughout the Passion events to guarantee their facticity (cf. 23:55; 24:10; 24:33ff.; Acts 1:11) are those "with Jesus" who will function as a control for what develops after the resurrection. Here we have it affirmed: Jesus really died.

Luke's account of the burial of Jesus by Joseph of Arimathea (vss. 50–56) has two significant variations from the story in Matthew and Mark furnishing clues to its main function in the gospel. First, in vs. 51, Luke says Joseph "had not consented to their purpose and deed." In other words, Joseph was a member of the Sanhedrin who thought Jesus was innocent. The declaration of Jesus' innocence has been a dominant thread in Luke 23: (a) Pilate—vs. 4; (b) Herod—vs. 15; (c) Pilate—vs. 14; (d) Pilate—vs. 22; (e) one of the crucified criminals—vs. 41; (f) the centurion—vs. 47; and now (g) Joseph of Arimathea—vs. 51—becomes Luke's final human witness to the innocence of Jesus. Second, in vs. 55, the evangelist not only indicates that some women saw where Jesus was buried but also specifies that they were those who had come with him from Galilee (cf. 8:1–3) and that they saw how his body was laid. In the Jerusalem events the evangelist is concerned to establish the corporeality of the one who dies, is buried, is raised, and ascends—hence the reference to Jesus' body. Luke is concerned to guarantee both the corporeality of the church's Lord and the continuity between the one who dies in Jerusalem and the one who worked in Galilee by having the Galileans present as witnesses to the Jerusalem events. Theologically this means that the one who was empowered is the one who dies. The death, moreover, is a real one. It was through the suffering of these things that Jesus' obedience was perfected. It was only on the other side of these sufferings that the empowered one entered into glory.

VICTORY, PRESENCE, AND MISSION

23:56b—24:53; 9:10-17

Luke 24 is, with one exception, composed of materials not found elsewhere in the synoptic tradition. The chapter consists of five major events (two empty tomb episodes; two major appearances; Jesus' departure) located in Jerusalem or its environs, which transpire on one long day (early morning on the first day of the week, 24:1; that same day, 24:13; that same hour, 24:33; then, 24:50). When one notes the Galilean orientation of the appearances in Matt 28:7, 10, 16-20; Mark 16:7; John 21, this exclusive focus on Jerusalem is seen as distinctive (cf. 24:47-49; Acts 1:4). The chapter as a whole is held together by an inclusion (23:56b; 24:53), both the introductory and concluding statements averring that Jesus' disciples are loyal, pious Jews (cf. 2:21ff.; Acts 3:1ff.; 5:12). There are at least three overriding functions of the resurrection chapter.

The first overriding function is to state the nature of Jesus' victory over death. The evangelist's view can only be grasped if seen in the context of early Christian understanding of Jesus' resurrection and the Lukan understanding of Jesus as a prototype of Christian existence. On the one hand, in earliest Christianity the resurrection of Jesus encompassed three different realities: (1) Jesus' victory over death; (2) his removal from human time and space into another dimension (that of God); and (3) his new function as cosmic Lord.

In Luke-Acts the unity of these three realities is broken and they become three separate events on a chronological time line. (1) The resurrection of Jesus is reduced to the reality of his victory over death. (2) The ascension becomes Jesus' removal to heaven. (3) The exaltation designates the moment of Jesus' new status as Lord and Christ. It may be said that this division of a unity into its parts, when done by Luke, is for "the sake of analysis": by taking the different pieces of a whole individually, the evangelist can focus on the meaning of each without distraction. This means, however, that in Luke-Acts the resurrection of Jesus refers only to Jesus' victory over death.

On the other hand, Jesus functions as a prototype of Christian existence. As we have seen, he is the pioneer who goes before, opening the Way for his disciples to follow. His existence, then, is a model for what his followers may expect. Given this, if Luke speaks about the nature of Jesus' victory over death, it must be taken as a comment about the nature of the victory over death for which Christians hope also. Against this double background we may investigate the resurrection traditions of Luke 24.

Both the first empty tomb tradition and the second appearance story witness to the corporeality of the risen Christ. (1) Luke 24:1–11 tells of the women finding the tomb empty (cf. Matt 28:1–10 // Mark 16:1–8), and has some emphases all its own. First, the evangelist emphasizes the priority of the women's own experience over the angels' words. Luke contrasts what the women found (the stone rolled away) with what they did not find (the body of Jesus). The focus on the absence of the body refers back to the women's observance of how Jesus' body was laid in the tomb (23:55). It is also echoed in a Lukan notice in the Emmaus account (24:23, "did not find his body"). The two angels' words (Luke 9:30; Acts 1:10) simply interpret the empirical data: "Why do you seek the living among the dead?[peculiar to Luke] He is not here but has risen" (24:5). Whatever the nature of Jesus' victory over death was, it involved the absence of his body from the tomb.

Such an assertion is buttressed in three ways by Luke. First, he mentions by name (vs. 10) the women who witnessed the absence of the body of Jesus, echoing the named ones at 8:1–3. This serves to link the Jerusalem witnesses to the career of Jesus from the very first— the same Galileans witnessed his burial in 23:55 and his crucifixion in 23:49 (cf. Acts 1:22; 10:37–41). These women told the disciples, the Eleven and "all the rest" (vs. 9; cf. 24:33), referring to those who were present so as to be qualified to be apostles (Acts 1:15–26) (J. Plevnik, "The Eleven and Those with Them according to Luke," *Catholic Biblical Quarterly* 40:205–11 [1978]): Galilean witnesses attest the absence of the body of Jesus from the tomb. Second, 24:12, if original, offers another empty tomb episode. The trend of recent research is to accept this verse as integral to the gospel (J. E. Alsup, *The Post-Resurrection Appearance Stories of the Gospel Tradition* [Stuttgart: Calver Verlag, 1975], p. 103): the style is Lukan, vs. 24 appears to be a cross-reference to vs. 12. It could have been omitted because it was thought to contradict vs. 34, but if it is accepted as part of the original text, then vs. 12 would function as a second witness to support the testimony of the women in 24:1–11 (cf. Num 35:30; Deut 17:6f.; 19:15; b. Sotah 2b; b. Sanhedrin 37b; b. Baba Bathra 31b; CD 9:16—10:3; Luke 23:1–16; 24:4; 2:25–38). The evangelist produces two sets of witnesses to the empty tomb (cf. 24:22–24). Given Jewish assumptions, the witness of the men would have been needed: Josephus (*Antiquities*, 4:8:15§219) says, "From women let not evidence be accepted, because of the levity and temerity of their sex" (cf. Mishna, *Rosh Hashana*, 1:8). In order to be persuasive in a Jewish context, the second episode was necessary to buttress the first. Third, 24:12 also aims to discredit any theory about the theft of the body as an explanation for the absence of Jesus' body: "He saw the linen cloths by themselves" (cf. Matt 28:11ff.; John 20:1ff. for similar concerns). In these three ways this gospel supports the tradition of the absence of Jesus' body from the tomb; it is a part of Luke's way of celebrating Jesus' victory over death.

(2) Luke 24:36–43 tells of an appearance of Jesus to the Eleven in Jerusalem; this also functions to establish the corporeality of the risen Christ (cf. 1 John 1:1; John 20:24–29). When Jesus appeared the disciples supposed they saw a spirit. The story combats such a belief with physical proof of two kinds: First, Jesus says, "See my hands and feet, that it is I myself; handle me, and see; for a spirit has not flesh and bones as you see that I have" (vs. 39; cf. 1 John 1:1–2); then he said to them, "Have you anything here to eat?" Luke adds, "They gave him a piece of broiled fish, and he took it and ate before them" (vss. 41–43; cf. Acts 1:4; 10:41). The significance of this action for the Jewish mind is clear: angels do not eat (e.g., Tob 12:19; Josephus, *Antiquities*, 1:9:2§197; Philo, *On Abraham*, 118). Only human beings eat. For Luke the risen Lord, no less than the pre-Easter Jesus, was flesh and bones, corporeal, truly human. The risen Jesus not only eats, he also can be seen (presumably even the wounds in his hands and feet) and touched.

These two stories say the same thing about the nature of Jesus' victory over death: it is not to be understood as an escape from this perishable frame but as a transformation of it; it is not to be understood as a transformation into a purely spiritual, angelic being, because Jesus remained flesh and bones, though immortal and not limited by time and space (24:31); it is no more the immortality of the soul while his body decayed than it is the survival of his shade (a pale shadow of the life on earth, cf. 1 Sam 28:8ff.). These views are presupposed in Paul's discussion of the Christians' resurrection in 1 Corinthians 15: "With what kind of body do they come?" (vs. 35b). Luke's answer is very much the same as Paul's, except he does not give an analytical answer, but gives his reply in the form of a narrative of the risen Christ who is understood as the prototype of Christian existence. In Luke 24 one sees the nature of Jesus' victory over death: it is the same victory for which his disciples hope (1 John 3:2).

The second overriding function of Luke 24 is to clarify the nature of the Eucharist, at least for the Lukan community. Proper appreciation of this appearance story comes only when we set it against the larger background of Jesus' meals in Luke-Acts. Jesus is frequently involved in meals: (1) with sinners (5:29–32; 15:1–2; 19:5–7); (2) with Pharisees (7:36–50; 11:37ff.; 14:1ff.); (3) with disciples (22:19–20; 24:30; 24:41–43; Acts 1:4—the term is literally "to take salt with someone" but the Latin, Syriac, and Coptic translations read, "to eat together"; Acts 10:41); (4) with the multitudes and disciples (9:11–17). Three of the meals in which the earthly and risen Jesus is involved mention the breaking of bread (9:11–17; 22:19–20; 24:30).

The first of these, Luke 9:10–17, echoes earlier elements in the narrative. In 1:53 Mary sings in celebration of the miraculous conception of Jesus and of the recognition of him as Lord by Elizabeth and by the yet unborn John: "He has filled the hungry with good things." This is doubtless the equivalent of the prophetic perfect in Hebrew, an utterance of such certainty that its content can be spoken of as already having happened. In 6:21 Jesus says, "Blessed are you that hunger now, for you shall be satisfied." Luke 9:10–17 picks up this theme and portrays Jesus as the one who satisfies the hungry, feeding them through his apostles.

That the symbolism of Jesus as the one who satisfies the hungry was intended by the evangelist is shown by Luke's location of the incident. While Matt 14:13 // Mark 6:31 locate the feeding in a lonely place (cf. Luke 9:12), Luke specifies Bethsaida, a main city of Philip's tetrarchy, located on the northern end of the lake across the Jordan from Herod's jurisdiction. Like the reference to the land of the Gerasenes (8:26), this location is geographically awkward because the feeding story demands a lonely place (9:12) rather than an urban area, but the use of the name Bethsaida is for its symbolic value—the name means "place of satisfaction." Luke 9:17 reinforces the point when it tells us that as a result of the feeding "all were satisfied." Again, Jesus is the one who satisfies the hungry.

In Acts we hear that the church was involved in breaking bread (2:42; 2:46; 20:7; 27:33–36—all but the last text in the setting of Christian worship). Since there are evidences of cultic meals in early Christianity with only bread and no mention of wine (e.g., Acts of John 106–10; Acts of Thomas 27, 49–50, 133), or with bread and salt (e.g., Pseudo-Clementines, *Recognitions* 4; *Homilies* 14:7), this seems to be the Lukan terminology for the Eucharist in Acts (P. H. Menoud, "The Acts of the Apostles and the Eucharist," in *Jesus Christ and the Faith,* trans. E. M. Paul [Pittsburgh: Pickwick Press, 1978], 84–106). If so, then for Luke's community the Eucharist is the cultic extension of the multiplication of the loaves and of the Last Supper, the continuation of the fellowship meals Jesus had with his disciples during his earthly life, done as a memorial of Jesus the martyr in obedience to his command (22:19). Such meals doubtless anticipated the messianic banquet (13:29; 14:15). It is in this context that 24:13–33, a resurrection appearance at mealtime where ritual actions are repeated, is to be understood. This story functions as a bridge between the meals of the earthly Jesus and the breaking of bread in the narrative of Acts.

In 24:30 the risen Christ "took bread and blessed, and broke it, and gave it to them." This action also echoes previous meals (9:16; 22:19). Although earlier they had been kept from recognizing him (vs. 16), now the disciples' eyes are opened and they do recognize him (vs. 31a; cf. Heb 6:4 where "enlightened" is an image of conversion; Mark 10:46–52; John 9). The table fellowship which was interrupted by Jesus' death is here resumed at the risen Jesus' initiative. Hereafter, the disciples will go on doing this in remembrance of him (22:19). That the evangelist wanted his readers to recognize the eucharistic overtones seems confirmed by the ending of the unit in vs. 35: "Then they told what had happened on the road, and how he was known to them in the breaking of the bread." This incident, moreover, is but one of several occasions when the risen Jesus ate with his followers (Acts 1:4; 10:41). This story not only serves as a bridge between the meals the earthly Jesus had with his disciples and the later church's Eucharist, it also says that at such meals the presence of the risen Lord was known: Jesus is alive and one place of his recognition is at the breaking of the bread.

The distinctiveness of this understanding of the Eucharist may be seen when it is compared with that of the fourth gospel and of Paul. In the fourth gospel the Eucharist is the cultic extension of the incarnation: through its physical elements one experiences contact with the divine world just as one did through the flesh of Jesus in the days of his incarnation (cf. John 6). In Paul the Lord's Supper is the moment in which one remembers (identifies with, participates in) Jesus' death much as the Israelites-Jews remembered (participated in) the events of the Exodus at their Passover meal (cf. 1 Corinthians 11). Luke sees the Supper as the extension of the meals with the earthly Jesus and in anticipation of the messianic banquet, a meal at which one experiences the presence of Christ as the disciples did after the resurrection.

The third overriding function of Luke 24 is to underscore the mission command of the risen Christ. Three components deserve attention. (1) The command itself is found in 24:46–48: "Thus it is written, that the Christ should suffer and on the third day rise from the dead, and that repentance and forgiveness of sins should be preached in his name to all nations, beginning from Jerusalem. You are witnesses of these things." The evangelist thinks that after Jesus' resurrection his trial is reopened and fresh evidence is presented by the apostles to get the Jews to change their verdict. The new evidence is the event of Jesus' resurrection. The condemnation of Christ had been done in ignorance (Acts 3:17; 13:27), but in raising Jesus God showed the Jews they had made a mistake: they had crucified the Christ (Acts 2:36). Now, however, the Jews are given a chance to change their minds, to repent (2:38; 3:19; 5:31). If they do not, then they themselves will be cut off from the people of God (Acts 3:22–23). The witnesses are to press for this decision (Allison Trites, *The New Testament Concept of Witness* [Cambridge: Cambridge University Press, 1977], 129–30). What is to begin in Jerusalem, however, is to be carried to all nations (cf. Acts 1:8).

(2) The authority for the mission command is twofold. On the one hand, the one who gives it speaks a compelling word. Twice in this chapter there is a reference to words spoken by the pre-Easter Jesus which have been fulfilled in the events of the Passion-resurrection. In vs. 6 the angels say, "Remember how he told you, *while he was still*

in Galilee, that the Son of Man must be delivered into the hands of sinful men, and be crucified, and on the third day rise." The reference is to the predictions in 9:22, 44 (cf. 17:25; 18:32–33). What Jesus prophesied has been fulfilled. In vs. 44 is a similar motif: "These are my words which I spoke to you, *while I was still with you,* that everything written about me . . . must be fulfilled." The events of Luke 22–24 have fulfilled Jesus' prophetic words. In the Lukan world, as we have noted, both pagans and Jews believed that the fulfillment of prophecy legitimated authority. Hence, if Jesus' words have been fulfilled, he is a true prophet who speaks with authority. This is the one who gives the mission command. On the other hand, vss. 46–47 not only indicate that the Christ's Passion is a fulfillment of scripture but so is the mission to Israel and the nations: the authoritative writings reinforce the mission command, understood as a divine necessity. This twofold emphasis upon the fulfillment of prophecy serves to give the authority for the new outreach by the disciples. Matt 28:16–20, the great commission, also gives a mission directive and underscores it with authority but in a different way: the Matthean Jesus says, "All authority has been given to me." By virtue of his resurrection-exaltation he rules over the cosmos. In Luke-Acts the exaltation comes later (Acts 2:36), so here the risen Christ appeals to the authority of fulfilled prophecy for his missionary directive.

(3) Jesus does not just give his mission command and then leave its accomplishment to his followers. He makes two provisions for his witnesses. On the one hand, the witnesses are to stay in Jerusalem until they are "clothed with power from on high" (24:49; cf. Acts 1:4–5; 1:8; 2:1ff.). Part of the reason for this rests in the Lukan belief that a valid testimony to Christ requires two prominent witnesses, in accordance with Deut 19:15, namely, the witness of the apostles and the witness of the Holy Spirit (cf. Acts 5:32—"we are witnesses to these things, and so is the Holy Spirit"). In part it is due to the belief that God has the initiative in salvation history so that what human beings do must be done in response to the divine leading and empowering. The gift of the Holy Spirit supplies that power and leading. The pentecostal gift of the Spirit is Jesus' first provision for his followers who are given a missionary directive. In Lukan theology this is prototypical: there is no evangelistic outreach without a prior empowering.

On the other hand, Jesus does not leave his disciples until he has put them under the protection of God. Luke 24:5–53 is a departure scene that takes place at night of the same Easter day. The evangelist often describes the departure of supernatural beings (1:38; 2:15; 9:33; 24:31, Acts 10:7; 12:10). This was a common motif among both pagan (Euripides, *Orestia,* 1496; Virgil, *Aeneid,* 9:657) and Jewish peoples (Gen 17:22; 35:13; Judg 6:21; 13:20; Tob 12:20f.; 2 Mac 3:34). Luke uses the typical departure motif to speak of Jesus' ascension into heaven: "He parted from them and was carried up into heaven" (vs. 51a). The inclusion of the words "and was carried up into heaven" is supported by the manuscript evidence, by Acts 1:2's recapitulation of what has been described in the gospel, and by the long ending of Mark (16:19f.), which seems to reflect a knowledge of the longer text here in Luke. Jesus did not leave his followers, however, until he first had blessed them: "While he blessed them, he parted from them" (vs. 51a). This act of blessing is like that of the high priest, Simon, in Sir 50:19–20. With a priestly act the risen Jesus puts his disciples under the protection of God before he leaves them (cf. Matt 28:20, "and lo, I am with you to the end of the Age; John 17:9–19). Just as the gospel began with the ministry of the priest Zechariah, so it ends with Jesus acting as priest for his flock (cf. Heb 2:17; 3:1; 6:19–20).

EXCURSUS A:
THE FULFILLMENT OF
PROPHECY IN LUKE-ACTS

The theme of the fulfillment of prophecy plays a major role in the Lukan narrative. Prophecy is understood in the sense of a prediction of things to come. Fulfillment means what was predicted has happened or is believed to have happened. Fulfilled prophecy in the Lukan narrative comes from three types of sources: (1) from the Jewish scriptures; (2) from a living prophet; (3) from a heavenly being. We will examine examples in each of these categories.

(1) OT prophecy. Two examples should suffice. (a) 4:16–21 says Jesus went into the synagogue at Nazareth, read from Isa 61:1–2; 58:6, and then said, "Today this scripture has been fulfilled in your hearing." The prophecy of Isaiah has been fulfilled in the narrative about Jesus' ministry. (b) Acts 13: 16–41 reports a speech by Paul in the synagogue at Antioch of Pisidia. Verse 23 says of David's posterity, "God has brought to Israel a Savior, Jesus, *as he promised.*" Verses 27, 29 continue the theme: "For those who live in Jerusalem and their rulers, because they did not recognize him nor understand the utterances of the prophets which are read every sabbath, fulfilled these by condemning him" (vs. 27). "And when they had fulfilled all that was written of him, they took him down from the tree . . ." (vs. 29). Verses 32–33 give the climax: "And we bring you the good news that what God promised to the fathers, this he fulfilled to us their children by raising Jesus; as also it is written in the second psalm. . . ." These two examples show Luke believed the career of Jesus fulfilled the prophecies of the Jewish scriptures.

(2) Prophecy of a living prophet. (a) Sometimes the living prophet is Jewish. For example, in 1:67–79 Zechariah prophesies. Part of what he says is about the future of his son, John the Baptist: "And you,

child, will be called the *prophet* of the Most High; for you will go before the Lord to *prepare his ways*" (vs. 76). Jesus asks, "What then did you go out to see? A *prophet?*" and answers, "Yes, I tell you, and more than a prophet. This is he of whom it is written, 'Behold, I send my messenger before thy face, who shall *prepare thy way* before thee'" (7:26–27). (b) At other times the living prophet is the earthly Jesus. Numerous examples present themselves. In 9:22, 44; 18:31–33 Jesus predicts his passion, which is fulfilled in the narrative of Luke 22—24. Jesus prophecies in 11:13 that the Father will give the Holy Spirit to those who ask him: this is fulfilled in the narrative of Acts 2:1ff. In 13:35b Jesus says the Jews will not see him until they say, "Blessed is he who comes in the name of the Lord," a prediction fulfilled at 19:38. Jesus says in 19:29–31 his disciples will find the desired colt in an opposite village and tells them what will be asked of them and how to answer: vss. 32–34 tell the fulfillment of his words. Luke 21:15 predicts that when the disciples are called upon to give testimony, they will be given "wisdom, which none of your adversaries will be able to withstand or contradict": This is fulfilled in the episode of Stephen in Acts 6:10. In 22:10–12 Jesus tells the disciples how to find the room where they will celebrate the Passover: it happened as he had told them in vs. 13. Jesus predicts Peter's denial (22:34), a prophecy fulfilled in 22:54–61. (c) On still other occasions the living prophet is a Christian. In Acts 11:27–28a Agabus predicts a famine: we hear that it occurred in vs. 28b. In Acts 21:10–11 Agabus predicts that Paul will be bound by the Jews and this is fulfilled in the narrative which follows. Paul predicts in Acts 27:22, 34 that no lives will be lost because of the storm at sea: vs. 44 says all escaped to land.

(3) Prophecy of a heavenly being. (a) Sometimes it is an angel who prophesies. In 1:13 the angel of the Lord tells Zechariah he will have a son: this prediction is fulfilled at 1:57, 63. An angel in 1:26–27, 31 tells Mary she will bear a son: in the narrative of 2:7, 21 this is fulfilled. In 2:8–12 the angel tells the shepherds they will find the babe wrapped in swaddling clothes and lying in a manger: they find this in 2:15–16. Acts 27:23–24 has an angel appear to Paul and tell him he will survive the storm at sea and will stand before Caesar: Paul escapes from the sea and ultimately arrives in Rome. (b) At other times the risen Christ makes predictions. In Luke 24:49 and Acts 1:4–5 he promises the gift of the Spirit, which is granted in Acts 2. He tells the disciples in Acts 1:8 that after their empowering they will be witnesses

to the ends of the earth: the rest of the narrative of Acts, of course, shows this to be true. In Acts 18:9–10 the Lord appears to Paul in a vision to promise him protection in Corinth: Acts 18:12–17 shows the fulfillment of this prophecy.

Whether it is a prophecy made in the OT by a living prophet or by a heavenly being, the evangelist takes pains to show its fulfillment in the course of his narrative. The question arises as to how this motif would have been understood by Luke's readers. In order to answer it is necessary to explore briefly the functions of prophecy in the Mediterranean world, both pagan and Jewish.

The notion that a divine necessity controls human history, shaping the course of its events, was a widespread belief in Mediterranean antiquity. (a) Polybius (b. 208 B.C.) realized early in his career that Roman power was irresistible. As a Stoic he believed the Roman order was part of a divine providence that ruled the world. This belief was expounded in his *Histories*. In I:4:1–2 he says, "Fortune (*hē tychē*) having guided almost all the affairs of the world in one direction and having forced them to incline towards one and the same end, a historian should bring before his readers under one synoptical view the operations by which she has accomplished her general purpose." (b) Josephus shared in this cultural belief, but as a Jew viewed the divine necessity as deriving from the personal will of a god who is a living person, not a neutral force. So, in *Antiquities* 10:8:2–33, 42, he tells of Jeremiah's prophecy of the fall of Jerusalem being fulfilled and says these events manifest the nature of God, "which foretells all which must (*dei*) take place, duly at the appointed hour." Pagan and Hellenistic Jew alike thought of history as unfolding according to a divine necessity or compulsion which could be expressed in terms of *dei* or *deon esti*. It was in these terms that Luke's language about the *dei* of events would have been understood (cf. 2:49; 4:43; 12:12; 13:14; 15:32; 18:1; 19:5; 22:7, 37).

The concept of history's fulfilling of oracles, whether written or oral, was also a cultural commonplace. Three examples from the pagan world will give a feel for this. (a) Lucian's *Alexander the False Prophet* tells of one Alexander who wanted to start a new religion. As a first step, he and a companion went to Chalcedon and buried bronze tablets which stated that in the near future Asclepios and his father, Apollo, would migrate to Pontus. These tablets were found and the people began building a temple. Alexander then went to Abonutichus, dressed as Perseus, declaiming an oracle which said he was a scion of Perseus. A Sibylline prophecy of his activity was then produced. As a result of one oral and two written prophecies, the stage was set—a new religion could emerge. (b) Suetonius' "Life of Vespasian" contains a section of omens which prophecy his ascendency to emperor. Among them are references not only to Josephus' declaration that he would soon be released by the same man who would then be emperor, but also to antique vases discovered by soothsayers which had on them an alleged image of Vespasian. (c) Apuleius' *Golden Ass* moves to its climax with Lucius trapped in the form of a donkey as a result of his experimentation with magic. Despairing over his plight, he cries to Isis to save him. The goddess appears by night and gives an oracle (11:7), which the next day Lucius follows exactly: he eats the roses that are part of the procession in Isis' honor and is miraculously changed back into a human being. Having been saved from his fate, Lucius is initiated into the Isis cult and says, "I was not deceived by the promise made to me" (11:13). In all three of these pagan examples the fulfillment of the oracle legitimates the religious or political authority of the person to whom the prophecy referred or of the god who gave it. In the strict sense this is proof-from-prophecy: what happened was in line with what the divine realm had revealed prior to the fact.

Three Jewish examples should also suffice. (a) The deuteronomic history (Deuteronomy through 2 Kings) uses the device of prophecy and fulfillment. For example, in Deuteronomy 28 Moses says that if Israel does not keep the covenant and obey the commandments, she will go away into exile (vss. 25, 36–37). In 2 Kings 17 the northern kingdom falls to the Assyrians and the Israelites are taken into bondage: The exile was because of Israel's sins (vs. 7); what was done was "as the Lord spoke by all his servants the prophets" (vs. 23). In 2 Kings 25 the southern kingdom is taken away into Babylonian exile: Moses' prophecy in Deuteronomy 28 is shown to have been fulfilled in the subsequent narrative of 2 Kings. This, in effect, legitimates the other things Moses said in Deuteronomy about how Israel should live. (b) At Qumran was a religious community that believed its own history was the fulfillment of the prophecies of the scriptures. In the commentaries on Isaiah, Micah, Psalm 37, and especially Habakkuk, are statements of the community's position. When it interprets the prophets and the Psalms as prophecies which are fulfilled in the wickedness of Qumran's enemies and in the righteousness of Qumran's covenanters, it is not only saying that the time of fulfillment has come, but also that it is the heir of the promises to Israel, the true people of God. This is in effect an argument for the continuity of the community with Israel of old. (c) Josephus, *Antiquities,* uses the motif of prophecy and its fulfillment as evidence for the providence of God (2:16:5 § 333): in 8:4:2 § 109–10 the fulfillment of David's prophecy makes clear the providence of God; in 1:11:7 § 278–81 the fulfillment of Daniel's prophecies of the destruction of Jerusalem by Antiochus Epiphanes and the Romans is said to demonstrate God's providence (against the Epicureans). The pattern of prophecy-fulfillment in the history of Israel constitutes evidence for belief in a providential God. The providence of God, moreover, consists primarily in his rewarding virtue and punishing vice (H. W. Attridge, *The Interpretation of Biblical History in the Antiquitates Judaicae of Flavious Josephus* [Missoula: Scholars, 1976]).

The Mediterranean mind-set which viewed history as the fulfillment of oracles also held that an oracle could be misunderstood as well as understood. The very act of misunderstanding could be the means by which the prophecy was fulfilled. Herodotus' *History* is a storehouse of examples, with the classic example being his story of Croesus who, after acknowledging the Delphic oracle to be the only true place of divination, asked if he should send an army against the Persians. The oracle replied that if he should send an army, he would destroy a great empire. Mistaking the meaning of the oracle, Croesus went to war against the Perisans and lost. Sending his chains to Delphi, Croesus asked if it were the manner of the Greek gods to be thankless. The priestess replied that the oracle was right. Croesus should have asked whether the god spoke of Croesus' or Cyrus' empire: "But he understood not that which was spoken, nor made further inquiry; wherefore now let him blame himself" (1:91). When Croesus received the answer he confessed the sin was not the god's but his own. The similarity of this way of thinking to Acts 13:27 would not be lost on Luke's original hearers: "those who live in Jerusalem and their rulers, because they did not understand the utterances of the prophets which are read every sabbath, fulfilled these by condemning him." Whether Luke's community was composed of former Jews or pagans—or both—his original readers would have found no surprises in the theme of history's course being determined by the fulfillment of oracles/prophecies.

The functions of a prophecy-fulfillment theme in the Mediterranean world match remarkably well with what we find in Luke-Acts. (a) As the pagan evidence showed prophecy made by a person or about a person, when fulfilled, legitimated the individual's religious or political status. It could evoke conversion to the one whose promise was kept. It is in this way that some prophetic utterances are used in Luke-Acts (e.g., prophecy made by Jesus, when fulfilled, legitimates his authority—Luke 9:22/Luke 22—24; 11:13/Acts 2; 12:11–12/Acts 5:29; prophecy made about Jesus, when fulfilled, legitimates him—Luke 1:31/1:42; 2:7/2:21). (b) As the evidence from the deuteronomic history showed, a prophetic promise, when fulfilled, can serve to legitimate the other things the prophet has said. When Jesus predicts the destruction of the temple (13:35a; 21:6) and the capture of Jerusalem by the Gentiles (19:43–44; 21:20–24; 23:28–31) and Luke's readers know of the events of A.D. 70, or when the risen Lord predicts the Gentile mission (Luke 24:47; Acts 1:8) and his readers are told of the progress of the gospel to Rome, these fulfilled words function to give authority to the other things Jesus said, like his parenetic sayings in 9:51—19:44. (c) As the evidence from Qumran showed, the claim that one's particular history and that of one's founder fulfilled the prophecies of the scriptures argues not only for the arrival of the eschaton but also for one's continuity with the history of Israel. As the heirs of the promises, Christians are the true descendents of Israel of old: the speech in Acts 13:16–41 seems especially emphatic in this regard. The argument emphasizes the continuity between Jesus and the history of ancient Israel, as well as showing his death and resurrection were in accord with the divine will. What we have not yet made clear, however, is exactly how such an argument on behalf of continuity would have been heard by Greek-speaking people, whether Jews or pagans.

It was a cultural commonplace in the Hellenistic age for a people to try to trace its own origins back to the remotest antiquity (e.g., Josephus, *Against Apion*, 2:152; Diodorus, 1:44:4; 1:96:2). This was in large measure due to the Greek belief that what was most ancient was most valuable. The Jews copied the practice (note the parallels between Josephus' *Antiquities* and the *Roman Antiquities* of Dionysius of Halicarnasus) and claimed their writings were the oldest. It was in terms of such a belief that the early Christian apologists and antiheretical writers often built their arguments. Tertullian, for example, in his *Apology* (21), claims, "Our religion is supported by the writings of the Jews, the oldest which exist." In *Against Marcion* (5:19) he says, "I am accustomed, in my prescription against all heresies, to fix my compendious criterion of truth in the testimony of time; claiming priority therein as our rule, and alleging lateness to be the characteristic of every heresy." Continuity between Christians and Israel and between the events of Jesus' career and the OT prophecies was important because it allowed Christians to appeal to the argument from antiquity, which would allow Greek-speaking Christians to feel not the least bit inferior to pagans with their cultural and religious claims allegedly rooted in antiquity.

(d) The evidence from Josephus showed the motif of prophecy-fulfillment in the history of Israel was used to provide evidence for the providence of God in human affairs—that is, that a personal God acts to reward virtue and punish vice. The promises that no harm would come to Paul (Acts 18:9–10; 27:23–24) and their fulfillment fit into this function: God cares for his own who work as missionaries. In Luke-Acts, therefore, the prophecy-fulfillment schema functions very much as it does in its Mediterranean milieu.

In 1:1–4 the evangelist speaks about the "things which have been accomplished/fulfilled among us." Given the importance of the theme of the fulfillment of prophecy in the two-volume work, it seems almost certain that the translation should be "fulfilled among us." The story of Jesus and the early church is one that fulfills the various prophecies made by the Jewish scriptures, by living prophets, and by heavenly beings. Insofar as the Christian story fulfilled the prophecies of the scriptures, it would be about those who had ancient roots. Insofar as it told of the fulfillment of the prophecies of Jesus and Christian prophets, it would depict them as being right. Taken together, having roots and being right would be highly persuasive. It would contribute to the certainty the evangelist wants to give Theophilus (vs. 4). The theme of the fulfillment of prophecy, then, would seem to be a legitimation device in the Lukan narrative, just as it was in Mediterranean antiquity generally.

EXCURSUS B:
MIRACLE IN LUKE-ACTS
AND IN THE LUKAN MILIEU

An appreciation of the Lukan attitude toward miracle is closely tied to an understanding of the attitudes toward miracle in the Lukan milieu: pagan, Jewish, and Christian.

(1) Pagan attitudes toward miracle range from very positive to very negative depending upon the context/circle in which an opinion is expressed. (a) In some circles the principle was fully accepted that miracle proved divinity. For example, Philostratus in the *Life of Apollonius*, 7:38, tells how, when Apollonius was in prison because of Domitian, to show his freedom to his companion Damis, he took his leg out of its shackles. Having done this, he then put his leg back again. At that moment, Damis said, he first understood clearly that Apollonius' nature was godlike and more than human. Again, Suetonius in his "Life of Vespasian," 7:2, tells us that Vespasian as yet lacked prestige and a certain divinity, since he was an unexpected and newly-made emperer. These, however, were soon given to him. In Alexandria two miracles were performed. Vespasian healed a man who was blind and a man who was lame was made to walk.

Since miracle had the power to prove deity, it was one means of winning converts to various religious cults. Ovid, *Metamorphoses*, 3:695ff., has a priest of Dionysius named Acoetes tell how he became a follower of the god when an epiphany was disclosed in a miraculous event. Philostratus, *Heroicus*, describes a conversion of a Phoenician trader brought about by a vinetender's telling what the hero had done for him. Apuleius, *Metamorphoses*, 11, says Lucius was changed back from a donkey to a human being by a miracle effected by Isis. As a result he became a devotee of the goddess and was initiated into her cult.

It was also likely that miracle was a means of encouraging the devotion of the adherents of a cult. Strabo (c. 801) tells that stories of miracles were collected for the Serapeum at Canopus. This would seem to be for the purpose of reinforcing those who were adherents of this religion.

(b) There were other circles, however, that discredited miracle. Lucian is a prime example. In his *Lovers of Lies* members of various philosophical schools are mocked for their desire to tell tales of wonder. Lucian professes himself baffled by the puzzle: why do serious people have an interest in lies about miracles? For Lucian, magic and miracle had become identical. In *Alexander the False Prophet* Lucian tells of a cult's origin via miracle and other things like fulfilled prophecy. The entire account, however, is told to discredit the oracle and its founder. Philostratus' *Life of Apollonius of Tyana* gives further evidence, being written to defend the philosopher against the charge of being a magician because he had worked miracles. In such circles as these, therefore, miracle was no proof; it was a problem.

(2) Jewish attitudes toward miracle show the same mixed reaction found in pagan circles. (a) In the period of Christian origins, miracle was widely regarded by Jews as the divine legitimation of a position, a person, or of God himself. In the first place, miracle was believed to legitimate the word or position of a prophet or rabbi. Sifre Deut 18:19 states that if a prophet who starts to prophesy gives evidence by signs and miracles, he is to be heeded; if not, he is not to be followed. This anonymous saying is early because a discussion between Jose ha-Gelili and Akiba presupposes the existence of such a statement (b. Sanh 90a; Sifre Deut 13:3). Josephus, *Antiquities*, 2:12:3 §280, reports God gave Moses three signs (rod became a serpent; leprous hand; water turned to blood) and said, "Make use of those signs, in order to obtain belief among all men, that you are sent by me and do all things according to my commands." The same motif is also found elsewhere in Josephus (e.g., *Ant.* 9:2:1 §23; 10:2:1 §28; 20:5:1 §168). In b. Ta'anith 23a, there is a tradition about the first century Honi who was effective in praying for rain. Once when there was a drought the people asked Honi to pray. He prayed and no rain fell. Then he drew a circle and stood within it and exclaimed before God, "I swear that I will not move from here until Thou hast mercy on Thy children." When it only dripped, he told God vehemently that this was not what he had asked. When it then rained so hard as to do damage, he strongly told God

that he had asked for rain of blessing not for rain to destroy life. When the normal rain continued so long that flooding became a problem, Honi again strongly told God it was time for the rain to stop. Immediately the clouds dispersed and the sun came out. Thereupon Simeon b. Shetah said, "Were it not that you are Honi, I would have placed you under the ban. But what shall I do to you who acts petulantly before God and He grants your desire?" Simeon's response means Honi's behavior should be rejected but since Honi's prayer produced the miracle of rain, his behavior was legitimated. This story shows that in the time of Honi the Circle Drawer matters of behavior toward God were settled by miracle. This is supported: a *bath qol* or voice from heaven was decisive in settling halakic questions in favor of Beth Hillel and against Beth Shammai at Jamnia not long after A.D. 70 (Alexander Guttmann, "The Significance of Miracles for Talmudic Judaism," *Hebrew Union College Annual,* 20 [1947]: 363–406, especially 369–71).

In the second place, miracle was believed to prove one's innocence or righteousness. In j. Berakoth 5:1 we hear that once when Rabbi Haninah b. Dosa was praying he was bitten by a snake but did not interrupt his prayer. Not only did the rabbi not feel the bite but also the snake was later found dead at the entrance to its den. The righteousness of the rabbi was vindicated by his immunity to a poisonous snakebite. In b. Baba Mezia 58b–59, after the excommunication of R. Eliezer, R. Gamaliel was traveling in a ship. When a huge wave arose to drown him, he said, "It appears to me that this is on account of none but R. Eliezer ben Hyrcannus." Thereupon he arose and cried, "Sovereign of the Universe, Thou knowest that I have not acted for my honor, nor for the honor of my paternal house, but for Thine, so that differences may not multiply in Israel." At that the raging sea subsided. Here the miracle of the sea's subsiding vindicates the rabbi's innocence.

The significance of deliverance from snakebite and storm at sea can only be understood if one is aware of the general cultural background. It was a common belief, pagan and Jewish, that divine forces in cooperation with nature (especially storms at sea) and the animal kingdom (especially snakes) punish wickedness. Homer, *Odyssey,* 12:127–41, 259–446, tells how Odysseus' crew were all destroyed in a shipwreck because they had slaughtered Helios' sacred cattle. Chariton's novel (3:3:10; 3:3:18; 3:4:9–10) also attests the belief that the polluted are drowned at sea while the just are delivered. An epitaph of Statyllus

Flaccus tells how the ship-wrecked sailor who had just escaped from the storm and raging sea lay stranded, naked, and destitute on a sandy beach in Lydia. Suddenly a poisonous snake bit him and killed him. The epitaph concludes, "Why did he struggle against the sea? He could not escape the lot that awaited him on the land" (H. Conzelmann, *Die Apostelgeschichte* [Tübingen: Mohr, 1963], p. 147). In the Tosefta, Sanhedrin 8:3, R. Simeon ben Shetah (c. 80 B.C.) said he saw a man with a sword running after a fellow. The two ran into a deserted building. When Simeon entered he found the one slain and the other with the sword dripping blood: "But he who knows the thoughts, he exacts vengeance from the guilty; for the murderer did not stir from the place before a serpent bit him so that he died." So certain was such punishment believed to be that in some circumstances the absence of destruction by storm or snakebite could be adduced as proof of innocence. The Athenian orator Antiphon (480–411 B.C.) wrote a speech for a client, one Helion, who on a sea journey was accused of murder. The speech says that although retribution comes on the guilty and those associated with him, "in my case the opposite is true on every count. For all those with whom I have sailed have enjoyed good voyages. I claim all this as great proof of the charge that the plaintiffs have accused me falsely" (G. B. Miles and G. Trompf, "Luke and Antiphon: The Theology of Acts 27–28 in the Light of Pagan Beliefs about Divine Retribution, Pollution, and Shipwreck," *Harvard Theological Review*, 69:259–67, esp. p. 262 [1976]). For a rabbi to escape death after the bite of a poisonous snake or in the midst of a storm at sea testifies to his innocence or righteousness (cf. Paul, Acts 27–28).

In the third place, miracle was believed sometimes to be effective in gaining acknowledgment of the superiority of Israel's God. In 2 Kgs 5: 15–19 Naaman the Syrian who had been healed of leprosy confesses his belief in Israel's God and asks indulgence as he is forced to go into the temple of the god of his land. In 2 Mac 3:35–39 Heliodorus makes a confession of the Jewish God's supremacy after experiencing a miracle.

(b) There was reluctance in many circles of Judaism after the end of the first century A.D., however, to allow miracle any legitimating power. The crucial point in time when miracle was disallowed as the authentication of a position in matters of *halakah* is recounted in b. Baba Mezia 58b–59b. In the period of the second generation of Tannaim, (A.D. 90–130) there was a debate between R. Eliezer and R.

Joshua which was resolved against Eliezer. This was done in spite of miracles supporting R. Eliezer's position (the uprooting of the carob tree; water flowing backwards; a *bath qol*) because the Torah had already been given on Sinai. In the following Tannaitic generation, the third, the principle "one should not mention miracles" makes its appearance. This was largely aimed at the miracles of rising Christianity. Furthermore, B. J. Bamberger's *Proselytism in the Talmudic Period* [reprint ed., New York: KTAV 1968] gives no examples of proselytes being made via miracle. In Judaism, therefore, after A.D. 100 miracle did not function as legitimation, as it had before.

(3) The ancient church also manifests a mixed attitude toward miracle. (a) On the one hand, many believed miracles were still happening in the life of the church (Justin, *Apology II*, 6; Irenaeus, *Against Heresies*, 2:48–49; 2:31:2; 2:32:4; Tertullian, *Apology*, 23; Origen, *Against Celsus*, 1:2:46; 3:24; Eusebius, *Church History*, 5:7; Augustine, *City of God*, 22:8; *Sermon*, 322). Further, miracles had or have an evangelistic-legitimating function (Quadratus [according to Eusebius, *HE*, 4:3:2]; Acts of Paul; Arnobius 2:12; Marcion [according to Tertullian, *Against Marcion*, 3:2–3]; Abgar legend [related by Eusebius, *HE*, 1:13]; Origen, *Against Celsus*, 1:46; Eusebius, *Church History*, 2:32).

(b) On the other hand, others believed miracles belonged to the first age of the church as a necessary prop to the rise of faith but were now unnecessary (John Chrysostom, *Homily in Matt* 12:2; 14:3; *Homily in John* 12:3; *Homily in 1 Cor* 6:2). Many believed miracles were either a problem or proved nothing: Theophilus of Antioch (*To Autolycus* 1:13) says if he were to provide an example of a man raised from the dead and alive, his adversary would not believe it. Furthermore, Jewish/pagan attacks on Christian miracles contended: 1) Christian miracles were no more remarkable than the wonders ascribed to other gods and heroes; 2) Christian miracle stories were fictitious; 3) Christian miracles were due to magic (G. W. H. Lampe, "Miracles and Early Christian Apologetic," in *Miracle*, ed. C. F. D. Moule [London: Mowbray, 1965], pp. 205–18). Considering these problems, it is not surprising some Christians made little use of miracle to legitimate their position.

In light of this sketch of the Lukan milieu it becomes possible to say something about Luke's attitude toward the role of miracle in Christian faith. (a) Luke-Acts has perhaps the most positive attitude toward miracle among the gospels. In the first place, as our discussion of 4:31—5:11 has shown, the evangelist believes miracle has an evangelistic function. It evokes faith (cf. also Acts 5:12–16; 8:6–7, 12; 9:32–35, 36–42; 13:6–12; 16:16–34; 19:11–20). In the second place, Luke believes miracle legitimates one's position or words. Acts 2:22 says Jesus was "attested to you by God with mighty works and wonders and signs which God did through him in your midst." This seems the case in passages like Luke 7:11–17, 18–23. Passages like 6:6–11 seem to settle the legal question of sabbath observance via miracle (cf. Honi's experience). In Acts 15:12 miracle plays a role in the church's decision about the inclusion of the Gentiles. In the third place, miracle, for Luke, establishes one's innocence or righteousness. In Acts 2:32–36; 3:14–15, the raising of Jesus from the dead vindicates him over against those who have rejected him. In Acts 27–28, Paul's deliverance from shipwreck and from snakebite attest his innocence.

(b) At the same time Luke is positive about miracle, he also is far from naive about its value. First, the evangelist, like pagan and Jewish critics of miracle, knows miracle is no proof that compels conversion (cf. 6:6–11; 8:26–39; 11:14ff.; Acts 4:16–21; 14:8–18; 16:16ff.). Second, miracle by itself is not an adequate guide. It needs to be supported by the OT and by Jesus' words (Acts 15:12, 13–19; 11:15–16; Luke 9:1–6; 10:9, 17–19). Third, miracle needs to be distinguished from magic by the good character of those who work miracles. Note that Luke 4:1–13 shows Jesus from the first as not self-indulgent or power hungry. The same point is made again in 23:35–39 in a threefold temptation echoing 4:1–13. Neither does Jesus use his miraculous power to harm anyone or anything. Plato (*Rep.* II:364) speaks of wandering soothsayers who promise to punish enemies in this world; certain Jews would like Honi to destroy their enemies and kill him when he will not; Apollonius of Tyana (*Life* 3:7) defends himself against the charge of being a magician by saying he does not harm people—it is surely significant that Luke omits the cursing of the fig tree. In Acts Peter is shown to be hostile to a magician who was motivated by gain (8:18–19). Paul also is shown to be hostile to a magician (13:6ff.) and to magic (19:18–19). Moreover, he is portrayed as not greedy (18:3; 20:33–35). Fourth, to have experienced a miracle, Luke believes, is not the same thing as having faith, being healed is not the same as being saved (Luke 17:11–19). Finally, in terms of priorities, having miraculous powers is secondary in importance to having experienced conversion (10:20).